MAUREEN STAPLETON

Maureen Stapleton as Birdie Hubbard in the 1981 Broadway revival of *The Little Foxes*. Photo by Martha Swope (© 1992).

MAUREEN STAPLETON

A Bio-Bibliography

Jeannie M. Woods

Bio-Bibliographies in the Performing Arts, Number 34

G P

Greenwood Press
Westport, Connecticut • London

Library of Congress Cataloging-in-Publication Data

Woods, Jeannie Marlin.
   Maureen Stapleton : a bio-bibliography / Jeannie M. Woods.
     p. cm.—(Bio-bibliographies in the performing arts, ISSN
  0892-5550 ; no. 34)
   Includes bibliographical references and index.
   ISBN 0-313-27761-3 (alk. paper)
   1. Stapleton, Maureen. 2. Stapleton, Maureen—Bibliography.
  3. Actors—United States—Biography.   I. Title.   II. Series.
  PN2287.S675W66 1992
  792'.028'092—dc20
  [B]   92-23787

British Library Cataloguing in Publication Data is available.

Library of Congress Catalog Card Number: 92-23787
ISBN: 0-313-27761-3
ISSN: 0892-5550

First published in 1992

Greenwood Press, 88 Post Road West, Westport, CT 06881
An imprint of Greenwood Publishing Group, Inc.

Printed in the United States of America

∞™

The paper used in this book complies with the
Permanent Paper Standard issued by the National
Information Standards Organization (Z39.48-1984).

10 9 8 7 6 5 4 3 2 1

This book is lovingly dedicated to Dan Woods

Contents

Preface

This book is intended to provide the reader with a complete reference volume on the diverse and accomplished career of the actress Maureen Stapleton. For almost fifty years this unique performing artist has brought her talent to the Broadway stage, the silver screen and the home screen. This volume is dedicated to exploring the panorama of that rich career.

The **Biography** introduces the reader to Ms. Stapleton and presents an overview of her life, from her early actor training with Herbert Berghof, her affiliation with The Actors Studio, and her rise to prominence in Tennessee Williams' play, *The Rose Tattoo,* on Broadway. The Biography traces the actress' artistic development and demonstrates the exciting, often eclectic variety of Ms. Stapleton's major performances.

A brief **Chronology** follows the Biography and summarizes the important highlights of Stapleton's public and private life. The Chronology is followed by three chapters that explore the three major arenas of her creative work: **Stage Performances, Television Performances** and **Film Performances.** Each entry in these three chapters describes a particular event in Stapleton's artistic career and each entry is given an individual number for convenience in cross-referencing within the text. The events are organized chronologically so that **S01** denotes her first major stage appearance (on Broadway in *The Playboy of the Western World*) and **S20** denotes her twentieth major stage appearance (on Broadway in *The Gingerbread Lady*). Film appearances begin with **F01** and television appearances begin with **T01.** Notations at the beginning of each chapter define the parameters of each section; thus, the chapter of Stage Performances refers the reader to the Biography for minor credits such as early summer stock appearances.

An **Appendix** follows the chapter on Film Performances. This appendix summarizes the nominations, awards, and honors which Ms. Stapleton has received during her career. An extensive **Bibliography** and detailed **Index** complete the volume. The **Bibliography** is divided into a section on books, articles and archival materials about Stapleton and another section listing selected reviews of her major performances. Entries in the Bibliography are discreetly numbered, **B01, B02,** etc. The **Index** provides an alphabetical listing of all of Stapleton's performances and any other important cross-references to the volume as a whole.

The author, date and page number of the sources are noted parenthetically and full references are given in the Bibliography. Where appropriate, special notations of abbreviations, chapter organization, and method of citation are given on the first page of the applicable chapter.

Acknowledgments

I wish to thank the many friends and colleagues who have been so generous with their time and assistance in compiling this work: Albert Bermel, Duncan and Jeanine Connell, Cynthia Contreras, Carla Craig, Lynn Doherty and Kathy Mets of the Theatre Collection of the Museum of the City of New York, Stuart Freedman, Sybil Huskey, Bennett Lentczner, Donald C. Lueder, Susana Powell, and to Walter Zvonchenko of the Performing Arts Library at the Kennedy Center. I am also grateful to Robert M. Gorman and the staff of Dacus Library for their kind assistance.

Special thanks goes to Wade Hobgood and the Research Council of Winthrop University for their essential support of this project.

MAUREEN STAPLETON

Biography

Maureen Stapleton is recognized as a major star of stage, screen and television. Her career spans more than four decades during which she has received the highest acclaim for her powerful performances and versatility. She has created many original characters and within each there has always been a fundamental core of honesty and earthiness, a seemingly ordinary person with extraordinary depths of passion and sensitivity.

Stapleton's early life was certainly as ordinary as could be. She was born Lois Maureen Stapleton on 21 June 1925 in Troy, New York. Her parents, John P. Stapleton and Irene Walsh Stapleton, were staunch Irish Catholics. However, John was an alcoholic and so when Maureen was very young (five or eight years old—accounts vary) her parents separated. After that she and her mother and younger brother, Jack, went to live with relatives in Troy (her maternal grandmother, three aunts and two uncles). Her mother worked as a clerk at the New York State Department of Unemployment Insurance.

Her childhood was not a happy one. The family was poor and the only person to encourage her was her favorite uncle, Vincent. She attended school at St. Mary's Catholic Grammar School and Central Catholic High. She did not become involved in theatre at school, except for playing roles in a couple of school plays. She played the mother in *Murder on a Ferris Wheel* and another mother in *Anne of Green Gables*. She was cast in such character roles because she was overweight, a condition that would plague her throughout her life.

Her low self-esteem led her to escape into fantasy and she became an avid film buff. She would go to the movies after school and stay until the last show. Seeing movies and collecting film magazines became her passion. In later interviews she would often relate how she had wanted to become a movie star because she thought she would magically transform herself into Jean Harlow and thus receive the adoration and riches that she craved.

When she graduated from high school in 1942 she took night classes at Siena College, a business school, while she worked to raise money to finance her career. Over the next year she held jobs at the Unemployment Insurance Department and at the Watervliet Arsenal in Schenectady. From these jobs she saved one hundred dollars. She was eighteen years old, 5'4" tall, with dark brown hair and green eyes, and she weighed 170 pounds when she left Troy to go to New York and become a star.

When she arrived in Manhattan in 1943, Stapleton worked at odd jobs and began her first theatre training. Her jobs included that of a billing clerk on the night shift at the Hotel New Yorker and that of an "ordinette" who gave lectures on war equipment at the Chrysler Exhibit of War Weapons. She also did stints as a clerk at Bonwit Teller and for a paint manufacturer. She first studied acting with Francis Robinson-Duff who taught the Delsarte method which divided the acting process into mental, emotional and physical arenas and dictated certain positions of the hands, eyes and body to relate different emotions. After several months, Stapleton decided to look for a different teacher. It was then that she met Herbert Berghof and began studying with him in night classes given at the New School.

It was meeting Berghof that led to Stapleton's first stage opportunities. In the summer of 1945, twenty-two of Berghof's pupils invested a hundred and fifty dollars apiece to start the Greenbush Summer Theatre in Blauvelt, New York. It was a trial by fire for the ardent young players. They did eight plays in eight weeks. Stapleton played only two parts, the grandmother in *Over Twenty-One* and a bear (!) in *Noah*.

It was to be the first of several summer stock seasons for the actress. In 1946 she went to Mount Kisco where she played a small role in *The Time of Your Life* at the Westchester Playhouse. She also understudied and performed one night in the leading role of Pegeen Mike in *The Playboy of the Western World*. Two summers later in 1948 she co-starred with Brian Aherne and John Merivale, in the role of Cherry in *The Beaux Stratagem* on Cape Cod and at the Westport Country Playhouse. Other summers took her to Gloucester, Massachusetts, and Metunuck, Rhode Island.

During the seasons in New York, Stapleton worked as secretary for Herbert Berghof who had now founded his own acting studio. She continued to study with Berghof there and with Mira Rostova who was to be one of her favorite teachers. She also modeled for painters Raphael Soyer and Reginald Marsh. Soyer did a portrait of her entitled *Maureen* and she appears as a burlesque queen in one of Marsh's genre paintings.

On 26 October 1946 Stapleton made her Broadway debut in the Guthrie McClintic production of *The Playboy of the Western World*. She had elbowed her way into the role by calling up McClintic directly and confronting him about who was to play Pegeen Mike (the role she had understudied in stock a few months earlier). McClintic must have been impressed with her boldness because he cast her as a village girl and as Pegeen's understudy. Her break came when the Irish star, Eithne Dunne, left the cast a week early and Stapleton was able to play Pegeen opposite Burgess Meredith as Christy. More significantly, she established a positive working relationship with McClintic and his wife, the great Broadway star Katharine Cornell. Stapleton was taken into the company for the Broadway production of *Antony and Cleopatra* and toured America with the 1947 revival of *The Barretts of Wimpole Street*. From these experiences she learned the basics of her craft.

In September 1947 there was another significant event in Stapleton's career when she became a charter member of the Actors Studio. The Studio was to become the most influential training ground for actors in America. It was established by directors Harold Clurman, Elia Kazan and Robert Lewis who wanted to create a workshop where actors could learn to perfect their craft in the tradition of the then defunct Group Theatre.

Kazan took the less experienced performers and Lewis the more experienced performers and they planned to rehearse scenes in private workshops where they would be free to explore the Stanislavsky techniques of subtext and character motivation.

Lewis' class included Maureen Stapleton, Eli Wallach, Marlon Brando, Montgomery Clift, Mildred Dunnock, Jerome Robbins, Herbert Berghof, Tom Ewell, John Forsythe, Anne Jackson, Sidney Lumet, Kevin McCarthy, Karl Malden, E. G. Marshall, Patricia Neal, Beatrice Straight, David Wayne and others—about fifty in all. They met in an abandoned church at first and the work included analyzing plays, staging scenes, and trying roles outside their usual range.

Stapleton benefitted from both the protected workshop environment of the Studio and from the personal contacts she made there. She would go on to work with almost all of the actors listed above, plus many others associated with the Studio. In the spring of 1948 she played Masha in a Studio performance of Chekhov's *The Seagull* which, like much of the Studio work, was performed for an audience of studio members and friends. Later that year Stapleton made her television debut in "Night Club," one of a series of dramas which the Actors Studio broadcast on ABC television.

Robert Lewis left the Studio shortly after *The Seagull* was staged. He had had a difference of opinion with Elia Kazan (which he details in his book, *Slings and Arrows*). Lewis' group was later directed by Joshua Logan and then by Lee Strasberg. Strasberg went on to take command there so that his name became synonymous with the Actors Studio. Stapleton never responded to his training techniques as she did with Lewis' method. In an interview with Esther Rosen, she explained her problems with Strasberg: "He talked too much for me . . . it's just that simple . . . . Also he had a kind of rigidity that I did not respond to . . . I didn't agree with much of that private moment and sense memory stuff, too. It was alright up to a point, but I saw too many people get hysterical and cry and carry on . . . I had great trepidations about it all" (1983, 15). Nevertheless, a hallmark of Stapleton's performance style is the absolute emotional truth of her character portraits and it is this element of acting which was emphasized at the Studio.

Stapleton has often been questioned about what came to be known as "The Method" but she has always avoided the debate and controversy that topic engenders. Like many of the early members of the Studio, she views her process as a craft—what all good actors do, even if they have never received the Studio training. In a 1961 interview she said "I'll tell you how the Method helps you. According to the Method, you see, you have to give yourself . . . . It's to be as true and real, and alive and fresh in the part each time. That's your job" (Funke and Booth 1961, 170-71). Robert Lewis once summed up Stapleton's personal talent when he said that she is a "true believer," that is an actress who can totally immerse herself in the part and the moment of the play. It is the essence of what Stanislavsky called the "Magic If" and for the rare actor who can make that leap of imagination, no technique or method is required—it is that achievement to which all technique aspires.

Stapleton's work at the Studio included a number of seminal performances. First was the private performance of *The Seagull* with a cast that included Thelma Schnef as Arkadina, Henry Barnard as Treplev,

David Wayne as Medvedenko, Joan Chandler as Nina, George Keane as Trigorin, Herbert Berghof as Dorn, Michael Strong as Shamrayev, William Hansen as Sorin and Mildred Dunnock as Paulina. In his book, *The Actors Studio, A Player's Place,* David Garfield says that this production "was one of the memorable events of the Studio's early history" (1984, 65). Stapleton would repeat her role, Masha, in the 1954 production at the Phoenix Theatre. Stapleton also did a reading of Tennessee Williams' *Twenty-Seven Wagons Full of Cotton* at the Studio. It was directed by Josh Logan who took over the advanced class after Lewis left. She would create the role of Flora Meighan on Broadway a few years later. She appeared in the Studio's *Hello from Bertha* with Anne Jackson and Margaret Phillips under the direction of Eli Wallach. She would film this short Williams play for television in 1961.

Perhaps the most intense experience Stapleton had at the Actors Studio was when she was cast in a workshop scene with Marilyn Monroe. Monroe was already a superstar and her presence at the Studio was unsettling. Initially the two actors were supposed to do a scene from a Noël Coward play, *Fallen Angels,* but they decided the material was not right for them. Instead they chose to do O'Neill's *Anna Christie* with Monroe in the role of Anna and Stapleton in the role of Marthy. According to Garfield, Monroe was so nervous she could not remember her lines, nor would she hold a script for reference during the performance. Therefore, Garfield says, "before the 'curtain' they eased their nerves with coffee laced with Jack Daniels" (1984, 122). Monroe was fine once the scene began. It was the only scene she ever did at the Studio.

Stapleton is a life member of the Actors Studio. She is one of the many artists featured in the documentary film, *Hello Actors Studio,* that was produced in 1987. Moreover, she is a recipient of the Actors Studio Award, a once in a lifetime honor that was granted to studio members in 1980 as recognition for their contribution to the American theatre.

As her work continued at the Studio, Stapleton returned to Broadway, playing a very small role in the immensely successful production of *Detective Story.* Meanwhile, during an audition for Kazan's production of *Death of a Salesman,* she met Max Allentuck, who was business manager and stage manager of that memorable production. So, in July 1949, between the matinee and evening performances of *Detective Story,* she and Allentuck dashed off to City Hall to get married. She was twenty-four, he was thirty-seven. Six months later she left that production to take the part of Emily in *The Bird Cage* and on 8 July 1950 she had her first child, Daniel Vincent Allentuck. By February of the next year she had achieved stardom.

The play that was to establish Maureen Stapleton as a true star was Tennessee Williams' lush drama of Sicilian passion on the Gulf coast—*The Rose Tattoo.* Williams had written the part of the young, earthy Sicilian widow for the Italian actress Anna Magnani. However, Magnani was not confident that her English was good enough to sustain a stage role in which the actress hardly leaves the stage. Numerous auditions were held to cast the roles of Serafina and Alvaro (the sensual but homely truck driver who renews Serafina's lust for life). Williams and producer Cheryl Crawford were familiar with the studio work of Stapleton and Eli Wallach because they had performed in several of Williams' short plays including *Hello from Bertha* (in which Wallach directed Stapleton) and *The Strangest Kind of Romance* (in which Wallach acted). In his book, *Memoirs,* Tennessee

Williams takes credit for casting Stapleton as Serafina: "It was I who found Maureen Stapleton for the part. Her reading convinced us all that, despite her youth, she could do it; she was a very young girl at the time but nevertheless I thought she was so brilliant in characterization that the obstacle of her youth could be overcome" (1975, 161-62).

Williams and Stapleton became fast friends. They affectionately referred to one another as "Maw" and "Paw." In the years to come he wrote three scripts for her, although she never appeared in any of them. The first was a play, *Kingdom of Earth*, which was staged in 1967 with Estelle Parsons in the role written for Stapleton. In the 1970s Williams wrote a television script entitled "A Second Epiphany" and then re-titled "Stopped Rocking," but it was never produced. Finally, he wrote the play *A Lovely Sunday for Creve Coeur* with her in mind for the leading role of Bodey, a protective busybody. It was produced under the title of *Creve Coeur* at the Spoleto Festival with Jan Miner in the lead, opening on 5 June 1978. On 21 January 1979, *A Lovely Sunday for Creve Coeur* premiered at the Hudson Theatre Guild in New York with Peg Murray as Bodey.

Although Stapleton never appeared in these plays, she was strongly connected with Williams and his heroines throughout her career. She was the first to create several Williams heroines on Broadway. In addition to creating Serafina in *The Rose Tattoo*, she was the first to play Lady Torrance in *Orpheus Descending*, and the first to to play Flora Meighan in *Twenty-Seven Wagons Full of Cotton*. She played Serafina also in the 1951-52 national touring production, in the 1966 Broadway revival, the 1967 sound recording of the play, and in regional theatre in 1973. When *Orpheus Descending* was made into the film, *The Fugitive Kind*, Stapleton portrayed Vee Talbott.

Stapleton also played Amanda Wingfield in *The Glass Menagerie* in the Broadway revival of 1965, in the off-Broadway revival at the Circle in the Square of 1975 and in regional productions in 1977 and 1982. She performed Amanda in a scene from *The Glass Menagerie* in a guest appearance for President Johnson at the White House and again in Harry Rasky's 1972 television documentary *Tennessee Williams' South*. Other television performances of Williams' plays included the 1961 *Play of the Week* in which she appeared in Williams' one-act, *Hello from Bertha*, and the 1976 television production of *Cat on a Hot Tin Roof* in which she co-starred with Laurence Olivier—she played Big Mama to his Big Daddy.

Stapleton won her first Tony Award for her performance in *The Rose Tattoo*. Her success in this production demonstrated her unique talent for immersing herself into the life of her character. The playwright Milan Stitt once made this observation about Stapleton's ability to take on a role: "Occasionally there are artists who can flash lightning into dark corners of human experience through their uncompromising vulnerability, openness to anguish. Maureen Stapleton has done this for me more often than any other living actress" (1978, 25). It is apparent from the critical response to *The Rose Tattoo* that Stapleton was able to achieve a complete identification with Serafina. No doubt it was a demanding role, too. Serafina is uncommonly passionate but also severely constrained by her religious and cultural customs. She is onstage through virtually the entire play and runs the gamut from fierce pride to outrage to breathless ardor. Although she was only twenty-four when she first played Serafina, this actress astounded her audiences with her emotional depth and ability to communicate her personal agony to each person present. The role rightfully made her a star.

Stardom, however, came with a price. She experienced severe stage fright—a fear that has continued throughout her career. In various interviews she has described how her fears were especially severe on opening night when she would burp and belch and her nerves would block out the memory of performance. She tried from time to time to dull the terror with alcohol. She claims she got drunk before one performance of *The Rose Tattoo* but learned her lesson and swore to never drink before a performance again. Nevertheless, Stapleton went on to battle alcoholism for many years. Also during the premiere production of *The Rose Tattoo*, the actress developed a paranoid fear that someone in the audience was going to kill her. The fear got so bad that she went into therapy to control it. By the time the production set off for the national tour, the paranoia had subsided. Over the years, however, she was besieged by other fears; for example, she developed a terror of flying and so she always travels by car, train or boat—never by plane.

After the tour of *The Rose Tattoo* ended it was a full year before she returned to the stage. In the interim she enjoyed her young son, Daniel, (who was now two years old) and she made some appearances in the emerging medium of television. In addition to her premiere appearance (with the Actors Studio in 1948), she was involved with an unsuccessful series pilot, *The Old Knickerbocker Music Hall,* for CBS in 1948. She appeared for several weeks on the celebrity panel of a new quiz show, *What Happened?* on NBC in 1952, and performed in a dramatic episode of the NBC series, *Curtain Call* the same year. Hereafter she would combine her stage appearances with television appearances.

In February 1953, Stapleton returned to the stage in a role very different from that of Serafina. This was Bella in George Tabori's play, *The Emperor's Clothes.* She played the wife of a Hungarian college professor. The role was less than satisfying for her, but it is significant in that it demonstrates Stapleton's unique persona that is decidedly European and matronly. Although this actress is from Irish Catholic stock, in her long career she has played an incredible range of women, including Irish, Hungarian, Jewish, Italian, English, Russian, Yugoslavian, Gypsy, German, and of course many women of the American south. Stapleton is the first to admit that she sees herself as outspoken, down-to-earth, even ordinary. She prides herself on enjoying a simple family-oriented life. (As early as 1955 her biography in the Broadway program for *All in One* says her outside interests are "being a housewife and taking care of the children.") This unassuming self-effacement has enhanced the credibility and authenticity of the very real women that she plays so brilliantly. The columnist Vernon Rice aptly described her "capacity for naturalness" and her "encompassing and expansive warmth" and observed "when she sits, she sits like a woman who has been shopping in Macy's all day in tight shoes. She collapses completely, with the hope and prayer that she'll never have to rise again" (8 June 1951).

Stapleton has, however, performed non-contemporary roles too. In 1953 and 1954 the actress appeared in Arthur Miller's controversial drama, *The Crucible,* in Shakespeare's *Richard III,* and in Chekhov's *The Seagull.* In *Richard III,* she played Anne opposite José Ferrer's Richard under the direction of Margaret Webster. In *The Seagull* she played Masha, as she had in the private performance of the play at the Actors Studio; this time the production was for the public at the Phoenix Theatre, under the direction of Norris Houghton. She played a scene from *Camille, or The Lady of the Camellias* in a celebrity benefit, *Highlights of the Empire* on 24 May 1953; José Reubens staged the scene and played Armand Duval and Janice Mars appeared as Nanine.

In October 1954 Stapleton had her second and last child, a daughter named Katherine. Then, as she had done after her first pregnancy, she returned to the stage a few months later in another Tennessee Williams play. This was the one-act play, *Twenty-Seven Wagons Full of Cotton*, which has already been mentioned as a work that began in a reading at the Actors Studio. In his biography of Williams, *Kindness of Strangers*, Donald Spoto writes that Williams chose Stapleton for the role of Flora, the simple-minded farmwife who is brutalized by a vindictive neighbor after her husband destroys his cotton gin. The production premiered at Tulane University and was re-staged on Broadway in the spring of 1955 with great success. She repeated the role once more in July 1956 at the Westport Country Playhouse in Westport, Connecticut; that production was directed by Peter Kass and also starred Jules Munshin as the husband, Jake, and John Cassavetes as the neighbor, Silva Vicarro.

During the 1950s Stapleton was also establishing herself in the emerging medium of television. She appeared in many live television dramas including "The Accident," "The Mother," and "Incident in July" on *The Philco Playhouse*, and "Track of Fear," an episode of the esteemed series *Justice*, in which she co-starred with Theodore Bikel. Stapleton also performed in a fact-based drama entitled "Minding Our Own Business" in which she played the wife of a newspaperman who moves to a small town in Washington and tries to start a small paper. For *The Armstrong Circle Theatre* she played a Yugoslavian immigrant who is reunited with her young son in "H.R. 8438—The Story of a Lost Boy."

In December 1956 Stapleton portrayed President Andrew Jackson's wife in "Rachel: A Love Story" for the series *Studio One*. She also appeared in a 1957 drama on *The Alcoa Hour* entitled "No License to Kill" in which she played a woman whose family is involved in a fatal car accident. The following year she gave a dramatic performance in an episode of John Houseman's drama anthology series, *The Seven Lively Arts*. In this episode, "Blast in Centralia No. 5," Stapleton portrayed a poor miner's wife who loses her husband and son in a mine disaster. A filmclip of that performance was included in the 1978 retrospective, "CBS on the Air: A Celebration of Fifty Years."

Stapleton's next experience onstage with a Tennessee Williams play was less positive only because the critical response to the play was subdued. The play was the 1957 premiere of *Orpheus Descending*. The script had developed from an earlier, weaker play which Williams had written in 1940, *Battle of Angels*. Stapleton herself received fine reviews for her portrayal of Lady Torrance, a role which Williams had written for the Italian actress, Anna Magnani (as he had written Serafina for her). Once again, Magnani declined the part and Stapleton was cast instead. That is how Stapleton came to be known as the "American Magnani." It was a title she always took with good grace. Even when *Orpheus Descending* was made into the film *The Fugitive Kind* (1960) and Magnani was cast as Lady Torrance, Stapleton (who also appeared in the film as Vee Talbott) was gracious and appreciative of Magnani's talent and content to play a different role.

In 1958 Stapleton received her first Emmy Award nomination and a second nomination for a Tony Award. The Emmy nomination was for her portrayal of Sadie Burke in the two-part dramatization of Robert Penn Warren's great political novel, *All the King's Men,* which aired in May 1958 on NBC-TV's *Kraft Television Theatre.* The Tony nomination was for her performance as Aunt Ida in S.N. Behrman's *The Cold Wind and the Warm.* Stapleton was immensely fond of this play, in which she again co-starred with her friend Eli Wallach. It was one of the few parts she had played at that point which was not hard work. The incorrigible Jewish matchmaker, Aunt Ida, is a far cry from the tortured Williams heroines for which Stapleton was known. Aunt Ida is a comforting, positive force in the play and much less physically demanding than Serafina or Lady.

It was lucky for Stapleton that *The Cold Wind and the Warm* was such a positive experience because during its run, from December 1958 through March 1959, her life was quite eventful. While enjoying the success of her Broadway show, she received her first nomination for an Academy Award as Best Supporting Actress for her portrayal of Fay Doyle, the nymphomaniac wife in *Lonelyhearts,* the film based on the novella by Nathanael West. This was to be the first of many films she would make. In addition to Broadway and Hollywood successes, Stapleton and co-star Eli Wallach also were cast in the *Playhouse 90* television adaptation of Hemingway's *For Whom the Bell Tolls.* Wallach played Rafael and Stapleton played Pilar, the gypsy, and they both had to shuttle back and forth between morning film shoots, theatre matinees, evening film shoots and evening performances. At the same time, her marriage with Max Allentuck ended in divorce.

After the close of *The Cold Wind and the Warm* in the spring of 1959, Stapleton apparently took some time for herself. She had a brief run in William Inge's drama *Come Back, Little Sheba* the next August at Philadelphia's Playhouse in the Park. She played Lola, the distraught wife of a recovering alcoholic. Myron McCormick co-starred as Doc under the direction of Albert Lipton.

In February 1960, Stapleton made a memorable return to Broadway when she played the vindictive sister, Carrie Berniers, in Lillian Hellman's drama, *Toys in the Attic.* Although Stapleton earned another nomination for a Tony Award, she would not appear again on the legitimate stage for five years.

From 1960 to 1965 Stapleton concentrated her efforts on film and television. Her film roles included Vee Talbott in *The Fugitive Kind,* which was released in April 1960, Beatrice Carbone in Arthur Miller's *A View from the Bridge,* and the hilarious portrayal of Mama in the film musical *Bye Bye Birdie.* Her television appearances in this period included two roles in dramatic episodes of *The Naked City,* a comic gypsy on an episode of *Car 54, Where Are You?,* a Tennessee Williams one-act play on *The Play of the Week,* an episode of *The Dupont Show* entitled "The Betrayal" in which she played a German scientist, a performance as the old Irish woman, Maurya, in a televised adaptation of Synge's *Riders to the Sea* for *The Robert Herridge Theater,* and a portrait of a homeless woman in the drama "One Drink at a Time," for the series *East Side/West Side.*

In July 1963 Stapleton remarried. Her second husband was the playwright David Rayfiel. The marriage lasted less than three years and ended in divorce.

Five years after her Broadway success in *Toys in the Attic* Stapleton was asked to perform another Tennessee Williams heroine, that of Amanda Wingfield in *The Glass Menagerie*. This revival came twenty years after the play's memorable debut with Laurette Taylor, but Stapleton was able to create a fresh image of Amanda and earned high praise from the critics. Her performance also garnered the Best Actress Award from Variety's Poll of New York Drama Critics. It took special courage for the actress to play Amanda because she was once again battling obesity. When the play opened she was nearing her fortieth birthday and weighed almost two hundred pounds. Nevertheless, the audiences responded warmly to Stapleton's Amanda and the play ran for 176 performances.

Stapleton was scheduled to play the lead role in *The Madwoman of Chaillot* in February 1965. This was to be the fourth show of the premiere season of the Lincoln Center Repertory Company in New York City. However, the departure of Robert Whitehead, who was the administrative head of the company, led to a controversial situation in which Arthur Miller and Elia Kazan also threatened to leave. In support of Whitehead, Stapleton dropped out of the production which led to the cancellation of it.

In 1966 she appeared with Eileen Heckart in a charming adaptation of Lorees Yorby's one-act play, *Save Me a Place at Forest Lawn,* which was broadcast on WNET's *New York Television Theatre* series. Heckart and Stapleton played two elderly friends who were planning their burial services. She also returned to Broadway in a popular 1966 revival of *The Rose Tattoo*. Stapleton once again found great success as Serafina, the role she had created on Broadway fifteen years earlier. This performance was captured in a sound recording on Caedmon Records—her first album.

The next few years of Stapleton's career reveal her range and diversity. Not only did she perform in various media (stage, screen, television, recording), but she also proved herself equally gifted in low comedy and high drama. At the end of 1967 Stapleton won her first Emmy Award for her performance in "Among the Paths to Eden," a Truman Capote story adapted for television. She played a middle-aged spinster who waits among the monuments in a cemetery in the hopes of finding a husband. The film was combined with two other Capote stories and released as a film in 1969 entitled *Truman Capote's Trilogy*. In each case, Stapleton was acclaimed for her sensitive performance.

Only two months after receiving the Emmy Award, the actress garnered another Tony Award nomination and rave reviews for her tour de force performances in three roles in the Broadway debut of Neil Simon's comedy, *Plaza Suite*. It was a new Maureen Stapleton who appeared on the stage of the Plymouth Theatre. Whereas she had weighed about 210 pounds only a year earlier (while undergoing the stress of a divorce), by the premiere of *Plaza Suite* she had trimmed down to a svelt 139 pounds. Thus she played the three parts of Karen Nash, Muriel Tate, and Norma Hubley in a fabulously successful run of more than a thousand performances. It was to be her longest Broadway run and she would share it with several fine leading men, including George C. Scott, Nicol Williamson and E. G. Marshall. In 1971, when *Plaza Suite* was made into a film, Walter Matthau played the three male roles but the female roles were split up so that Stapleton played Karen Nash and Lee Grant and Barbara Harris played the other women's roles.

In the wake of her success with *Plaza Suite*, Stapleton was considered for other comic roles. In 1969 she appeared in *Johnny Carson's Repertory Company in an Evening of Comedy* on NBC-TV and teamed up again with George C. Scott for a television comedy, *Mirror, Mirror, Off the Wall*. She was then cast in a funny cameo role in a Broadway play by Ron Clark and Sam Bobrick, *Norman, Is That You?* It closed, however, after only twelve performances.

Stapleton returned to dramatic roles in her next film, *Airport*, which opened in March 1970. Her wrenching performance as the despondent wife of the man who wants to blow up the airplane earned her a second Oscar (Academy Award) nomination and also a nomination for a Golden Globe Award. The film was a huge commercial success and led to the popularity of disaster films in the 1970s.

After Stapleton's sparkling success in Neil Simon's comedy, *Plaza Suite*, Simon chose to write a play for her. That play was *The Gingerbread Lady*. It is a mark of success to have a play written for a particular actor. Stapleton was so honored throughout the decade of the 1970s. The scripts by Tennessee Williams have already been mentioned but one must also add the role of Evy Meara in Simon's *The Gingerbread Lady*, written in 1970, the title role in *The Secret Affairs of Mildred Wild*, written by Paul Zindel in 1982, the part of Gladys Boughton in *The Club Champion's Widow*, written by John Ford Noonan for her in 1978, and the role of Mrs. Shandig in Milan Stitt's *The Runner Stumbles* in 1979. Zindel had also written his first two plays for Stapleton, although she did not appear in either of them; these were *And Miss Reardon Drinks a Little* and *The Effect of Gamma Rays on Man-in-the-Moon Marigolds* (which won the Pulitzer Prize).

Perhaps the role most closely modelled on Maureen Stapleton's own personality, however, is that of Evy Meara. The part is that of a recovering alcoholic cabaret singer who is divorced and trying to get her life together, trying to be there for her teenage daughter. At the start of the play Evy has just returned from a drunk tank, has lost lots of weight and is apparently on the upswing. Stapleton once said that Simon must have been listening under her bed when he wrote the script. One aspect of her personality that Simon accurately captured is Stapleton's colorful vocabulary. In his book, *All People Are Famous*, Harold Clurman made this observation about it: "Maureen Stapleton's 'fishwife' vocabulary—an 'impediment of speech,' Neil Simon wittily called it—makes it difficult to give credence to the fact that she is a constant reader of Keats and Yeats. But it is so. She must have been a victim in her early life of some nameless wound; to heal it she requires the escape of acting, the solace of close embrace and constant companionable reassurance" (1974, 245).

Stapleton's performance of Evy Meara earned her many accolades, including the Tony Award for Best Actress, the Drama Desk Award and the New York Drama Critics Poll. It is unfortunate that the film was not made until eleven years later and that Stapleton's performance of Evy Meara was not recorded. Instead, Marsha Mason played the role of Evy in the 1981 film.

The Gingerbread Lady was a high point in Stapleton's career, but many accomplishments still lay ahead of her. In May 1971, just as the run of the play was ending, she had two films released, *Plaza Suite* and

Summer of '42 in which only her voice was heard as that of Hermie's mother. In the same film Stapleton's daughter, Kathy, made her film debut as Aggie, the young girlfriend of Hermie. That same year Stapleton co-starred with Jason Robards in a revival of *The Country Girl* which originated at the Kennedy Center and moved to Broadway where she received favorable reviews.

In 1972 Stapleton returned to Broadway in another comedy that had been written for her, *The Secret Affairs of Mildred Wild*. This fantasy by the Pulitzer Prize winning author, Paul Zindel, was a disappointment in many ways. It seemed a perfect role for Stapleton because it was about an unassuming woman who is obsessed with the movies, as Stapleton had been for years in her youth. Stapleton received much support and sympathy for being mired in such insubstantial material and the farce closed after twenty-three performances. It would be almost six years before she would return to the Broadway stage.

In the interim, she performed in regional theatre, on television and film and made several sound recordings. On stage she repeated her famous roles, playing Evy Meara at the North Shore Theatre in Massachusetts, Serafina at the Walnut Theatre for the Philadelphia Drama Guild, and Amanda Wingfield at the Circle in the Square Theatre, off-Broadway, and in Chicago. She also appeared in Los Angeles as Juno in the Mark Taper Forum's production of *Juno and the Paycock* with co-stars Walter Matthau and Jack Lemmon.

In 1976 she was a guest artist at the College of Santa Fe where she agreed to appear in a play directed by her good friend, Kim Stanley. The play, amazingly enough, was *Waiting for Godot* by Samuel Beckett. Stapleton played Estragon in a cross-cast production directed by Stanley. Estragon and Pozzo are male roles that Stanley changed to female roles. The rest of the cast were students: William Jones (Vladimir), Sue Goodson (Pozzo), Jamie O'Neill (Lucky) and Herman Varos (boy). The play ran for four performances, 18 to 21 November 1976, in the Greer Garson Theatre. John C. Weckesser was producer; Larry Schultz designed the sets and costumes. This production was the only time Stapleton ever ventured into absurdist material and she admitted that it was not her cup of tea, although it was interesting to explore a Beckett play.

While she was away from the neon of Broadway, Stapleton also began to make several sound recordings and do voiceovers for animated features. Stapleton's raspy, honeyed voice had already been captured in the 1967 sound recording of the revival of *The Rose Tattoo* and as the voice of Hermie's mother in the film *Summer of '42*. In 1972 she was one of the voices in Faith Hubley's animated special about earth's geology, *Dig*, and in 1974 she and Pat Hingle made two recordings for the Caedmon label: *A Book of Americans* is a collection of light verse by Stephen Vincent Benet and Rosemary Benet and *Journeys: Prose by Children* consists of readings from the writings of children, directed by Marianne Mantell.

In 1975 Stapleton received her only nomination for a Grammy Award for her reading of *To Kill a Mockingbird*, Margaret Albrecht's adaptation of Harper Lee's novel about a lawyer's defense of a black man in a small town in Alabama in the thirties. Paul Kresh directed Stapleton in this reading; the album was produced by Miller-Brody Productions. Other recordings include Stapleton as the voice of Mother Earth in *The Cosmic Eye* (another Hubley animated feature produced in 1985 by Walt Disney Home Video) and two 1976 albums for Caedmon, *"The Lottery" and Other Stories* and *"Summer People" and "The Little House"*—on both of these albums Stapleton read stories by Shirley Jackson. Stapleton has had an opportunity to sing on stage but she has only made one recording of songs. On an album titled *Ben Bagley's Vincent Youmans Revisited* she sings "Keeping Myself for You" and "I'm Glad I Waited."

During the 1970s Maureen Stapleton also made some memorable appearances on the small screen. In 1974, for the *GE Theatre*, she played a housewife who starts a consciousness-raising group in Fay Kanin's award-winning teleplay, "Tell Me Where It Hurts." And she played yet another Tennessee Williams' part, that of Big Mama, in NBC's 1976 broadcast of *Cat on a Hot Tin Roof.* Laurence Olivier produced the play and starred in the role of Big Daddy; Maggie and Brick were portrayed by Natalie Wood and Robert Wagner. In 1975 and 1977 Stapleton received two more nominations for Emmy Awards. The first was for her performance in the made-for-tv movie, *Queen of the Stardust Ballroom,* in which she co-starred with Charles Durning as a lonely couple who meet and fall in love in a ballroom dance hall. (The movie became the basis for the Broadway musical, *Ballroom.*) The second Emmy nomination was for her portrayal of Kate Thornton in "The Gathering" for *ABC Theatre*, a teleplay that won the Emmy for Best Special of 1977-78.

Stapleton also made another television series pilot in 1977. This one, *There's Always Room,* called for her to play an eccentric, well-to-do woman who opens her Los Angeles home as a boarding house. Like her other pilots, *The Old Knickerbocker Music Hall* and *Private Sessions, There's Always Room* was promising but did not develop into a series.

Robert Lewis, who had been Stapleton's first teacher at the Actors Studio, enlisted the actress' participation in a venture he started in 1976. Lewis began an actor's workshop to prove that American actors were as adept at playing highly stylized or classical roles as they were at playing modern realistic drama. The workshop developed into the Robert Lewis Acting Company, which produced a season of plays at the College of New Rochelle, New York. Stapleton offered to appear in the first production and John Ford Noonan (a playwright who had studied at Yale Drama School where Lewis had headed the theatre program) came forward with an original script he had written for Stapleton. This was *The Club Champion's Widow* which was staged in January 1978. The production was fairly well received, but the company did not survive the first season, so it was Stapleton's only opportunity to work with them. Lewis remembers the occasion fondly and observes

> it also afforded me the great pleasure of directing Maureen again and watching her work. Some actors want to analyze and understand their characters completely in their heads first, make choices from that understanding, and gradually fill those choices in with justified experience and behavior. Maureen adopts a more instinctive approach. Without deciding on any specific path, she allows the character to grow day by day, using her extraordinary ability to believe in the situations of her part as they're revealed to her in rehearsal. Fellow actors as well as audience members sense this complete identification Maureen can make with the character she's playing (1984, 320-21).

In 1978 Stapleton returned to the Broadway stage when she and E. G. Marshall replaced Hume Cronyn and Jessica Tandy in *The Gin Game*. It had been six full years since she had appeared on Broadway. She would appear again in 1981 in the revival of *The Little Foxes*, a production that grabbed lots of attention from the press because it was the American stage debut of superstar Elizabeth Taylor. Nevertheless, Stapleton distinguished herself as the pathetic Birdie Hubbard and received accolades from all sides. In 1981 Maureen Stapleton was inducted into the Theatre Hall of Fame at the Uris Theatre.

Over the years Stapleton found the demands of live performance more and more taxing so that she frequently admitted that she preferred making films. In March 1978 she appeared in an educational film short produced by Phoenix Films, *Sunday Dinner*, in which she played a pushcart lady who is homeless. After that, however, she concentrated her efforts on major releases.

In August 1978 Stapleton won the New York Film Critics Circle Award, the Los Angeles Film Critics Association Award and earned another Oscar nomination as Best Supporting Actress for her portrayal of Pearl in Woody Allen's unique film *Interiors*. Although this was her ninth film, in the next ten years she would make fourteen more major releases. Stapleton has always been a character actress and by the late seventies, when she was in her fifties, she began to play a remarkable range of women. Whereas her early stage and screen career was predominantly dramatic roles, Stapleton established herself as a versatile comedienne, playing such roles as the Irish washer-woman and gangster's mother in *Johnny Dangerously*, the sweet little bag lady in *On the Right Track*, the looney real estate crook in *The Money Pit*, and the endearing Aunt Lisa in *Made in Heaven*. Of course she was among a whole crop of charming senior citizens (including Jessica Tandy, Hume Cronyn, Jack Gilford, Gwen Verdon and Don Ameche) in *Cocoon* and its sequel, *Cocoon: The Return*.

Stapleton's dramatic roles in film were even more impressive. In spite of the bold sensationalism of *The Fan*, Stapleton's portrayal of the pragmatic secretary, who is victimized as a warning to her celebrity employer, was chillingly effective. So was her convincing performance as the priest's illiterate housekeeper, Mrs. Shandig, in *The Runner Stumbles*, a role created for her by Milan Stitt. In Barbra Streisand's dramatic screen adaptation of the stage play, *Nuts*, Stapleton created a sensitive portrait of the tortured woman who learns her daughter has been abused by her step-father.

However, her most outstanding performances in recent years have been in two films that are impressive in vastly different ways. The first was a "sleeper"—a film which found its audience in spite of its notable lack of violence, sex, or controversy. This was *Sweet Lorraine*, a film in which Stapleton starred in 1987. The Lorraine is a summer resort hotel in the Catskills and Stapleton played the aging proprietor who has raised her family and fostered the tradition of a decent family-run establishment until she just cannot carry on anymore. It was a film that revolved around the persona of Stapleton, who brought a subtle dignity and wisdom to the role of Lillian Garber.

Stapleton's most exciting film portrayal was that of Emma Goldman in *Reds*—Warren Beatty's 1981 epic about the lives of John Reed and Louise

Bryant. Stapleton won the Academy Award as Best Supporting Actress, the National Society of Film Critics Award and the British Academy Award for this incisive, authentic performance.

The actress is now semi-retired but continues to work in television or film, as the opportunity presents itself. Over the last few years she's played a robot in *The Electric Grandmother,* a Ray Bradbury story filmed for NBC, the Red Queen (opposite Colleen Dewhurst) in *Alice in Wonderland,* and a variety of mothers, aunts and eccentrics in television dramas and sitcoms. Most recently, Stapleton gave an impressive performance in the television docudrama, *Last Wish,* in which she played a terminal cancer patient who chooses to commit suicide.

Today Stapleton, who is known to close friends as "Mo," gives first priority to her family, friends and to her own needs. She is a grandmother and enjoys spending time with her children and grandchildren. Throughout her career, Stapleton has reiterated the importance of her family. She has often worked out of necessity and regrets not having had more time for them. Now that she can choose, she chooses to be a homebody.

Stapleton's career has been rich and eclectic. Although she has never been a superstar, she has always been a star—one who has scaled emotional heights on the stage and screen and in her personal life. She has sometimes anchored inferior material, making it seem better than it was but she has also had her moments of glory. Moreover, she has always inspired the casts and audiences who partake of her unique talent for creating living, breathing, three-dimensional characters. Her great friend, Tennessee Williams, said, "Maureen Stapleton, I think is an absolute genius and one of the total innocents of the world, you know. Very self-destructive. She's a genius because her talent doesn't seem to come from anywhere. It just comes out of her fingertips and her toes and her kneecaps" (cited by Reed 1974, 37). That ineffable talent has made her a truly original American artist who has made a significant contribution to the stage, cinema and television.

Chronology

This **Chronology** demonstrates how effortlessly Maureen Stapleton has made the transition from the stage to the silver screen to the home screen. Listed below are significant events from her personal life and her major performances which are cross-indexed to later sections of this book. Stage performances are indexed with the letter S followed by a number (e.g., **S03**); film performances are indexed with the letter F followed by a number (e.g., **F03**); television performances are indexed with the letter T followed by a number (e.g., **T03**).

21 June 1925	(Lois) Maureen Stapleton was born in Troy, New York. Her parents were John P. Stapleton and Irene Walsh Stapleton.
26 October 1946	Made her Broadway debut in Guthrie McClintic's production of *The Playboy of the Western World* (**S01**).
September 1947	Became a charter member of the Actors Studio where she trained with Robert Lewis and Lee Strasberg.
3 October 1948	Made her television debut in a series of live dramas presented by the Actors Studio for ABC (**T01**).
July 1949	Married Max Allentuck, general manager to producer Kermit Bloomgarden.
22 February 1950	Received favorable notices for her portrayal of Emily in Arthur Laurents' *The Bird Cage* at the Coronet Theatre, New York (**S05**).
8 July 1950	Had her first child, Daniel Vincent Allentuck.
3 February 1951	Achieved stardom as Serafina Delle Rose in Tennessee Williams' *The Rose Tattoo* (**S06**). The play ran for three hundred performances before a

	six-month national tour (**S07**). Stapleton received her first Tony Award for Best Actress.
3 May 1953	Made the first of several appearances on the *Philco Playhouse* on NBC-TV (**T05, T06, T07**).
9 December 1953	Stapleton co-starred with José Ferrer in Margaret Webster's production of *Richard III* at City Center Theatre, New York. Stapleton received fine reviews for her portrayal of Anne (**S10**).
11 May 1954	Received excellent critical response for her performance as Masha in *The Seagull* at the Phoenix Theatre, New York (**S11**).
16 October 1954	Daughter Katherine born.
January -May 1955	Stapleton had another success in a Tennessee Williams' role when she played Flora Meighan in the world premiere of *Twenty-Seven Wagons Full of Cotton* (**S12**).
21 March 1957	Highly praised for her creation of Lady Torrance in Tennessee Williams' *Orpheus Descending* in the play's Broadway premiere (**S13**). The play itself received mixed reviews.
14 and 21 May 1958	Received her first Emmy nomination for her portrayal of Sadie Burke in the two-part dramatization of *All the King's Men* for the *Kraft Television Theatre* on NBC-TV (**T15**).
8 December 1958	Co-starred with Eli Wallach in *The Cold Wind and the Warm* on Broadway (**S14**). She received a nomination for a Tony Award for Best Actress.
February 1959	Marriage with Max Allentuck ended in divorce.
4 March 1959	Received her first Academy Award nomination as Best Supporting Actress for her film debut in *Lonelyhearts* (**F01**).
12 and 29 March 1959	Portrayed Pilar the Gypsy in the *Playhouse 90* dramatization of Hemingway's *For Whom the Bell Tolls* (**T16**).
25 February 1960	Portrayed Carrie Berniers in *Toys in the Attic* at the Hudson Theatre (**S15**). For the second time in as many years she received a Tony Award nomination for Best Actress. Nevertheless, this was to be her last appearance on stage for the next five years.

14 April 1960	The film of *Orpheus Descending* opened under the title of *The Fugitive Kind* (**F02**). The role of Lady Torrance, which Stapleton had originated on Broadway three years earlier, was given to Anna Magnani and Stapleton was cast as Vee Talbott.
22 January 1962	Stapleton's third film, *A View from the Bridge*, opened to generally positive reviews (**F03**).
4 April 1963	Film, *Bye Bye Birdie*, offered Stapleton a chance to show her comic talents as the incorrigible mother of Dick Van Dyke who played a timid, would-be songwriter (**F04**).
July 1963	Married playwright David Rayfiel.
4 May 1965	Stapleton returned to the stage as Amanda Wingfield in the revival of *The Glass Menagerie* at the Brooks Atkinson Theatre. She won the Best Actress Award from *Variety's* Poll of New York Drama Critics (**S16**).
June 1966	Marriage to David Rayfiel ended in divorce.
20 October 1966	Returned to her most famous role, that of Serafina, in the revival of Williams' *The Rose Tattoo* at the City Center Theatre. The production moved to the Billy Rose Theatre, where it played through the end of the year (**S17**). She also made a sound recording of this performance for the Caedmon label.
17 December 1967	Stapleton earned her first Emmy Award for her portrayal of Mary O'Meaghan in Truman Capote's story, "Among the Paths to Eden," which was produced on ABC-TV as a *Xerox Special* (**T27**). This story was combined with other Capote dramas in the 1969 film *Truman Capote's Trilogy* (**F05**).
14 February 1968	Played three roles in Neil Simon's comedy, *Plaza Suite*. Her co-star was George C. Scott. Stapleton received rave reviews and a Tony Award nomination for Best Actress (**S18**).
5 March 1970	Film *Airport* opened and became a huge commercial success. Stapleton was nominated for another Academy Award (this was her second Oscar nomination) and for a Golden Globe Award for Best Supporting Actress (**F06**).

13 December 1970	Stapleton's performance as the alcoholic Evy Meara in Neil Simon's *The Gingerbread Lady* earned her a Tony Award for Best Actress. She also won the Drama Desk Award and the New York Drama Critics Poll (**S20**).
12 November 1971	Co-starred with Jason Robards in Odets' *The Country Girl*. The production opened at the Kennedy Center and moved to Broadway (**S21**).
12 March 1974	Played a housewife who starts a consciousness-raising group in Fay Kanin's Emmy Award-winning teleplay, "Tell Me Where It Hurts" on the *GE Theatre* (**T31**).
7 November 1974	Played Juno in the Mark Taper Forum's production of *Juno and the Paycock* in Los Angeles in a cast that included Walter Matthau and Jack Lemmon (**S24**).
1975	Was nominated for a Grammy Award for her sound recording of *To Kill a Mockingbird*.
13 February 1975	Stapleton and her co-star, Charles Durning, both received Emmy nominations for their performances as a couple who meet and fall in love in a ballroom dance hall in *Queen of the Stardust Ballroom* on CBS-TV (**T32**).
6 December 1976	Played Big Mama in NBC-TV's broadcast of *Cat on a Hot Tin Roof*. Her co-star was Laurence Olivier in the role of Big Daddy (**T33**).
4 December 1977	Received another Emmy nomination for her performance in *The Gathering,* a made-for-television movie which also starred Ed Asner (**T35**). The telefilm was so popular a sequel was made two years later entitled *The Gathering: Part II* (**T37**).
2 August 1978	Film *Interiors* opened (**F09**). Stapleton received another Academy Award nomination in the Best Supporting Actress category. She also received Best Supporting Actress Awards from the New York Film Critics Circle and the Los Angeles Film Critics Association.
16 November 1979	Stapleton received acclaim for her portrayal of Mrs. Shandig in the film, *The Runner Stumbles* (**F11**).

5 April 1981	Stapleton was inducted into the Theatre Hall of Fame at the Uris Theatre.
7 May 1981	Gave a heart-rending portrayal of Birdie Hubbard in the Broadway revival of *The Little Foxes* (**S28**) that starred Elizabeth Taylor. This was to be Stapleton's last stage appearance in the decade; hereafter she concentrated her efforts in film and television.
4 December 1981	Stapleton won the Academy Award for Best Supporting Actress for her portrayal of Emma Goldman in *Reds*. She also won the National Society of Film Critics Award and the British Academy Award for this performance (**F14**).
3 October 1983	Colleen Dewhurst and Maureen Stapleton played the Red and White Queens in a televised production of "Alice in Wonderland" (**T40**).
21 December 1984	Film, *Johnny Dangerously*, opened with generally positive reviews (**F15**).
21 June 1985	Film, *Cocoon*, released. Stapleton was among a stellar cast of character actors, including Hume Cronyn, Jessica Tandy and Jack Gilford, in this sci-fi fantasy about a kind of fountain of youth (**F16**).
26 March 1986	Played a lovable crook in the film, *The Money Pit*, which opened with favorable reviews (**F17**).
6 May 1987	Stapleton starred in the film, *Sweet Lorraine*, about a kind and wise woman proprietor of a summer resort hotel in the Catskills. It was a gentle film which, nevertheless found its audience (**F19**).
6 November 1987	Stapleton delighted audiences as Aunt Lisa in the film, *Made in Heaven*, which featured Kelly McGillis and Timothy Hutton. The film received excellent reviews (**F20**).
20 November 1987	Barbra Streisand produced and starred as Claudia Draper, a call girl who has murdered a client, in the film, *Nuts*. Stapleton gave a dramatic performance as Claudia's mother (**F21**).
23 November 1988	Stapleton was among the all-star cast to return in *Cocoon: The Return* (the sequel of *Cocoon*). The latter film received less critical acclaim, but was still quite a commercial success (**F23**).

12 January 1992   Stapleton gave an impressive performance in *Last Wish*, a made-for-television movie which explored the controversial issue of the right-to-die (**T48**).

Stage Performances

In this section, **Stage Performances**, the major stage appearances of Maureen Stapleton are listed in chronological order with the name of the theatre, opening and closing dates, production credits, cast, synopsis, reviews and commentary. Productions which had more than one venue will be found under the Broadway listing unless the cast is significantly changed, then that production will be listed separately.

Stapleton's summer stock credits, her private performances at the Actors Studio and other minor performances are described in the **Biography** section of this book.

Date and page numbers are provided for reviews from the *New York Times*, and popular magazines like *Newsweek* which are widely available in libraries. For other newspapers, such as the *New York Post* or *Herald Tribune*, the reader is referred to *The New York Theatre Critic Reviews* (see **B44**), which is available in many libraries and has reprints of the reviews cited, compiled into volumes by chronological date.

S01   *THE PLAYBOY OF THE WESTERN WORLD*

Revival staged at the Booth Theatre, New York
Opened 26 October 1946
Closed 4 January 1947
Number of Performances: 81

Credits
Playwright: John Millington Synge. Producer: Theatre Incorporated. Director: Guthrie McClintic. Scenery and Costumes: John Boyt. Stage Managers: James Neilson and Mary T. Walker. Production Supervision: Norris Houghton. Managing Director: Richard Aldrich. Press: Francis Robinson and William Fields.

Cast
Margaret Flaherty, called Pegeen Mike	Eithne Dunne
Shawn Keogh	Dennis King, Jr.
Michael James Flaherty	J. M. Kerrigan
Philly Cullen	Barry Macollum

Jimmy Farrell	J. C. Nugent
Christopher Mahon	Burgess Meredith
Widow Quin	Mildred Natwick
Susan Brady	Mary Diveny
Honor Blake	Sheila Keddy
Nelly	Julie Harris
Sara Tansey	**Maureen Stapleton** (also understudy for Eithne Dunne)
Old Mahon	Fred Johnson

And Robin Humphrey, Mary Lou Taylor, Mary T. Walker, Paul Anderson, James L. O'Neil, Ford Rainey, Edith Shayne, Elmer Barlab and Charles Martin.

Synopsis

Synge's comedy is set in a village pub in an isolated coastal area of Ireland. Pegeen Mike is the hot-tempered daughter of pub owner Michael James Flaherty. She is also the unwilling object of the affection of the miserable Shawn Keogh. When a handsome young stranger arrives in the village, bragging about how he has murdered his brutal, alcoholic father, even the fiercely independent Pegeen joins the village girls in their abject adoration of the hero.

The young stranger, Christy Mahon, wins Pegeen's love only to be shamed when his "dead" father arrives and tells the villagers how his son had cracked his skull. Christy is exposed as a dreamer and charlatan with a gift for blarney. Pegeen sees him for what he is and the "playboy" reacts with an attempt to make his fantasy true by initiating another violent attack on his dad. This time the villagers are sure the blow is fatal but Christy is saved from hanging by his father's miraculous recovery.

The son and his father are reconciled and leave the village together, as Pegeen mourns the loss of her lover.

Reviews and Commentary

The Playboy of the Western World premiered at the Abbey Theatre in Dublin Ireland on 26 January 1907. That premiere and subsequent stagings in New York, Boston and Philadelphia caused riots in the audiences who objected to Synge's portrayal of Irish countryfolk. The play has, nevertheless, been revived frequently.

The Irish Players (from the Abbey Theatre) brought *Playboy* to New York in 1911 and at regular intervals after that. Guthrie McClintic's 1946 revival was the ninth production staged in New York. There was no out-of-town tryout, which was unusual for this time.

In McClintic's hands Synge's lyrical fantasy was reduced to a literal realism that some critics felt ill-served the play. Brooks Atkinson's review in the *New York Times* observes that "the performance is literal, as though 'The Playboy' were a naturalistic drama about country people instead of a vibrant dramatic poem edged with laughter at the tip of the wings" (28 October 1946, 18). George Jean Nathan concurred saying that the revival "rids the fine play of all its lyricism, all its great comic gusto, and all its normal effect." Nathan goes on to say that "Mr. McClintic missed entirely the intrinsic ironic nature of the comedy and staged it much as if it were half naturalistic problem drama, half literal melodrama" (1947, 138).

Other critics thought the production was more successful. Indeed, its run was extended beyond the planned closing date. The biggest failing seemed to be in the contrasting styles and Irish dialects of the players. The cast was a mixture of actors from Hollywood, Broadway and Ireland. Eithne Dunne (of Dublin's Gate Theatre) made her New York debut in the role of Pegeen opposite Burgess Meredith in the role of Christy. The cast also featured Mildred Natwick as the Widow Quin and Fred Johnson (an alumnus of the Abbey) as Old Mahon.

Maureen Stapleton made her Broadway debut in this production playing the minor role of the village girl, Sara Tansey. Stapleton also understudied Dunne and had the opportunity to play Pegeen Mike for a full week at the end of the run. So *Playboy* was an auspicious beginning for the actress. She continued to work with McClintic's company and at the Actors Studio and only four years after her role in this production she would take New York by storm in *The Rose Tattoo*.

*****

S02   *THE BARRETTS OF WIMPOLE STREET*

1947 Tour
Opened at the Cass Theatre, Detroit on 7 April 1947
Closed at the Geary Theatre, San Francisco on 7 June 1947

Credits
Playwright: Rudolf Besier.   Producer: Katharine Cornell.   Director: Guthrie McClintic.   Settings and Costumes: Jo Mielziner.   Stage Managers: James Neilson and David Stewart.   General Manager: Gertrude Macy.   Press: Lorella Val-Mery.

Cast

Doctor Chambers	Edward Cooper
Elizabeth Barrett Moulton-Barrett	Katharine Cornell
Wilson	**Maureen Stapleton**
Henrietta Moulton-Barrett	Emily Lawrence
Arabel Moulton-Barrett	Margaret Barker
Octavius Moulton-Barrett	Tony Randall
Septimus Moulton-Barrett	David Stewart
Alfred Moulton-Barrett	Richard Hylton
Charles Moulton-Barrett	Robert Duke
Henry Moulton-Barrett	Walter Craig
George Moulton-Barrett	James Grudier
Edward Moulton-Barrett	Wilfrid Lawson
	(replaced during tour by Sir Cedric Hardwicke)
Bella Hedley	Anne Jackson
Henry Bevan	Oliver Cliff
Robert Browning	Brian Aherne
Doctor Ford-Waterlow	Ivan Simpson
Captain Surtees Cook	David Orrick
Flush	Himself

Synopsis

The romance of Elizabeth Barrett and Robert Browning opens in Elizabeth's bed-sitting room in her father's home, 50 Wimpole Street, London, England. The year is 1845. Under a doctor's constant care, the frail poetess is confined to her couch, unable to walk unassisted. The house teems with Victorian gloom and Elizabeth's oppressive illness is worsened by family strife. The household is run by her father, Edward Moulton-Barrett. He is a disagreeable man, a dictator who forces his nine children to obey him in every regard. He specifically refuses to let any of them marry.

The opening scene establishes the family's devotion to Elizabeth and their fear and hatred of Barrett. In the second scene Elizabeth is expecting a visit from Robert Browning. It is to be their first meeting following a long correspondence. Browning arrives and confesses his deep devotion to Elizabeth. She is likewise taken with the handsome young poet. Over the next few months their mutual regard restores her strength.

Elizabeth's doctors prescribe a trip to Italy but her father refuses to give his consent. That crisis prompts Robert and Elizabeth to declare their love for each other. Barrett decides to move his family to the country in order to get his daughters, Elizabeth and Henrietta, away from their suitors. Elizabeth and Robert decide to marry but she hesitates to incur her father's wrath. When Barrett violently chastises Henrietta for asking permission to marry her own love, Elizabeth confronts her father. She then calls in Wilson, her devoted maid, and arranges her own secret marriage and escape to Italy.

On the day of the planned elopement Barrett unexpectedly returns to the house. He pleads with her, telling her how he needs her constant devotion. He reveals his total lack of love for his deceased wife and their other children. Elizabeth is moved to make her escape. She dashes off to the church with Wilson to meet and marry Robert.

Hours later the family convenes and learns of her escape. Barrett seethes with fury and orders her beloved pet dog, Flush, to be destroyed. However, Henrietta joyously announces that Flush has also escaped the dreadful household and gone with Elizabeth and Robert to Italy.

Reviews and Commentary

This play was perhaps the most famous of the productions of producer-actress Katharine Cornell and her husband, stage director Guthrie McClintic. Cornell's portrayal of the frail poetess thrilled audiences around the world for years. McClintic first staged the production in 1931 and the couple revived it on Broadway and toured regularly including a most successful tour for the troops in Europe during World War II. It is due to the role of Elizabeth and to the title roles in *Candida* and in *St. Joan* that Cornell earned her reputation as one of the First Ladies of the Theatre.

The tour traveled throughout America and included stops in Detroit, Des Moines, Omaha, Salt Lake City, Vancouver, Victoria, San Francisco and Los Angeles. During the tour Sir Cedric Hardwicke took over the role of the tyrannical father.

For Stapleton the tour was an important training ground, as she explained in an interview with Lillian Ross: "It was the best time of my life, going across the country, seeing all the big cities, and working with Miss Cornell and Mr. McClintic. I felt intoxicated all the time just being with the company . . . . Miss Cornell and Mr. McClintic did things in a way that was always considerate, always kind, always thoughtful. Sort of old fashioned ways . . . . They treated actors like people" (1961, 300).

*****

S03 *ANTONY AND CLEOPATRA*

Revival staged at the Martin Beck Theatre, New York
Opened 26 November 1947
Closed 13 March 1948
Number of Performances: 126

Credits
Playwright: William Shakespeare. Producer: Katharine Cornell. Director: Guthrie McClintic. Settings: Leo Kerz. Ladies' Costumes: Valentina. Men's Costumes: John Boyt. Music: Paul Nordoff. Stage Managers: James Neilson, Windsor Lewis and James Grudier. General Manager: Gertrude Macy. Company Manager: William G. Tisdale. Press: Francis Robinson and Lorella Val-Mery.

Cast

Philo, soldier of Antony	Alan Shayne
Demetrius, soldier of Antony	Theodore Marcuse
Antony, a triumvir	Godfrey Tearle
Cleopatra, Queen of Egypt	Katharine Cornell
A Messenger	David J. Stewart
Dolabella, soldier of Caesar	Robert Duke
Proculeius, soldier of Caesar	Charlton Heston
Iras, attendant on Cleopatra	**Maureen Stapleton**
Charmian, attendant on Cleopatra	Lenore Ulric
Alexas, attendant on Cleopatra	Oliver Cliff
Diomedes, a soothsayer	Eli Wallach
Enobarbus, friend to Antony	Kent Smith
Mardian, attendant on Cleopatra	Joseph Wiseman
Octavius Caesar, a triumvir	Ralph Clanton
Lepidus, a triumvir	Ivan Simpson
Agrippa, soldier of Caesar	David Orrick
Pompey, a pirate	Joseph Holland

And Martin Kingsley, Barnet Biro, Bruce Gordon, Betty Low, Dayton Lummis, Douglass Watson, Charles Nolte, Robert Carricart, Gilbert Reade, Rudulph Watson, Bruce Gordon, Anthony Randall, Ernest Rowan, Martin Kingsley, Oliver Cliff, John Russo, Peter Barno, Drummond Erskine, Milfred Hull, Orrin Redfield, Charles Holt, James Grudier and Lawrence Perron.

Synopsis

The play begins in the year 40 B.C. One of the triumvirs of Rome, Antony, grows tired of his political responsibilities and succumbs to the charms of the quintessential seductress, Cleopatra, Queen of Egypt. When trouble arises in Rome and Pompey threatens rebellion, Antony is forced to return home to quell the disturbance.   Octavius Caesar arranges a marriage between his sister, Octavia, and Antony in the hopes of strengthening the alliance and preventing Antony's return to Cleopatra.

The triumvirs (Antony, Caesar and Lepidus) meet with Pompey and agree to peace, which they celebrate in a drunken party aboard Pompey's galley. The peace is short-lived. As Enobarbus, Antony's closest friend, predicts, Antony cannot forget the charms of the Egyptian queen. Caesar takes power when he defeats Pompey and brings Lepidus up on conspiracy charges. Angered by Antony's desertion of Octavia, Caesar declares war on Antony.

Cleopatra urges Antony to meet Caesar at sea near Actium where she has her fleet. During the battle Cleopatra flees in her galley and Antony shamefully abandons the field to follow her. His friend Enobarbus then deserts Antony for Caesar. When Antony tries to make amends, Enobarbus commits suicide.

Antony and Caesar confront one another on land and Antony is betrayed by the Egyptians. When Cleopatra is charged with treachery, she hides and sends Antony word of her death. In his grief, Antony stabs himself only to receive word that Cleopatra lives. He is brought to her side where he dies in her arms. Caesar wins the day and captures Cleopatra, but is not able to restrain her from taking her own life.

Reviews and Commentary

Shakespeare's tragedy first appeared on a New York stage on 27 April 1846 at the Park Theatre. New York was to witness many great actors playing the Queen of Egypt: Helen Modjeska played Cleopatra in 1889, Julia Marlowe played her in 1909, Jane Cowl was highly praised for her performance in 1924 and Tallulah Bankhead played her in the 1937 production.

Katharine Cornell was producer of the 1947 production which was directed by her husband, Guthrie McClintic, and which featured herself as Cleopatra. Cornell's co-star, Godfrey Tearle, had performed the role of Antony earlier that year in the London production with Edith Evans. The Broadway performances were preceded by an out-of-town tour which began in Buffalo (Erlanger Theatre, 8 October 1947) and included stops in Cleveland (Hanna Theatre), Pittsburgh (Nixon Theatre), Detroit (Cass Theatre) and Toronto (Royal Alexandria Theatre). Stapleton apparently joined the cast on the road, as her name first appears in the program for the Cass Theatre.

The critics greatly applauded the grandeur and beauty of this production. The photographs of Cornell are a tribute to the majesty and classic style of her performance. Also laudable was McClintic's staging and his courage in presenting a virtually uncut text. However, the formality of the production diminished other elements in the play, as *New York Times'* critic Brooks Atkinson explains, "Miss Cornell's Cleopatra is formal, good-mannered, a little fastidious. This is what well-bred people would like to think a Shakespeare tragedy is. It is pictorial, but drafty . . . .

[the production is] a stately ritual which is admirable but detached and scholarly" (27 November 1947, 49).

*****

S04 *DETECTIVE STORY*

Broadway premiere at the Hudson Theatre, New York
Opened 23 March 1949
Moved to the Broadhurst Theatre on 3 July 1950
Closed 12 August 1950
Number of Performances: 581

Credits
Playwright and Director: Sidney Kingsley. Producers: Howard Lindsay and Russel Crouse. Settings: Boris Aronson. Costumes: Millie Sutherland. Stage Managers: David Gray, Jr. and Arthur Hughes. General Manager: Herman Bernstein. Company Manager: Warren P. Munsell, Jr. Press: Leo Freedman and Abner D. Klipstein.

Cast

Detective Dakis	Robert Strauss
Shoplifter	Lee Grant
Detective Gallagher	Edward Binns
Mrs. Farragut	Jean Adair
Joe Feinson	Lou Gilbert
Detective Callahan	Patrick McVey
Detective O'Brien	John Boyd
Detective Brody	James Westerfield
Mr. Sims	Les Tremayne
Detective McLeod	Ralph Bellamy
Arthur Kindred	Warren Stevens
Patrolman Barnes	Earl Sydnor
1st Burglar, Charlie	Joseph Wiseman
2nd Burglar, Lewis	Michael Strong
Mrs. Bagatelle	Michelette Burani
Dr. Schneider	Harry Worth
Lt. Monoghan	Horace McMahon
Susan Carmichael	Joan Copeland
Patrolman Keogh	Byron C. Halstead
Patrolman Baker	Joe Roberts
Willy	Carl Griscom
Miss Hatch	**Maureen Stapleton**
Mrs. Feeney	Sarah Grable
Mr. Feeney	Jim Flynn
Crumb-Bum	Archie Benson
Mr. Gallantz	Garney Wilson
Mr. Pritchett	James Maloney
Mary McLeod	Meg Mundy

And Alexander Scourby, Michael Lewin, Ruth Storm, John Alberts, Joseph Ancona and Jacqueline Paige.

Synopsis

Kingsley's play is best described as a crime melodrama. He uses the setting of a New York police station as a breeding ground for pathos, humor and tragedy. The play revolves around Detective McLeod who takes it upon himself to mete out justice. McLeod is both a man of high principles and an embittered, sadistic public servant. He has suffered from an alcoholic, abusive father and so sees the world in blacks and whites.

Several story lines converge in the play to lead it to a tragic end. McLeod is determined to prosecute a young man, Arthur Kindred, who has stolen money from his boss. McLeod's fanatical compulsion to make the criminal pay for his crime blinds him to the extenuating circumstances of Arthur's case: he is a war-hero who took the money to impress his girlfriend; he regrets his actions and his boss agrees to drop the charges; even the pleas of the girl's sister fail to move the hard-boiled detective.

McLeod is even sterner with Dr. Schneider, a back-alley abortionist who has cost the lives of at least two women. Schneider's lawyer, Endicott Sims, warns McLeod against venting his hostility on his client. McLeod turns his attention to two burglars, Charlie and Lewis, who have been brought into the station house. As Lewis reveals their guilt, Charlie grows more unstable.

McLeod's self-righteousness is pushed to the breaking point when he learns that a potential witness against Dr. Schneider has died as a result of the surgery he performed on her. Although he has no proof, McLeod beats up the doctor. Sims suggests to the police lieutenant, Monoghan, that McLeod's fury is a personal vendetta. At first McLeod does not understand but then his wife, Mary arrives. She is the one fine thing in his life—at least until the truth comes out that Schneider had performed an abortion on Mary before she knew McLeod.

McLeod is overwhelmed with disgust and is unable to hide it from Mary. His lack of compassion moves her to leave him. Suddenly the burglar, Charlie, manages to get a gun. McLeod finds the solution to his anguish by wresting the gun away and getting fatally wounded in the process. Before the detective dies, however, he exhibits a measure of compassion by excusing Arthur for his mistake.

Reviews and Commentary

Sidney Kingsley wrote and directed his own play with great success. The production had only one brief tryout, nine performances at the Locust Street Theatre in Philadelphia, before going to Broadway for almost two years and 581 performances.

Critics were ecstatic about the play, its staging and its performance. A good bit of the credit went to designer Boris Aronson whose settings precisely captured the run-down Manhattan squad room. Uniform praise was also given to the entire cast. For example, Brooks Atkinson wrote in the *New York Times*, "the part of McLeod is magnificently played by Ralph Bellamy with a kind of tired, lumbering, introspective passion" (24 March 1949); and Richard Watts, Jr., critic for the *New York Post*, exclaimed: "splendidly played by Ralph Bellamy, who here gives the finest performance

I have ever seen him offer, McLeod has stature and dignity, evoking pity as well as terror" (24 March 1949).

Meg Mundy, who played Mary McLeod, and Lee Grant, who did a small turn as a shoplifter, were also applauded as were Les Tremayne, Harry Worth, and Warren Stevens, among others. Stapleton, however, played a very small role and was not mentioned although most reviews remarked on the excellence and fine ensemble playing of the entire cast.

*****

S05   *THE BIRD CAGE*

Broadway premiere at the Coronet Theatre, New York
Opened 22 February 1950
Closed 11 March 1950
Number of Performances: 21

Credits
Playwright: Arthur Laurents. Producers: Walter Fried and Lars Nordenson. Director: Harold Clurman. Settings and Lighting: Boris Aronson. Music Composer: Alec Wilder. Costumes: Ben Edwards. Stage Managers: James Gelb, David White and Russell Dennis. Press: Gerald Goode.

Cast

Frank	Mike Kellin
Cork	John Shellie
Eloise	Kate Harkin
India Grey	Eleanor Lynn
Ferdy	Sanford Meisner
Mr. Ripley	Heywood Hale Broun
Pearl	Jean Carson
Wally Williams	Melvyn Douglas
Vic	Laurence Hugo
Emily Williams	**Maureen Stapleton**
Renie Renay	Rita Duncan
Joe Williams	Wright King
Mr. Mack	Rudy Bond

Synopsis
The title of the play is taken from the name of the Manhattan night club, "The Bird Cage," where the action takes place. The central figure is club-owner Wally Williams, an ambitious and cruel man who will take any measures to retain control of the flashy club. Williams is opposed by his partner, Ferdy, who knows that Williams resorted to blackmail in order to obtain the club. Ferdy also fears that his daughter's deafness is somehow tied to the double-dealings that led to the partnership.

Unable to convince Ferdy from pulling out of the partnership, Williams double-crosses him. The third partner is Vic, the piano-player in the club. Williams takes care of him by crushing his hand in the piano.

Williams is estranged from his family—Emily, his socialite wife who has succumbed to alcohol and a teenage son, Joe. The club-owner takes advantage of the showgirls who need a job. Only one resists his advances— the lovely entertainer, India Gray. When Williams finds he cannot have India, he takes his revenge by sending his son to seduce her.

When his friends and family have all turned against him, Williams turns his anger on that which he loves the most—the Bird Cage itself. He sets fire to the club and so takes his own life.

Reviews and Commentary

Laurents' play opened out of town at the Shubert Theatre, New Haven, on 2 February 1950. It played also at the Locust Street Theatre in Philadelphia before coming into New York.

In spite of clear admiration for the acting and a fabulous, two-tiered revolving setting (designed by Boris Aronson), the critics condemned the play as a transparent melodrama. Laurents was aiming to present the nightclub as a microcosm of a villainous world crippled with fear, but his characterization of Williams left little room for self-awareness. As Richard Watts, Jr. observes, the play "is so artificially wrought that it never succeeds in being the pointed and ironic comment on life which he intended. And even as melodrama it has the grave fault of being so elaborately fabricated that it is, in the end, too artificial to have any genuine emotion or credibility about it" (23 February 1950).

Stapleton received unanimously good reviews for her portrayal of Emily, the defeated, alcoholic wife. The role of Emily was originally intended for Stella Adler, director Clurman's wife; Adler, however, was unavailable to do the show. Brooks Atkinson said that Stapleton "plays her big scene with warmth and candor" (23 February 1950, 32).

*****

S06   *THE ROSE TATTOO*

Broadway premiere at the Martin Beck Theatre, New York
Opened 3 February 1951
Closed 27 October 1951
Number of Performances: 300

Credits

Playwright: Tennessee Williams. Producer: Cheryl Crawford. Director: Daniel Mann. Settings: Boris Aronson. Costumes: Rose Bogdanoff. Incidental Music: David Diamond. Lighting: Charles Elson. Production Associate: Bea Lawrence. Stage Manager: Ralph DeLauney. General Manager for C. Crawford: John Yorke. Press: Wolfe Kaufman and Merle Debuskey.

Cast

Salvatore	Salvatore Mineo
Vivi	Judy Ratner
Bruno	Salvatore Taormina
Assunta	Ludmilla Toretzka

Rosa Delle Rose	Phyllis Love
Serafina Delle Rose	**Maureen Stapleton**
Estelle Hohengarten	Sonia Sorel
The Strega	Daisy Belmore
Giuseppina	Rossana San Marco
Peppina	Augusta Merighi
Violetta	Vivian Nathan
Mariella	Penny Santon
Teresa	Nancy Franklin
Father De Leo	Robert Carricart
Doctor	Andrew Duggan
Miss Yorke	Dorrit Kelton
Flora	Jane Hoffman
Bessie	Florence Sundstrom
Jack Hunter	Don Murray
Salesman	Eddie Hyans
Alvaro Mangiacavallo	Eli Wallach
Man	David Stewart
Man	Martin Balsam

Synopsis

Set in a village of Sicilian immigrants on the Gulf Coast, *The Rose Tattoo* is the story of Serafina Delle Rose. She is a proud, plump little seamstress with a twelve-year-old daughter and is pregnant with her second child. Her husband, Rosario, is a Sicilian of a good family who drives a truck in which he smuggles contraband. To Serafina this man (who has a rose tattooed on his chest) is an incomparable lover of mythic stature. She prides herself on their passionate relationship and claims the emblem of a rose briefly appeared on her breast the night she conceived the baby. This evening Rosario fails to return and when Serafina learns he has died in an accident, she loses the baby.

Three years later the widow has become an object of ridicule in the village. She wears a dirty old slip and displays her husband's ashes in a religious shrine. She is tormented by rumors that Rosario had been unfaithful to her and she has locked up her daughter, Rosa, so she cannot see Jack, a young sailor that Rosa met at a dance. Miss Yorke, the high school teacher, arrives to intercede for Rosa and get her to her high school graduation. Soon after Serafina is told that Rosario had had a long-term affair with a local woman blackjack dealer.

Serafina is devastated and, refusing to believe the lie, begs God for a sign. Almost at once a man appears—also a Sicilian truck driver—who resembles her late husband from the neck down only he has a clownish face and disposition and explains that his name, Alvaro Mangiacavallo, means "eat a horse." He is the son of the village idiot. They talk and she invites him back that evening.

When Alvaro returns he reveals that he, too, has a tattoo of a rose on his chest. Serafina is affronted but when she is given proof that her husband betrayed her she smashes his urn and takes Alvaro to her bed. Meanwhile Jack and Rosa return to the house and Rosa confesses her love and desire for the boy. With difficulty, Jack leaves, as Rosa promises to meet with him before he ships out.

Before daylight Alvaro emerges from Serafina's room and finds Rosa asleep on the sofa. He is huddled over her when Serafina enters and viciously attacks him pretending that he is an intruder. Rosa sizes up the situation and tells her mother to make him leave quietly before the neighbors are awakened. After his departure Serafina gives Rosa leave to go and meet Jack. She then confides to her friend that she felt the burning rose upon her breast once more. She joyfully goes to meet Alvaro.

Reviews and Commentary

The Rose Tattoo was the play which propelled Maureen Stapleton to stardom. In the role of Serafina, Stapleton demonstrated her gift for creating wildly emotional characters with great truth and compassion. The play premiered at the Erlanger Theatre in Chicago on 29 December 1950 and moved on to a lengthy Broadway run and extensive tour.

Some critics found Williams' play much too earthy and overtly sexual in spite of the fine acting. Others felt that the village characters weakened the construction. Audiences, however, responded favorably and so did many of the reviewers. Otis L. Guernsey, Jr., critic of the *New York Herald Tribune,* judged *The Rose Tattoo* to be the best new American play of the season. *New York Times'* critic Brooks Atkinson commended the fantasy and lyrical romanticism of what he called Williams' "folk comedy."

Stapleton received accolades from all sides. William Hawkins said "Miss Stapleton gives one of the most honest performances I remember ever witnessing. She hypnotizes herself into moving and even looking like this character whom she physically resembles not in the least" (5 February 1951). Brooks Atkinson wrote: "Maureen Stapleton's performance is triumphant. The widow is unlearned and superstitious and becomes something of a harridan after her husband dies. Miss Stapleton does not evade the coarseness of the part. But neither does she miss its exaltation. For Mr. Williams has sprinkled a little stardust over the widow's shoulders and Miss Stapleton has kept the part sparkling through all the fury and tumult of the emotion" (5 February 1951, 19).

Stapleton won the Tony Award for Best Actress for her portrayal of Serafina. It was her first Tony. The production also garnered Tony Awards for Best Play, Best Actor (Eli Wallach), Best Producer and Best Scenic Designer.

Stapleton's triumph as Serafina was all the more impressive since she was the second choice for the role. Serafina had originally been offered to the Italian actress Anna Magnani, but she was concerned that her English was insufficient and did not want to commit to a long run. It was a role that Stapleton would play again and again. Nevertheless, Magnani took the part when the play was made into a film.

*****

S07   *THE ROSE TATTOO*

Six-month North American tour
Opened at His Majesty's Theatre, Montreal on 29 October 1951
Closed at the Curran Theatre, San Francisco on 5 April 1952

Credits
Playwright: Tennessee Williams. Producer: Cheryl Crawford. Director: Daniel Mann. Setting Design: Boris Aronson. Costume Design: Rose Bogdanoff. Lighting: Charles Elson. Stage Managers: Paul A. Foley, William Krot and Claude Akins. Company Manager: Max Allentuck. Press: Wolfe Kaufman and Ned Armstrong.

Cast

Street Singer	Alfonso Cancelmo
Vivi	Dorothy Estler
Bruno	Sal Taormina
Assunta	Ludmilla Toretzka
Rosa Delle Rose	Sally Hester
Serafina Delle Rose	**Maureen Stapleton**
Estelle Hohengarten	Lila Paris
The Strega	Pearl Somner
Giuseppina	Rossana San Marco
Peppina	Augusta Merighi
Mariella	Sybil Levenson
Father De Leo	Martin Balsam
Doctor	William Major
Miss Yorke	Dorrit Kelton
Flora	Connie Davis
Bessie	Camila Ashland
Jack Hunter	Don Murray
Salesman	Claude Akins
Alvaro Mangiacavallo	Eli Wallach
Man	William Krot
Man	Bill Froelich

Synopsis
See **S06**.

Reviews and Commentary
The Rose Tattoo continued its success on this long tour. Stapleton was hereafter identified with the character of Serafina. She starred in revivals of *The Rose Tattoo* in 1966 and again in 1973.

*****

S08   *THE EMPEROR'S CLOTHES*

Broadway premiere at the Ethel Barrymore Theatre, New York
Opened 9 February 1953
Closed 21 February 1953
Number of Performances: 16

Credits
Playwright: George Tabori. Producers: Robert Whitehead and The Playwrights' Company. Director: Harold Clurman. Setting and Lighting: Lester Polakov. Costumes: Ben Edwards. Company Manager: Max

Allentuck. Stage Managers: Frederic de Wilde, Howard H. Fischer and
Chris Mahan. Press: Barry Hyams and Martin Schwartz.

Cast

Elek Odry	Lee J. Cobb
Bella, his wife	**Maureen Stapleton**
Ferike, his son	Brandon de Wilde
Peter, his brother	Anthony Ross
Granny	Tamara Daykarhanova
The Baron	Esmond Knight
1st Rottenbiller Brother	Michael Strong
2nd Rottenbiller Brother	Mike Kellin
The Fat Hugo	Philip Rodd
Mr. Schmitz	Howard H. Fischer
Mrs. Schmitz	Nydia Westman
The Man Without Shoes	David Clarke
A Boy	Richard Case
Milkman	Allan Rich
Policeman; Singer	John Anderson

Synopsis

Elek Odry is a professor of the classics in Budapest in 1930 but he has
lost his job for making politically inexpedient speeches and is condemned to
proofreading trashy Western novels to make a living. His thirteen-year-old
son, Ferike, idolizes him. When the boy realizes his father cannot afford a
Christmas tree, he cons his neighborhood chum, Fat Hugo, into
relinquishing the milk money in exchange for a membership in Ferike's
secret society, The Illegal Party of Boys. As Ferike rushes off to buy a tree,
Hugo's mother calls the police.

Elek and his devoted wife, Bella, reminisce about better days. Bella
convinces Elek to call her old beau, the Baron, who has connections to get
Elek another teaching position. The Baron arrives and it is evident he has
more interest in Bella's welfare than Elek's. However, he offers Elek a job
teaching high school. Elek swallows his pride and accepts although he
must sign a letter of apology. Ferike is disappointed in his father but before
Elek can explain, Ferike is arrested.

Elek, Bella and Elek's brother Peter all struggle to find some way to
help Ferike. When warned by the Baron that the house will be searched,
Elek hysterically begins burning his books. Ferike suddenly returns in the
hands of the twin special police, the Rottenbiller Brothers. The detectives
grill Elek about the stories Ferike has told them asking him to tell them
who is Hoot Gibson, Sherlock Holmes and the Scarlet Pimpernal. Elek tries
to explain they are characters from films and books, but the Rottenbillers
insist he must go with them. He gets a moment to talk to his son and uses
it to destroy the hero the son has imagined him to be. The boy shouts "Liar!"
as his father is taken away.

As the family waits for word of Elek, the Baron offers to take Bella
and the boy away to safety. She furiously refuses and waits for word from
Elek. When he comes home she and Ferike receive him coldly until he
describes what happened. They realize he has been tortured and has stood
up for his principles. The boy regains his hero and the father regains his
honor.

Reviews and Commentary

Critics drew parallels with other dramas of the year such as *The Children's Hour, The Crucible,* and *The Emperor's Clothes* because these plays all deal with children and their perception of truth, but Tabori's play was both praised and panned. Brooks Atkinson echoed much of the critical response when he wrote that "Mr. Tabori likes to write at random, putting in an amusing bit here and a trenchant bit there—hoping to make a dramatic point through indirection . . . . Although it looks profound, it is basically superficial, and too glib to get under the skin of its material" (10 February 1953, 24).

Stapleton received mixed reviews as well for her portrayal of the wife, Bella. Walter Kerr, writing in the *New York Herald Tribune,* said, "Maureen Stapleton, as a bewildered mother, suffers most from this rambling, impressionistic and utterly untheatrical literary style" (10 February 1953). William Hawkins disagreed, saying, "as the mother, she plays authentically a Chekhovian creature of gentleness and fantasy" (10 February 1953).

As for Stapleton's feelings about the play, this may have been her least favorite experience on stage. In interviews she has said that she thought she was terribly wrong for the role. Her disappointment was short-lived, however, as the production only ran for sixteen performances.

*****

S09   *THE CRUCIBLE*

Broadway premiere at the Martin Beck Theatre, New York
Opened 22 January 1953
Re-staged with cast changes; re-opened 1 July 1953
Closed 11 July 1953
Number of Performances: 197

Credits

Playwright: Arthur Miller. Producer: Kermit Bloomgarden. Director: Jed Harris. Set Design: Boris Aronson. Costume Design: Edith Lutyens. Music: Anne Ronnell and Alex Miller. Stage Managers: Del Hughes, Leonard Patrick and Donald Marye. Company Manager: S. M. Handelsman. Press: James Proctor, Merle Debuskey and Maxine Keith.

Original Cast

Betty Parris	Janet Alexander
Tituba	Jacqueline Andre
Rev. Samuel Parris	Fred Stewart
Abigail Williams	Madeleine Sherwood
Susana Walcott	Barbara Stanton
Mrs. Ann Putnam	Jane Hoffman
Thomas Putnam	Raymond Bramley
Mercy Lewis	Dorothy Jolliffe
Mary Warren	Jenny Egan
John Proctor	Arthur Kennedy

Rebecca Nurse	Jean Adair
Giles Corey	Joseph Sweeney
Rev. John Hale	E. G. Marshall
Elizabeth Proctor	Beatrice Straight
Francis Nurse	Graham Velsey
Ezekiel Cheever	Don McHenry
John Willard	George Mitchell
Judge Hathorne	Philip Coolidge
Deputy-Governor Danforth	Walter Hampden
Sarah Good	Adele Fortin
Hopkins	Donald Marye

Revised Cast (only roles that changed are listed; the others are as above)

Betty Parris	Judy Ratner
Rev. Samuel Parris	Donald Marye
Thomas Putnam	William Hussig
John Proctor	E.G. Marshall
Rebecca Nurse	Neil Harrison
Rev. John Hale	Del Hughes
Elizabeth Proctor	**Maureen Stapleton**
John Willard	Chris Gampel
Judge Hathorne	Ralph Bell
Deputy-Governor Danforth	Philip Coolidge
Hopkins	Edwin Gordon

Synopsis

The Salem witch trials of 1692 are the subject of Miller's play. The action begins in the home of Reverend Parris, the local preacher who has recently taken over the church at Salem and has offended some of his parishioners with his fire-and-brimstone sermons. Parris' daughter, Betty, and some of the other village girls have been discovered dancing around a fire at night with the black slave, Tituba. Fearing reprisals, Betty pretends to be under the influence of a spell. The prospect of witchcraft lures the local farmers and their wives who convene to pray while the preacher sends for the Reverend Hale, who is more experienced in the inexplicable doings of the devil.

The specter of witchcraft exacerbates tensions and hard feelings already within the community. Abigail, a beautiful but vicious girl, uses the circumstances to try to blackmail her former lover, John Proctor, into leaving his wife for her. John rejects her and Abigail gets revenge on Elizabeth Proctor (and all the other village women who she feels have slighted her) by bringing accusations of witchcraft against them.

Proctor can only weakly defend his family because he has avoided church and devotion out of distaste for Parris' religious leadership. Other villagers find the witchcraft charge a convenient solution to land disputes and other disagreements and soon the jails are bursting with women, old and young, devout and deluded. The action peaks in a scene where the girls demonstrate their possession by spirits. The authorities offer Proctor his life if he will sign a false confession. At first Proctor agrees, but in the final moment he decides his good name is more valuable than his life and he goes to the gallows with the other men and women who have also maintained their innocence. Abigail, having completed her deadly game, silently slips out of the town.

Reviews and Commentary

The Crucible opened on 22 January 1953 with Beatrice Straight and Arthur Kennedy in the leading roles of Elizabeth and John Proctor. After a six-month run, the play was re-staged with E.G. Marshall and Maureen Stapleton in those roles. (Marshall had played Reverend Hale in the premiere production.) This was the first opportunity for Stapleton to work with Marshall. She would later co-star with him in the stage versions of *Plaza Suite* and *The Gin Game* and in the film *Interiors*.

Miller's historical drama followed in the wake of his masterpiece, *Death of a Salesman*, which won the Pulitzer Prize and Drama Critics Award. It was, however, the political parallels of *The Crucible* which sparked the most interest in the play. *The Crucible* came to Broadway during the painful era of McCarthyism in which many theatre and film artists were blacklisted as suspected communists. The rampant accusations and presumed guilt of the accused were themes being played out in life and on the stage.

The parallels between Senator Joseph McCarthy's "witch hunt" and the witch hunt in the play may have colored the critics' opinions of the premiere. The gist of the response is that the first production was more intellectual than emotional or, as Richard Watts Jr. put it, Miller's characters "tend to be dramatized points of view, or points of emotional hysteria, rather than the human beings that would have made them more striking in the theatre" (23 January 1953).

The second version of the production apparently grew out of disagreements between Arthur Miller and director Jed Harris. Miller re-staged much of the play and added a scene between Proctor and Abigail that illuminates their prior relationship. Aronson also simplified the staging. The changes, according to Brooks Atkinson improved the play which, the critic said, "has acquired a certain human warmth that it lacked amid the shrill excitements of the original version" (2 July 1953, 20). Atkinson credited this change of focus, from the intellect to the heart to the performances of Stapleton and Marshall. Nevertheless, the play lasted less than two weeks in its new version.

*****

S10   *RICHARD III*

Revival staged at the New York City Center
Opened 9 December 1953
Closed 20 December 1953
Number of Performances: 15

Credits

Playwright: William Shakespeare. Producer: New York City Theatre Company. Director: Margaret Webster. Production Design: Richard Whorf. Production Supervision: Jean Dalrymple. Costume Design: Emeline Roche. Music Composed and Conducted by Alex North. Stage

Managers: Buford Armitage and Jess Kimmel.   Company Manager:
Gilman Haskell. Press: Reginald Denenholz.

Cast

Richard, Duke of Gloucester, (later Richard III)	José Ferrer
George, Duke of Clarence	Staats Cotsworth
Brackenbury	Paul Ballantyne
Lord Hastings	William Post, Jr.
Anne	**Maureen Stapleton**
Tressel	Tom Tryon
Berkeley	Benedict MacQuarrie
A Priest	G. Wood
Queen Elizabeth	Jessie Royce Landis
Earl Rivers	Philip Huston
Lord Grey	Bert Whitley
Duke of Buckingham	Vincent Price
Lord Stanley	John Straub
Marquis of Dorset	Robert Lansing
Queen Margaret	Florence Reed
Catesby	Eugene Stuckmann
1st Murderer	Martin Kingsley
2nd Murderer	Jack Bittner
Edward IV	Norman Roland
Young Clarence	John Glennon
Dowager Duchess of York	Margaret Wycherly
1st Citizen	Stanley Carlson
2nd Citizen	Jack Fletcher
3rd Citizen	Will Davis
Richard, Duke of York	Charles Taylor
Edward, Prince of Wales	John Connoughton
Lord Mayor of London	Leopold Badia
Bishop of Ely	James Arenton
Another Bishop	Wallace Widdecombe
A Messenger	Dehl Berti
Duke of Norfolk	Charles Summers
Sir Richard Ratcliff	Jay Barney
Lord Lovel	Robinson Stone
A Scrivener	Bill Butler
A Page	Sandy Campbell
Sir James Tyrell	Kendall Clark
1st Messenger	Peter Harris
2nd Messenger	Richard Cowdery
3rd Messenger	Robert Ludlum
Henry, Earl of Richmond	Douglas Watson
Sir James Blunt	Bill Butler
Sir William Brandon	Vincent Donahue
Earl of Oxford	John Glennon

And Jack Betts, Dehl Berti, Jack Bittner, Marc Breaux, Peter Buchan, Bill
Butler, David Post, Sandy Campbell, Stanley Carlson, Wyatt Cooper, Garry
Cowan, Will Davis, John Devoe, Vincent Donahue, Jack Fletcher, John

Glennon, Martin Kingsley, Walter Lawrence, Benedict MacQuarrie, Ray MacDonnel, Phil Prindle, Ray Rizzo, Kenneth Sleeper, Stanley Tannen, Tom Tryon, Bruce Webster, Bert Whitley, G. Wood, David Wright and Stefan Olsen.

Synopsis

Shakespeare's tragedy offers one of the greatest stage villains of all time, "that bottled spider, that foul bunch-back'd toad," Richard the Third. The action of the play is that Richard wants to be King of England and he methodically kills off every person in his way to obtain the crown.

His first obstacles are his two brothers, George, Duke of Clarence, and the present king, Edward IV. Richard turns Edward against Clarence who is then imprisoned in the Tower where Richard arranges his murder—drowning in a butt of malmsey wine. Meanwhile, Richard interrupts the funeral procession of the former king, Henry VI, and professes love to the Lady Anne (Henry's daughter). Anne gives in to Richard's malevolent charisma, even though he admittedly murdered both her father and her beloved husband.

King Edward takes ill and dies and Richard joins forces with the Duke of Buckingham to secure the throne. They imprison the supporters of Edward's queen (Elizabeth) and contrive to get the king's two young sons sent to the Tower. The queen's supporters are executed at Pomfret Castle and Buckingham convinces the populace to offer the crown to Richard.

Buckingham loses his nerve, however, when Richard suggests that he murder the little princes. Richard has Tyrell execute the children and proceeds to remove all other threats in his way. He imprisons the son of Clarence and arranges a convenient marriage for the daughter of Clarence. He also strengthens his claim on the throne when he has Anne murdered and proposes to marry his niece (Edward's daughter, Princess Elizabeth).

Meanwhile Buckingham has fled to align himself with Richard's enemy, Richmond. Richmond arrives with an army and is joined by English nobles. Buckingham is captured by Richard and executed. The final confrontation occurs on Bosworth Field. The night before the battle Richard is besieged by the ghosts of those he has sent to their untimely deaths. The next day Richard is killed by Richmond who accepts the crown and the hand of Elizabeth. Richmond becomes Henry VII and peace returns to England.

Reviews and Commentary

This *Richard III* was the third of a four-play series starring José Ferrer at the City Center Theatre. Ferrer's Richard came on the heels of *Cyrano de Bergerac* and *The Shrike*. Ferrer was supported by a rich array of talent, including Vincent Price in the role of Buckingham, Margaret Wycherly as the Dowager Duchess and Maureen Stapleton as the unfortunate Lady Anne.

Critics praised the production, especially the effective staging by Margaret Webster, but they found Ferrer's performance less laudatory than his other roles in this series. Brooks Atkinson said in the *New York Times* that this Richard was "prosaic" and "undistinguished" (10 December 1953, 65) and William Hawkins, writing in the *New York World-Telegram,* said Ferrer's Richard lacked clear motivation for his dastardly deeds.

Other actors fared better at the critics' hands.   Hawkins said "Maureen Stapleton has energetic excitement for the strange and difficult scene of Anne" (10 December 1953) and other critics also singled her out for praise.   The biggest failing in the production was lack of time to develop a coherent performance style among the many talents involved.

*****

S11   *THE SEAGULL*

Revival staged at the Phoenix Theatre, New York
Opened 11 May 1954
Closed 13 June 1954
Number of Performances: 40

Credits

Playwright: Anton Chekhov. Adaptation: Mira Rostova, Kevin McCarthy and Montgomery Clift.   Producers: T. Edward Hambleton and Norris Houghton.   Director: Norris Houghton.   Settings: Duane McKinney. Costumes: Alvin Colt.   Lighting: Klaus Holm.   Music Arranger: Max Marlin.   Stage Managers: Robert Woods, John Cornell and Karl Light. General Manager: Carl Fisher. Press: Samuel J. Friedman and Max Gendel.

Cast

Madame Irina Arkadina	Judith Evelyn
Constantin Treplev	Montgomery Clift
Peter Sorin	Sam Jaffe
Nina Zarechnaya	Mira Rostova
Shamrayev	Will Geer
Paulina	June Walker
Masha	**Maureen Stapleton**
Boris Trigorin	Kevin McCarthy
Dr. Dorn	George Voskovec
Medvedenko	John Fiedler
Yakov	Karl Light
Cook	Lou Polan
Housemaid	Sarah Marshall

Synopsis

Chekhov's play is a chamber piece of unrequited love.   The action takes place at a country estate in nineteenth century Russia.   Constantin Treplev, the high-strung son of the glamorous and beguiling actress Irina Arkadina, is a fledgling author who stands in the shadow of his mother's lover, Boris Trigorin.   Trigorin is a highly successful author who is, at age forty, as cynical as Treplev is idealistic.

Trigorin, Arkadina and her brother, Sorin (who owns the estate) are invited to a performance of Treplev's experimental play.   Other guests at the performance include Shamrayev and Paulina (who manage Sorin's estate), their daughter, Masha, the philosophic physician Dr. Dorn, and Medvedenko, the hapless, boring schoolteacher.   Almost every character loves someone who does not love him or her in return. Masha dresses in black and is "in mourning for her life" out of love for Treplev. Paulina loves Dr. Dorn who maintains affection for Arkadina. Medvedenko pines for Masha and Treplev showers his affection on the beautiful Nina, a young girl from the neighboring estate who is acting in his play.

At the performance of Treplev's "decadent" play Arkadina interrupts and makes fun of the play, to the great shame and embarrassment of her son, who stops the performance and runs into the forest. Treplev's rejection as an artist is deepened when Nina falls under the spell of Trigorin's ruthless charm. Treplev presents Nina with a seagull he has murdered—the symbol of his injured heart. When Nina shows the dead thing to Trigorin, it inspires him to write a story about a young girl casually destroyed by a man. Treplev's tries to shoot himself, but fails that too. Trigorin proceeds to seduce the innocent Nina who runs away to become an actress and Trigorin's mistress.

Two years later the characters come together again at the estate. Little has changed. Masha has married Medvedenko but is as unhappy as ever. Treplev has become a successful author but is still devout in his affections for Nina. Nina has come to realize that she has no talent for the stage; she has had a baby by Trigorin, but it died and Trigorin tired of her and returned to the indomitable Arkadina. Defiled and abandoned, Nina returns to Sorin's estate where Treplev waits for her. Nina's grip on reality is tenuous at best. She tells Treplev she is the seagull and that she is sorry but she still is passionately in love with Trigorin. After she flees into the night Treplev follows her. A shot is heard and word comes that Treplev has killed himself.

Reviews and Commentary

This was the fourth and final production of the first season of the Phoenix Theatre. The adaptation from the Russian was written by three actors in the cast, Clift, McCarthy and Rostova. Prior to the Phoenix production New York had seen several productions of *The Seagull* including a 1916 production by the Washington Square Players, a 1929 production by the Civic Repertory Company which featured Eva LeGallienne and Jacob Ben-Ami and the 1938 revival with Alfred Lunt and Lynn Fontanne.

The critics judged the 1954 production an ambitious, impressive but not entirely successful venture. Director Norris Houghton brought together many talented professionals who, nevertheless, had strongly conflicting performance styles. In his book, *Lies Like Truth,* Harold Clurman said that the play was "signally miscast in several important parts. I refer not only to individual actors but to a lack of homogeneity and correlation in the ensemble" (1958, 132). Clurman went on to criticize the clash of dialects and accents of the cast.

Montgomery Clift was praised for his sensitive, if overly American, portrayal of Treplev. Mira Rostova was faulted for her heavy Russian accent and insubstantial vocal projection. Walter Kerr commented that "young and well-meaning actors are always playing Chekhov to improve themselves. It seems to me that they should first improve themselves, and then play Chekhov" (12 May 1954). Stapleton, however, was highly acclaimed for her performance as Masha, a role she had played six years before at the Actors Studio. Kerr says that, although Masha is "given to lightly tragic posturing, she is earthy, pungent, and sharply aware. Miss Stapleton outlines these

contrasts very graphically, then ties them together into a believable whole."
For Stapleton *The Seagull* was an opportunity to perform with her favorite
acting teacher, Mira Rostova.

*****

S12   *TWENTY-SEVEN WAGONS FULL OF COTTON*

Broadway premiere at The Playhouse Theatre on a triple bill entitled
All in One
Opened 19 April 1955
Closed 28 May 1955
Number of Performances: 49

Production Credits
Playwright: Tennessee Williams.   Director: Vincent J. Donohue.
Producers: Charles Bowden and Richard Barr. Sets/Lighting: Eldon Elder.
Costumes: Pat Campbell.   Stage Managers: Barnett Owen and Neil
Laurence. Company Manager: Lawrence Farrell. Press: Phillip Bloom.

Cast
Flora Meighan	**Maureen Stapleton**
Jake Meighan	Myron McCormick
Silva Vicarro	Felice Orlandi

Synopsis
Flora and Jake Meighan live in a small house in Blue Mountain,
Mississippi. Jake is about sixty and is a corpulent, uncouth owner of an
independent cotton gin. His wife Flora is a younger, plump, simple-
minded woman who is victimized by the men in the play.
The action takes place on the front porch of the house which Jake
shares with his "baby doll" wife. Jake is seen exiting with a can of
flammable liquid and on his return Flora learns the Syndicate Plantation
has caught on fire. Jake explains that the fire will make money for them
because the Syndicate's cotton gin has been destroyed. He turns abusive
when he insists that Flora provide an alibi for him. Flora only weakly
resists Jake's rough treatment, suggesting a sadomasochistic bond
between them.
In the second scene the plantation superintendent, an Italian named
Silva Vicarro, arrives at the house. Jake assures Vicarro that he would be
glad to gin the plantation cotton for him. Jake also humiliates Flora about
her weight, then leaves to do the "neighborly thing" and process the cotton.
Vicarro begins to flirt with Flora in order to obtain information about the
fire. When Flora unwittingly destroys Jake's alibi Vicarro takes his
revenge by bedding the wife of the arsonist.
That evening the front porch is bathed in garish moonlight when
Flora, ravaged and beaten, enters almost as if in a trance. Jake returns
singing and seeming immensely pleased with himself. In spite of Flora's
suggestions, Jake is oblivious to what has occurred. The play ends with a
smiling Flora cradling her white kid purse—an implication that Vicarro
has impregnated her.

Reviews and Commentary

Williams' one-act play, *Twenty-Seven Wagons Full of Cotton,* had its world premiere on 17 January 1955 at Tulane University in Louisiana. It is representative of his early work, as it was first published in 1945. The play was on a double bill with a one-act opera by Williams and Raffaello de Banfield entitled *Lord Byron's Love Letter*. Paul Ballantyne played Jake in that production and Stapleton and Orlandi originated the roles they later played in New York. The production was directed by Edward Ludlum and produced by James Elliott and the New Orleans Opera Guild.

The New York production, *All in One,* consisted of the Williams' play and a comic one-act opera by Leonard Bernstein, *Trouble in Tahiti,* which featured Alice Ghostly as a bored suburban housewife. Also on the bill was a series of theatrical and humorous dance pieces by Paul Draper. This production of Williams' one-act play placed less emphasis on the brutality of the Meighan's relationship and stressed the rustic humor of the couple's relationship. Perhaps this was due to the other pieces it followed on the triple bill.

The reviews of the Broadway production were very favorable and acknowledged that the fascination of the story and characters transcended their basic viciousness. Stapleton brought humor and insight to Flora. Richard Watts, Jr., writing in the *New York Post,* described her performance as "astonishingly brilliant" and he added that she "doesn't mind emphasizing the utter foolishness of the woman or the role's leeringly comic aspects, and yet she succeeds in making the part utterly believable, honestly pathetic and even strangely touching. I think it is the finest portrayal I have seen this admirable actress give, and one of the season's best" (20 April 1955).

Twenty-Seven Wagons Full of Cotton furthered Stapleton's reputation as an ideal portrayer of Williams' heroines. She performed Flora Meighan a third time in a 1956 summer stock production at the Westport Country Playhouse. However, when the play was made into the film (*Baby Doll*) Stapleton was again overlooked and Carroll Baker was cast as Flora.

*****

S13   *ORPHEUS DESCENDING*

Broadway premiere at the Martin Beck Theatre, New York
Opened 21 March 1957
Closed 18 May 1957
Number of Performances: 67

Credits
Playwright: Tennessee Williams. Producers: The Producers Theatre and Robert Whitehead. Director: Harold Clurman. Design: Boris Aronson. Costumes: Lucinda Ballard. Lighting: Feder. Incidental Music: Chuck Wayne. Music Arrangement: John Mehegan. Song "Heavenly Grass": Paul Bowles and Tennessee Williams. Stage Managers: James Gelb, Norman Kean and Beau Tilden. Company Manager: Leonard Field. Press: Ben Kornzweig and Robert Ganshaw.

Cast

Dolly Hamma	Elizabeth Eustis
Beulah Binnings	Jane Rose
Pee Wee Binnings	Warren Kemmerling
Dog Hamma	David Clarke
Carol Cutrere	Lois Smith
Eva Temple	Nell Harrison
Sister Temple	Mary Farrell
Uncle Pleasant	John Marriott
Val Xavier	Cliff Robertson
Vee Talbott	Joanna Roos
Lady Torrance	**Maureen Stapleton**
Jabe Torrance	Crahan Denton
Sheriff Talbott	R. G. Armstrong
Mr. Dubinsky	Beau Tilden
Woman	Janice Mars
David Cutrere	Robert Webber
Nurse Porter	Virgilia Chew
First Man	Albert Henderson
Second Man	Charles Tyner

Synopsis

The play is set in a small Southern town in a dry goods store with an adjacent "confectionary" which is presently in disuse. Some local women await the return of the store owner, Jabe Torrance, who has been away while undergoing treatment for cancer. We learn that his wife is an Italian woman, Lady Torrance, who has led a tormented existence in the town. Fifteen years ago Lady was seduced by David Cutrere, a man of good social standing, who then abandoned her for a more socially acceptable marriage. At the same time Lady's father, an immigrant wine-maker, died in a fire. The fire was set by the "Mystic Crew"—locals outraged that he sold liquor to Negroes.

Soon David's sister, Carol Cutrere, enters. She is a pale, barefoot wraith whose blatant sexuality and amorality has made her a social outcast. We learn that Carol is planning to leave town but before she can do so Val Xavier appears in the store looking for a job. Val is a newcomer to the town and his arrival will affect the lives of all the main characters. This Orpheus is clad in a snakeskin jacket and has his guitar over his shoulder. He is young, handsome and sensual.

Lady arrives with Jabe. She is thirty-ish, still attractive, but on the verge of hysteria. Jabe shows his violent temper before being taken up to his room. Soon after, Lady agrees to hire Val. She reveals that she is going to re-open the confectionary to have a place like her father's wine-garden.

Carol stays in town, warning Val he is in danger there. Vee Talbott is caught talking to Val by her husband, the local Sheriff, who becomes suspicious of their relationship, although it is innocent. Meanwhile, Lady has fallen for the handsome stranger and suggests that he move into a small room at the back of the store. Val resents the idea of becoming "a store-clerk days and a stud nights" and starts to leave, but Lady's passionate pleas soften his resolve and he stays on.

One morning Jabe appears downstairs and flies into a rage at Lady's plans for the confectionary. He lets it slip that he was part of the Mystic Crew that took her father's life. Following his outburst, Jabe turns gravely ill. Against the backdrop of Jabe's dying, Talbott again finds Vee with Val and tells him to clear out of town. Lady enters in a low-cut dress, with arms full of party favors, determined to re-open the confectionary and thus take her revenge on Jabe. When Val starts to leave, Lady panics. As she clings to Val, Jabe enters and shoots her. Then he shouts out that Val is robbing the store and Val is dragged off by the lynch mob.

Reviews and Commentary

Tennessee Williams wrote *Battle of Angels* in 1940 but the problematic play did not make it to Broadway. Williams shelved it and found success with *The Glass Menagerie, The Rose Tattoo,* and other plays. However, he kept working on the script and he presented it at the Shubert Theatre in Washington, D.C. on 28 February 1957 under the title of *Something Wild in the Country.* It played four performances before moving to the Walnut Theatre in Philadelphia on 5 March 1957. When it opened on Broadway on 21 March the title was changed to *Orpheus Descending.*

The critics admired the cast and the direction of Harold Clurman. However, they were divided on the effectiveness of Williams' script. Some felt the lyricism and passion of the play redeemed it. Others felt that the Mississippi town Williams imagined was too much like an insane asylum of sadists and pathetic victims. Richard Watts, Jr. compared it to Jacobean drama: "it is steeped in passion, hatred, frustration, bitterness and violence, and it ends in a welter of blood and death worthy of one of the Elizabethan tragedies . . . And, splendidly acted and staged, it is a drama of notable power, grim poetic insight and disturbing fascination" (22 March 1957). In general there seemed to be a lack of cohesion in the script, an aimlessness that may reflect the lack of direction of the characters themselves.

Stapleton's performance, however, received unanimous praise. Brooks Atkinson wrote "as the shopkeeper Maureen Stapleton gives a remarkable performance that has all the strength, the honesty and the power of her best work" (22 March 1957, 28). This was the third time Stapleton created a new Williams heroine. Lady Torrance follows her portrayals of Serafina Delle Rose (*The Rose Tattoo,* S06) and Flora Meighan (*Twenty-Seven Wagons Full of Cotton,* S12).

Lady Torrance is, indeed, a character very akin to Serafina. Both are passionate Italian women, neither young nor old, who succumb to the charms of a sensual stranger and rejoice in their impregnation. As was the case with *The Rose Tattoo,* Stapleton's role of Lady Torrance was first offered to Italian actress Anna Magnani but she declined the part. Magnani did, however, play Lady Torrance in the movie version entitled *The Fugitive Kind.* Stapleton played Vee Talbott in that film (see **F02**). These connections between Magnani and Stapleton led to Stapleton's title as "the American Magnani."

S14   *THE COLD WIND AND THE WARM*

Broadway premiere at the Morosco Theatre, New York
Opened 8 December 1958
Closed 21 March 1959
Number of Performances: 120

Credits
Playwright: S. N. Behrman. Producer: The Producers Theatre and Robert Whitehead. Director: Harold Clurman. Settings: Boris Aronson. Costumes: Motley. Lighting: Feder. Stage Managers: James Gelb and Walter Neal. General Manager: Oscar Olesen. Company Manager: Robert Hector. Press: Barry Hyams, Lila Glaser, Shirley E. Herz and Bob Ullman.

Cast
Tobey	Timmy Everett
Willie	Eli Wallach
Jim Nightingale	Vincent Gardenia
Ida	**Maureen Stapleton**
Ren	Jada Rowland
Myra	Carol Grace
Aaron	Peter Trytler
Rappaport	Sig Arno
Mr. Sacher	Morris Carnovsky
Dan	Sidney Armus
Leah	Suzanne Pleshette
Norbert Mandel	Sanford Meisner

Synopsis
The story begins in a Jewish neighborhood in Worcester, Massachusetts in 1908 and traces the friendship of two boys over a period of years. Willie and Tobey are twelve years old when the play begins. They are mystified by life and their place in it. Tobey is the son of a grocer, Mr. Sacher, who is also a wise scholar of the Talmud. Willie often comes to Mr. Sacher for advice, but seldom takes it.

Tobey and Willie's world revolves around the family and friends in the neighborhood. There is Tobey's incorrigible Aunt Ida who is a "finder" or matchmaker. Ida has her own sights set on the rich neighbor, Mr. Mandel, a polished dandy who ignores her. Ida also takes in Leah, a quiet young seamstress from Fitchburg for whom Ida has promised to find a husband. Willie and Tobey learn from Jim, the local doctor, that a mutual friend, Dan, has diabetes. Willie is tempted to tell Myra, Dan's fiancé, because he is infatuated with Myra himself.

Two years later Tobey's mother has died and Ida now looks after Mr. Sacher and Tobey. As anticipated, Myra is now a young widow. Willie confesses his love for her. Myra, however, throws off her widow's weeds, turns her back on custom and takes off for New York City to become an entertainer. Mr. Mandel has decided that he must marry Leah but she has fallen in love with Willie. Willie responds to Leah's affection only to abruptly leave Worcester to follow the flighty Myra.

Five years later the friends have moved to New York City. Tobey is now an aspiring young composer and Willie has just completed his law exams. Ida and her daughter have also moved to the city. When Ida learns that Leah is coming to town she arranges a dinner with Tobey, Willie and Myra. Before the dinner Mr. Mandel arrives. He has heard that Leah adopted a baby in Chicago and feels she needs a husband and it should be him. Leah and Ida reject him and, after he leaves, Ida learns that Leah's "adopted" baby is really Willie's child.

Ida tells Tobey the news so Tobey can relate it to Willie. Willie has just realized that his affections for Myra are actually part of his obsession with the unattainable and has decided he needs to give up his law career and go to work in a factory, where he can confront cold reality. Tobey confronts Willie with the reality of his responsibilities to Leah and urges Willie to accept the love of Leah and the simple pleasures of life. Willie accepts and proposes, but suddenly commits suicide.

The final episode finds Tobey back in Worcester, trying to make sense of Willie's death.

Reviews and Commentary

Behrman's play was adapted from a series of magazine sketches which were later published in a book entitled *The Worcester Account.* Harold Clurman directed the production which premiered 4 November 1958 at the New Locust Theatre in Philadelphia. The production then played two weeks at the Colonial Theatre in Boston before coming to New York.

The play received favorable reviews, although it was evident that the episodic nature of the original material carried over into the script of the play. Some critics mentioned that the play does not resolve, that there is no one central character. However, director Clurman developed a lovely, evocative production, as these comments of Brooks Atkinson, critic for the *New York Times*, reveal: "The Congreve of the American theatre writes with a suppleness and ease that give distinction to things that are ordinary and that can shift the mood without changing the pace. Under the sensitive direction of Harold Clurman, the play is lightly expressed in its own terms without effort or contriving" (9 December 1958, 55).

In addition to Clurman's perceptive direction, the play owed its success to the dynamic performances of the very talented cast which included Eli Wallach as Willie, Maureen Stapleton as Aunt Ida, Morris Carnovsky as Tobey's father, Vincent Gardenia as Jim, Sanford Meisner as Norbert Mandel and Suzanne Pleshette as Leah. Walter Kerr wrote that "it is an honest and expansive pleasure to watch Maureen Stapleton, as matchmaker for a Jewish neighborhood and foster-mother to practically everyone in sight, turn a speculative eye on an attractive and available spinster, invent a handful of splendid lies to account for the failure of a promised suitor to show up, and, in a burst of breathless efficiency, hustle the lass off to the corner drugstore where there are prospects with every milk shake" (9 December 1958).

The Cold Wind and the Warm offered Stapleton a rare chance to play a character that was not in turmoil. Aunt Ida drew upon Stapleton's natural talents for being involved with and giving support to those around her. Her portrayal of the well-meaning meddler was humorous and heart-warming, adding to the overall beauty of the play. Stapleton received a Tony Award nomination for Best Actress for her portrait of Aunt Ida.

S15   *TOYS IN THE ATTIC*

Broadway premiere at the Hudson Theatre, New York
Opened 25 February 1960
Closed 8 April 1961
Number of Performances: 556

Credits
Playwright: Lillian Hellman. Producer: Kermit Bloomgarden. Director:
Arthur Penn. Setting & Lighting: Howard Bay. Costumes: Ruth Morley.
Music: Marc Blitzstein. Stage Managers: Kermit Kegley, Clifford Cothren
and William Hawley. Company Manager: Richard Seader. Press: Arthur
Cantor, Gertrude Kirschner, Tony Geiss and Violet Welles.

Cast

Carrie Berniers	**Maureen Stapleton**
Anna Berniers	Anne Revere
Gus	Charles McRae
Albertine Prine	Irene Worth
Henry Simpson	Percy Rodriguez
Julian Berniers	Jason Robards, Jr.
Lily Berniers	Rochelle Oliver
Taxi Driver	William Hawley
Moving Men	Clifford Cothren
	Tom Manley
	Maurice Ellis

Synopsis
Carrie and Anna Berniers are middle-aged sisters in New Orleans
who have chosen to spend their lives looking after their ne'er-do-well
brother, Julian. They work unsatisfying jobs and defer their dreams of
travelling to Europe or moving out of the house they detest so that Julian
will be able to pursue various schemes. Julian, however, marries a young
rich girl, Lily Prine. Lily and Julian move to Chicago where he buys a
factory which, like all his other attempts, fails to bring him fortune.

At the outset of the play Julian and Lily have been married a year
and the spinsters have accrued enough savings to take their long-awaited
tour. However, Julian returns to New Orleans with Lily bringing lavish
presents and surprises to the sisters. He has apparently struck it rich in
some kind of deal but Lily and his sisters are unhappy with the change in
Julian because they all feel he no longer needs them.

Lily's mother, the elegant and wise Albertine Prine, tries to reassure
her daughter and keep her from making mistakes. Albertine and Henry (a
black man who is her friend and lover) deduce that Julian's money is
coming from buying some swamp land and selling it back to the investor
who must have it at any price. Julian's partner in the deal is Charlotte, the
investor's wife, who needs the money to escape from her abusive husband.

Carrie, the younger sister, harbors incestuous feelings about her
brother. In the crisis precipitated by Julian's new fortune, Anna accuses
Carrie of this unnatural affection and she decides to leave the house and

depart for Europe alone. Meanwhile, Carrie learns about the deal and manipulates Lily to warn the investor. The result is that Julian and the other woman are badly beaten and all the money is stolen. Reduced to his former dependence on the women, the wife and sisters go about making Julian comfortable and cheerfully pick up their lives again.

Reviews and Commentary

Toys in the Attic premiered in Boston at the Wilbur Theatre on 3 February 1960 and then moved on to New York. It was Lillian Hellman's first play in nine years and it received rave reviews from the New York critics. They praised the writing, the direction by Arthur Penn, and the brilliant acting. The drama was evidently spell-binding, in spite of the nasty natures of some of the characters. Jason Robards, Jr. played Julian Berniers with a definitive charm and style. Irene Worth was impressive as the refined Albertine. Rochelle Oliver made an auspicious debut in the role of Lily.

Stapleton was highly praised for her portrayal of Carrie Berniers. In an interview conducted after this production, Stapleton admits that she originally wanted to play the part of Albertine because she so admired the honesty in the relationship between Albertine and Henry. Stapleton agreed to read for the role. Hellman was not impressed but she asked the actress to stay and read for Carrie and that is how she was cast. Brooks Atkinson wrote "the acting is superb. Especially Miss Stapleton's acting of the more possessive of the sisters: it is comic, disarming, awkward and pathetic all at once. Her breathless, high-pressured, plaintive-voiced portrait is the most vital element in the play and also the most thoroughly resolved characterization in terms of gesture, movement, inflection and timing" (26 February 1960, 23). John McClain agreed, saying "nobody in the theatre today could attempt to top Maureen Stapleton in the role of the dumpy, aging sister whose whole life has been devoted to this brother for whom she has a well-buried physical attraction" (26 February 1960).

Stapleton received another Tony Award nomination (Best Actress) for her portrayal of Carrie. Anne Revere, who played Anna, won the Tony Award (Best Actress, Supporting or Featured). The production also received Tony Award nominations for Best Play and Best Actor (Jason Robards). *Toys in the Attic* ran for more than a year on Broadway.

*****

S16   *THE GLASS MENAGERIE*

Revival staged at the Brooks Atkinson Theatre, New York
Opened 4 May 1965
Closed 2 October 1965
Number of Performances: 176

Credits

Playwright: Tennessee Williams. Producers: Claude Giroux and Orrin Christy, Jr. Director: George Keathley. Setting Design: Robert T. Williams. Setting Supervision: James A. Taylor. Costumes: Patton Campbell. Lighting: V. C. Fuqua. Music: Paul Bowles. Stage Managers:

Wade Miller and Donald Bumgardner. General Manager: George Banyai. Company Manager: Richard Grayson. Press: John Springer Associates, Walter Alford and Mary Ward.

Cast

The Mother	**Maureen Stapleton**
Her Son	George Grizzard
Her Daughter	Piper Laurie
The Gentleman Caller	Pat Hingle

Synopsis

Williams' memory play is set in an alley and its adjacent apartment in a lower middle-class neighborhood in St. Louis in the 1930s. Tom Wingfield, the narrator, leads us back to this time and place to tell the story of how he left his mother and sister to find a world beyond this apartment's dingy walls.

Tom is a poet working in a shoe factory. His mother has scratched out a living since the children's father "fell in love with long distance" and abandoned them. Tom's sister Laura is an pathologically shy girl due to a slightly crippled leg which makes her terribly self-conscious. She spends her days listening to records and playing with her collection of glass animals, her "glass menagerie." Their mother, Amanda, is a faded Southern belle whose claim to fame is having been courted once by seventeen "gentleman callers."

A crisis occurs in the household when Amanda learns that Laura has dropped out of her classes at the business college and has for months been walking in the park or going to movies so her mother would not find out. Amanda panics when she realizes Laura cannot have a career and so she determines to provide for her daughter the only way she can—she decides to find a husband for her.

Tom is prevailed upon to bring home a "gentleman caller." The visit goes better than anyone can hope. The "caller" is a likeable, energetic young man who is able to set Laura at ease. At the end of a romantic evening, however, he tells her he is engaged to another. Amanda lashes out at Tom, unable to believe that he did not know this information and Tom is forced to finally break away from home and follow his own star.

Reviews and Commentary

This revival, which was staged twenty years after the premiere production, originated in New Jersey at the Paper Mill Playhouse where it played from 30 March to 11 April 1965. The production then moved to New York for an anticipated eight-week run but was so popular it ran for four months.

There were inevitable comparisons between the revival and the first production in which Laurette Taylor established a lasting image of Amanda Wingfield. Maureen Stapleton was commended by the critics for challenging that memory in this quintessential memory play. Stapleton looked nothing like Taylor in the role—where Taylor was a slender wraith of a Southern Belle, Stapleton was far more homey and matronly. Nevertheless, Stapleton's enormous capacity for producing heartfelt emotion won over every critic.

Howard Taubman summed up the critical opinion in this observation in the *New York Times*: "Maureen Stapleton does not cause one to forget Miss Taylor; she makes one remember her own conception. Her Amanda is pitiful and touching in a distinctive way. Through the magic of her own sensitivity, she gives Amanda a strong, binding thread of sadness and tenderness" (5 May 1965, 53).

Stapleton's accomplished performance as Amanda earned her the Best Actress Award from *Variety's* Poll of New York Drama Critics. This role also complimented her many successes in other Tennessee Williams' plays including Serafina in *The Rose Tattoo,* Flora Meighan in *Twenty-Seven Wagons Full of Cotton,* and Lady Torrance and Vee Talbott in *Orpheus Descending.* Amanda Wingfield was also a role that Stapleton would play again and again for almost the next twenty years. (See **S25** and **Biography** for details.)

*****

S17   *THE ROSE TATTOO*

Revival stage at the New York City Center, New York
Opened 20 October 1966
Closed 30 October 1966
Number of Performances: 14 (limited engagement)
Moved to the Billy Rose Theatre 9 November 1966
Closed 31 December 1966
Number of Performances: 61 (and one preview)

Credits
Playwright: Tennessee Williams. Producer: City Center Drama Company. Company Director: Jean Dalrymple. Director: Milton Katselas. Scenery: David Ballou. Costumes: Frank Thompson. Lighting: Peggy Clark. Stage Managers: Ray Laine and Phil King. General Manager: Homer Poupart. Company Manager, City Center: George Zorn. Company Manager, Billy Rose: Irving Cooper. Press, City Center: Jean Dalrymple and John Clugstone. Press, Billy Rose: Arthur Cantor and Artie Solomon.

Cast

Salvatore	Sonny Rocco
Vivi	Elena Christi
Bruno	Peter Falzone
Assunta	Nina Varela
Rosa Delle Rose	Maria Tucci
Serafina Delle Rose	**Maureen Stapleton**
Estelle Hohengarten	Marcie Hubert
The Strega	Georgia Simmons
Giuseppina	Rosetta Veneziani
Peppina	Jo Flores Chase
Violetta	Ruth Manning
Mariella	Ann Berger Malatzky
Teresa	Honey Sanders
Father De Leo	Dino Terranova

A Doctor	Kevin O'Morrison
Miss Yorke	Barbara Townsend
Flora	Gina Collens
Bessie	Peggy Pope
Jack Hunter	Christopher Walken
Salesman	L. M. Gibbons
Alvaro Mangiacavallo	Harry Guardino
Lucia	Gloria Tofano
Giovana	Dorothy Raymond
Children	Joanna Sandra Malatzky
	Susan Carol Malatzky

Synopsis
See S06.

Reviews and Commentary
Fifteen years after her first major Broadway success, Maureen Stapleton returned to Broadway to play Serafina Delle Rose in this revival of *The Rose Tattoo*. This time Stapleton's performance was compared to both her own original creation and to that of Anna Magnani in the film version of the play. Once again Stapleton held her own. *New York Times* critic Dan Sullivan made this observation of Stapleton's 1966 performance: "In general she is daintier and subtler than Miss Magnani was—less awe-inspiring, perhaps, but more sympathetic . . . . because she seems more the victim, less the prisoner of her plight" (21 October 1966, 36). Leo Mishkin of the *New York Morning Telegraph* said "if, as reports have had it, the part was originally written for Anna Magnani . . . Miss Stapleton now seems to have captured it for her own. And she makes a fine, glowing thing out of it too" (22 October 1966).

The overall production also received excellent reviews. The revival had a very strong cast, including Maria Tucci as Rosa, Harry Guardino as Alvaro, and Christopher Walken as the young sailor, Jack Hunter. This fine production was preserved on a sound recording distributed by Caedmon Records.

*****

S18   *PLAZA SUITE*

Broadway premiere at the Plymouth Theatre, New York
Opened 14 February 1968
Closed 3 October 1970
Number of Performances: 1,097

Credits
Playwright: Neil Simon. Producers: Saint-Subber and Nancy Enterprises, Inc. Director: Mike Nichols. Scenic Production: Oliver Smith. Costumes: Patricia Zipprodt. Lighting: Jean Rosenthal. Hairstyles: Ernest Adler. Stage Managers: Harvey Medlinsky and Wisner Washam. General Manager: C. Edwin Knill. Company Manager: William Craver. Press: Harvey B. Sabinson, Lee Solters and Harry Nigro.

Cast: *Visitor from Mamaroneck*

Bellhop	Bob Balaban
Karen Nash	**Maureen Stapleton**
Sam Nash	George C. Scott
Waiter	José Ocasio
Jean McCormack	Claudette Nevins

Cast: *Visitor from Hollywood*

Waiter	José Ocasio
Jesse Kiplinger	George C. Scott
Muriel Tate	**Maureen Stapleton**

Cast: *Visitor from Forest Hills*

Norma Hubley	**Maureen Stapleton**
Roy Hubley	George C. Scott
Borden Eisler	Bob Balaban
Mimsey Hubley	Claudette Nevins

Synopsis

The Plaza Hotel in New York is the setting for this Neil Simon comedy. Each act occurs in the same opulent hotel suite but concerns a different couple. Unlike a *Grand Hotel* plot, however, the stories do not intersect; the only thing they have in common is that they occur in the same room.

The first story concerns a married couple who reserve a room at the hotel because their apartment is being painted. However, the wife (Karen) has intentionally reserved the same room where she and husband Sam celebrated their honeymoon almost twenty-five years earlier. She has ordered champagne and Sam's favorite dinner in the hopes of renewing the spark of their marriage. Sam, however, is preoccupied with problems at work and tries to avoid Karen's romantic plans. Intuitively Karen perceives that Sam's real interest at the office is his young secretary. Yet she is shocked when Sam admits that the secretary is his mistress. He defends himself by expressing his fears of growing old. In the end Sam leaves for the office but the possibility is open that Sam and Karen might find reconciliation in the future.

The second story concerns Jesse Kiplinger, a glitzy Hollywood producer who has blown into town for a few hours and calls up his high school sweetheart, Muriel Tate, for a spontaneous reunion. Muriel is now a conventional New Jersey housewife, but she dashes to the hotel to see her old flame. Jesse wows Muriel with vodka and stories of Hollywood. She claims she has a perfect marriage and fends off Jesse's amorous advances until he learns Muriel's weakness is an infatuation with movie stars. He then sweet-talks her right into bed with the names of the rich and famous.

The final story in this hotel room concerns the middle-aged parents of a bride-to-be who has locked herself in the bathroom and called off the wedding. The parents undergo great trials, including sending Dad out on the window ledge in his frock coat, trying to get the daughter to reconsider. When all efforts have failed and the parents have been thoroughly disheveled and disgruntled, the groom enters, gives a sharp command and the bride emerges, ready for the ceremony.

Reviews and Commentary

The world premiere of *Plaza Suite* was at the Shubert Theatre in New Haven, Connecticut on 17 January 1968. This comedy became one of Stapleton's longest Broadway runs. The play ran more than a thousand performances; except for a four month leave in early 1969, Stapleton performed into January 1970. During that time she starred with George C. Scott, E.G. Marshall and Nicol Williamson. She also played the part of Karen Nash in the film version (see **F08**).

This was the third collaboration between playwright Neil Simon and director Mike Nichols and it proved as successful as its predecessors (*Barefoot in the Park* and *The Odd Couple*). The reviews were so good, it seemed as though the critics were helpless to find fault with that dynamic duo. Nichols won the Tony Award for Best Director and Simon received a nomination for Best Play.

The playwright and director were ably served by the stars. For Stapleton (who received a Tony nomination for Best Actress) *Plaza Suite* was an opportunity to display her range and versatility. Richard P. Cooke wrote in the *Wall St. Journal* that "Miss Stapleton, about as far as possible from her characterization in *The Rose Tattoo,* here plays a succession of suburban matrons with stimulating gusto. She is a warm rather than a brittle comedienne, which is all to the good' (16 February 1968). And Martin Gottfried exclaimed that the ensemble-playing between Stapleton and Scott proved "for the first time to me that an Actors Studio-trained actor can play comedy" (15 February 1968).

*****

S19   *NORMAN, IS THAT YOU?*

Broadway premiere at the Lyceum Theatre, New York
Opened 19 February 1970
Closed 28 February 1970
Number of Performances: 12 (and 20 previews)

Credits
Playwrights: Ron Clark and Sam Bobrick. Producer: Harold D. Cohen. Produced by arrangement with Augustus Productions. Director: George Abbott. Scenery: William and Jean Eckart. Costumes: Florence Klotz. Lighting: Fred Allison. Hair Styles: Rusty Buonaccorso. Stage Managers: Bernard Pollock and Sean Simpson. General Manager: Richard Horner. Company Manager: Al Jones. Press: Lee Solters, Harvey B. Sabinson and Jay Russell.

Cast
Norman Chambers	Martin Huston
Garson Hobart	Walter Willison
Ben Chambers	Lou Jacobi
Mary	Dorothy Emmerson
Beatrice Chambers	**Maureen Stapleton**

Synopsis

Ben Chambers is a midwestern dry cleaner whose wife, Beatrice, has just run off to Montreal with his own brother. In desperation this middle class Jewish father heads to New York seeking sympathy from his only son, Norman. There he is confronted with the fact that Norman has become a window-dresser and shares his lavender-walled apartment with Garson, a girlish boy sporting a Saks negligee. Ben is besieged by nightmares of being chosen the homosexuals' father of the year. Unable to come to terms with his son's homosexuality, Ben hires a prostitute to reform him. Despite her best professional efforts, Norman is not persuaded.

Beatrice, meanwhile, has grown disenchanted with her fling and arrives in New York as well. Ben leaves in a huff. In the "happy" ending Norman is suddenly drafted and Beatrice takes Garson under her wing. Together they follow Ben home to Ohio.

Reviews and Commentary

This insubstantial comedy was written by two television comedy writers and was their first venture onto Broadway. In spite of a tour de force performance by Lou Jacobi as the beleaguered father, the play was soundly drubbed and lasted for only ten days. It then went on to play in community theatres across America.

This production was number 113 for director George Abbott. Critic Martin Gottfried criticized Abbott's direction which "treated the play as if it were farce—a fundamental misunderstanding that undercut the performances more than the speedy action was worth" (20 February 1970).

Stapleton received favorable reviews for a miniscule part. (Beatrice shows up only briefly at the end of the play.) Clive Barnes, critic for the *New York Times,* described her as someone who "always manages to look gloriously trampled upon, as if she had just stumbled off a rush-hour subway, laddered her stocking, broken her bra-strap and stubbed her heart" (20 February 1970, 30). Another critic offered Stapleton condolences for even appearing in the play and expressed hope that the actress was well paid for the imposition.

*****

S20   *THE GINGERBREAD LADY*

Broadway premiere at the Plymouth Theatre, New York
Opened 13 December 1970
Closed 29 May 1971
Number of Performances: 193

Credits

Playwright: Neil Simon. Producers: Saint-Subber and Nancy Enterprises & Footlight Productions, Inc. Director: Robert Moore. Setting: David Hays. Costumes: Frank Thompson. Lighting: Martin Aronstein. Hairstyle: Phyllis Sagnelli. Stage Managers: Tom Porter and George Rondo. General Manager: C. Edwin Knill. Company Manager: James Turner. Press: Harvey B. Sabinson, Lee Solters, Cheryl Sue Dolby and Edie Kean.

Cast

Jimmy Perry	Michael Lombard
Manuel	Alex Colon
Toby Landau	Betsy von Furstenberg
Evy Meara	**Maureen Stapleton**
Polly Meara	Ayn Ruymen
Lou Tanner	Charles Siebert

Synopsis

Evy Meara is forty-three, an attractive divorcee, a cabaret singer who has battled addiction to alcohol for years. The play takes place in her brownstone apartment in Manhattan's west seventies on a late afternoon in mid-November. Evy's good friend, Jimmy Perry, an unsuccessful actor who is a homosexual, is waiting for Evy to return from a three-month stint in a Long Island drunk tank. Toby Landau, Evy's other best friend, soon arrives as well. Toby is about Evy's age and has devoted her life to making herself attractive to men.

Evy arrives and looks terrific. She's lost forty-two pounds and is elated to be home. Her seventeen-year-old daughter, Polly, drops by and announces she is going to move in so they can now be together. Evy's former boyfriend, a guitar player named Lou Tanner, also comes to see her but she now has the courage to send him packing.

Three weeks later, Evy enters with bottles of champagne which she tells Polly are to celebrate Toby's birthday. However, Jimmy arrives in a state of crisis, having been fired from a Broadway play three days before opening. Then Toby comes in, also in crisis, because she has learned her husband wants a divorce. Evy consoles them both with champagne. Both friends indulge themselves, unaware that Evy is sliding off the wagon with them. When they realize what is happening, an argument ensues and Jimmy and Toby angrily leave. Polly retires to the bedroom as Evy first celebrates alone, then calls up Lou for company.

When Evy returns the next morning, she has a black eye. Toby and Jimmy return to make amends. Evy tries to convince Polly that it would be better if she went to live with her dad, but Polly stands her ground and convinces Evy that it would be better for both of them to stay together and work through the problems.

Reviews and Commentary

Neil Simon wrote *The Gingerbread Lady* after numerous successful comedies. The play premiered 3 November 1970 at the Shubert Theatre in New Haven, Connecticut. It was originally titled *It Only Hurts When I Laugh*. The second tryout was at the Colonial Theatre in Boston, Massachusetts, 10 to 28 November 1970. Some reports indicate that Simon tried to prevent the Broadway opening but gave into pressure because of the advance sales. The reviews of the play were extremely mixed, although the run was creditable. For Stapleton, *The Gingerbread Lady* earned her a second Tony Award (Best Actress).

Much was made of the fact that this was Simon's first "serious" play. Most of the critics seemed to think Simon's mixture of hearty one-liners and deep-seated emotional problems proved a basic weakness in the writing. As Richard Watts observed, Simon "has combined an amusing comedy with an atmosphere of great sadness . . . . But that sadness, instead of bolstering the humor, interferes with it and the contrast weakens both aspects" (14 December 1970).

The critics did agree that the cast turned in excellent performances, especially Betsy von Furstenberg as the aging beauty queen, Toby. Stapleton received some of her finest reviews such as this rave from Clive Barnes: "Maureen Stapleton as the battered, baffled lush thrush has probably the part of her career and she is quite wonderful . . . . Childlike, innocent, confused, sly but trusting—Miss Stapleton plays her game of solitaire with no card unturned" (14 December 1970, 58).

Simon wrote the play specifically for Maureen Stapleton and interviews conducted during the run draw parallels between the public and private lives of Evy Meara and Stapleton. Milton Goldman (Stapleton's agent at the time) reported that Stapleton read the script and exclaimed "the son of a bitch must have had a tape recorder under my bed" (cited by Giosa 1978, 45). The quote reflects language typical of both Evy—who claims she has "an impediment of speech"—and of Maureen Stapleton. Other similarities between the character and the actress are their battles with obesity and alcohol. Stapleton, however, stresses an important difference: alcoholism prevents Evy from working; Stapleton says her drinking never interfered with her work.

For her portrayal of Evy Meara Stapleton won the Tony for Best Actress, the Drama Desk Award for Outstanding Performance and the *Variety* Poll of New York Drama Critics award for Best Female Lead in a Straight Play.

In 1981 *The Gingerbread Lady* was made into a film with the title *Only When I Laugh*. Marsha Mason played Evy Meara.

*****

S21   THE COUNTRY GIRL

Revival staged at the Eisenhower Theatre, John F. Kennedy Center for the Performing Arts, Washington, D.C.
Opened 12 November 1971
Closed 18 December 1971
Moved to the Billy Rose Theatre, New York
Opened 15 March 1972
Closed 6 May 1972
Number of Performances: 62 (and 4 previews)

Credits
Playwright: Clifford Odets. Producers: Roger L. Stevens and Hugh O'Brian. Director: John Houseman. Settings & Lighting: Douglas W. Schmidt. Lighting Consultant: James Waring. Costumes: Frank Thompson. Production Supervision, Washington: Frank Cassidy. Production Supervision, New York: Max Allentuck. Stage Managers: Allen Leicht and Julia Fremon. Press, New York: Michael Sean O'Shea and Leonard Traube.

Cast
Bernie Dodd   George Grizzard
Larry   James Karen

Phil Cook	Martin Wolfson (replaced by Roland Winters in New York production)
Paul Unger	Joe Ponazecki
Nancy Stoddard	Eda Zahl
Frank Elgin	Jason Robards
Georgie Elgin	**Maureen Stapleton**
Ralph	William Shust

Synopsis

Frank Elgin is an alcoholic and former stage star who has been cast in a small role in a new play. When the idealistic and ambitious young director of the play, Bernie Dodd, offers Frank the leading role, the aging star gets one last chance to make a come-back. Frank hurries home to tell Georgie, his wife, of his stroke of luck. He fails to notice that she was just preparing to walk out on the marriage and the news motivates her to stay and see him through the terrifying challenge he faces.

As Odets' play develops we get two perspectives on Georgie. Frank confides to Bernie that Georgie was an alcoholic, that she brought havoc to their lives which made him begin drinking. Bernie, who is fiercely adamant in his faith in Frank, grows antagonistic towards Georgie and sets out to separate her from Frank.

Georgie, however, is on very familiar ground. When Frank's terrors block his ability to learn lines and he succumbs to the comfort of the bottle, Georgie is there to dry him out, set him on his feet again and get him through the opening night. It is only at this point that Bernie realizes his view of Georgie is a fiction created by Frank and that the character description Frank has given him of Georgie is, in fact, the scripted lines of his last great role. When her true character is revealed Bernie falls in love with the real Georgie, a woman of quiet integrity and steadfast devotion. However, Georgie chooses to stand by Frank. She is at his side for his big success and it is clear she will be there as long as he needs her.

Reviews and Commentary

This revival originated at the Kennedy Center in Washington and moved on to Broadway and then to the Huntington Hartford in Los Angeles. The production received extremely mixed reviews in New York. The critics all agreed that the play was a sentimental, melodramatic soap opera—but they disagreed on whether that meant that it was a great play or a terrible one.

The one point that the reviewers did agree upon was the performance of Jason Robards in the role of Frank Elgin. He was universally praised for his multi-faceted characterization. Stapleton and Robards had co-starred before in the 1960 *Toys in the Attic*. Stapleton received some criticism for her matronly appearance in a role that demands physical appeal but, as Martin Gottfried observed, she made up for it: "She introduced a depth and dignity that a lesser actress would never have found in the gross lines" (17 March 1972). *Time* critic T. E. Kalem summed up Stapleton's performance saying "she is all theater, and—bless it—so is *The Country Girl*" (27 March 1972).

S22 *THE SECRET AFFAIRS OF MILDRED WILD*

Broadway premiere at the Ambassador Theatre, New York
Opened 14 November 1972
Closed 2 December 1972
Number of Performances: 23 (and 5 previews)

Credits
Playwright: Paul Zindel. Producers: James B. McKenzie and Spofford J.
Beadle. Director: Jeff Bleckner. Setting: Santo Loquasto. Lighting:
Thomas Skelton. Costumes: Carrie F. Robbins. Hairstyles: Ernest Adler.
Sound: James Reichert. Special Music Arrangements: Rudolph Bennett.
Choreography: Edward Roll. Stage Managers: Frank Hartenstein and Bill
McIntyre. General Manager: Ralph Roseman. Press: Solters/ Sabinson/
Roskin, Inc. and Sandra Manley.

Cast

Mildred Wild	**Maureen Stapleton**
Roy Wild	Lee Wallace
Bertha Gale	Florence Stanley
Helen Wild	Elizabeth Wilson
Carroll Chatham	Neil Flanagan
Sister Cecelia	Joan Pape
Miss Manley	Doris Roberts
Rex Bulby	Bill McIntyre
Louis Garibaldi	Pat Corley
Warren, TV Host	Paul DeWitt
Evelyn, TV Hostess	Joan Pape

Synopsis
      Mildred Wild is a housewife obsessed with the movies. She lives with
her husband, Roy, in the rear of a candy store in Greenwich Village. By
day she surrounds herself with hundreds of movie magazines and by night
she goes to the movies with her friend, Neil Flanagan, the homosexual
neighborhood butcher. While her diabetic husband is perfecting his strudel
dough and passing out from overdoses of Baby Ruths, Mildred retreats into
fantasies of appearing on the silver screen. She becomes Scarlett O'Hara,
Faye Ray and tap dances her way through a Shirley Temple musical.
      These "secret affairs" of Mildred are a coping mechanism to protect
her from the real world in which she has to cope with a nagging sister-in-
law and the landlady who has an eye for her husband. Mildred's dream of
being a Hollywood star almost comes true when she wins a contest on the
TV show, Hollywood Matinee. When she finds her husband in the clutch of
the landlady, the dream proves to be ephemeral and Mildred comes down to
earth.

Reviews and Commentary
      Before he penned *The Secret Affairs of Mildred Wild* Paul Zindel won
the Pulitzer Prize for his touching drama, *The Effect of Gamma Rays on
Man-in-the-Moon Marigolds.* That play and the second Zindel success, *And
Miss Reardon Drinks a Little,* had been written for Maureen Stapleton. She

did not, however, appear in either play. When Zindel wrote his third play for Stapleton (*Mildred Wild*), he created an outrageous farce about a woman who devours movie magazines (a habit Stapleton has had since childhood). She accepted Zindel's comedy; the critical response was that she should have turned it down.

The play previewed at the Shubert Theatre in New Haven and at the Colonial Theatre in Boston before opening at the Ambassador in New York. The play was panned by almost everyone. This comment from *Newsweek* critic Jack Kroll explains why: "In *The Secret Affairs of Mildred Wild* [Zindel] has written so far down to the audience that he's fallen right through it and is at this moment plummeting straight to hell, where his Pulitzer citation will be used to set fire to a copy of the collected plays of Neil Simon, which will then be dropped eternally into Zindel's pants" (27 November 1972).

In spite of the attacks on the play, Stapleton received favorable notices and many condolences. The critics recognized that a great talent was fighting a losing battle. She did not have to fight long—the play closed in its third week.

*****

S23   *THE ROSE TATTOO*

Revival staged at the Walnut Street Theatre, Philadelphia, PA
Opened 29 November 1973
Closed 16 December 1973

Credits
Playwright: Tennessee Williams. Producers: Philadelphia Drama Guild and Sidney S. Bloom. Artistic Director: William Ross. Stage Director: Jeff Bleckner. Settings and Lighting: Clarke Dunham. Costumes: Joseph F. Bella. Stage Managers: Michael Sinclair and David Gold. Press: William Wright.

Cast

Salvatore	Bret Kratchman
Vivi	Lisa Levinson
Bruno	Barry Kratchman
Maria	Karen Kratchman
Rosa Delle Rose	Laurie Heineman
Serafina Delle Rose	**Maureen Stapleton**
Assunta	Miriam Goldina
Estelle Hohengarten	Ellen Hanley
The Strega	Lisa Wolfson
Giuseppina	Gloria Matthews
Peppina	Antonia Rey
Violetta	Dimitra Arliss
Mariella	Nancy Zala
Teresa	Anita Dangler
Father De Leo	Victor Rendina
A Doctor	Elek Hartman
Miss Yorke	Joan Pape

Flora	Anita Dangler
Bessie	Nancy Zala
Jack Hunter	Kristoffer Tabori
Salesman	Bill McIntyre
Alvaro Mangiacavallo	Jerry Orbach

Synopsis
See **S06**.

Reviews and Commentary
Stapleton first appeared in *The Rose Tattoo* in 1951 at the age of twenty-five. She played Serafina again in the 1966 revival of the play in New York. This production, staged in 1973 by the Philadelphia Drama Guild, was her third and final revival of the role at age forty-eight. Once again the critics praised Stapleton for lusty portrayal of the little widow. Jerry Orbach also received fine notices for his portrait of Alvaro.

*****

S24   *JUNO AND THE PAYCOCK*

Revival staged at the Mark Taper Forum, Los Angeles, CA
Opened 7 November 1974
Closed 22 December 1974

Credits
Playwright: Sean O'Casey. Director: George Seaton. Set Design: John Conklin. Costume Design: Dorothy Jenkins. Lighting Design: Donald Harris. Artistic Director: Gordon Davidson. General Manager: Frank von Zerneck. Production Manager: John DeSantis. Technical Director: Robert Calhoun. Stage Managers: David Barber, Don Winton and Madeline Puzo. Press: Richard Kitzrow, Thomas Brocato and Dennis Hammer.

Cast

Mary Boyle	Laurie Prange
Johnny Boyle	John Glover
Juno Boyle	**Maureen Stapleton**
Jerry Devine	Dennis Robertson
"Captain" Jack Boyle	Walter Matthau
"Joxer" Daly	Jack Lemmon
A Sewing Machine Man	Charles Thomas Murphy
A Coal-Block Vendor	Anthony Auer
Charles Bentham, N.T.	Nicholas Hammond
Mrs. Maisie Madigan	Mary Wicks
Mrs. Tancred	Mary Jackson
Neighbors	Peggy Rea
	Duchess Dale
"Needle" Nugent	William Glover

And Martin Speer, Sandy McCallum, Sean McClory, Victor Vitartas and Charles Thomas Murphy.

Synopsis

Juno is the long-suffering matriarch of the Boyle family which lives in a squalid tenement in Dublin in the 1920s. Juno and her daughter, Mary, work to support the family. "Captain" Jack Boyle is the good-for-nothing husband of Juno who went to sea once and who is allergic to employment. Their son, Johnny, is a one-armed youth who is passionately involved with the "troubles"—fighting for the IRA. The Captain spends his days drinking and carousing with his talkative parasitic friend, Joxer.

When the Boyles receive word of an unexpected inheritance from a distant cousin, their lives seem to turn around. The attractive young Englishman who brings the good tidings, Charles Bentham, turns a favorable eye on Mary who, desperate to find a way out of the Dublin slum, is quick to leave her former fiancé and return Bentham's affection. Juno grabs the chance to brighten their surroundings by re-decorating the apartment on credit.

The Boyles' joyful prosperity lasts only a few months. Bentham realizes he has made an error in drafting the will so the anticipated fortune will not materialize. After discovering his error, he rapidly skips town, leaving Mary single and pregnant. This misfortune is followed by others—the furniture is repossessed and Johnny is executed for leading his fellow rebels into an ambush.

As the Captain and Joxer get rip-roaring drunk, Juno abandons him and takes Mary away to start a new life.

Reviews and Commentary

This revival sparked both interest and speculation long before the production opened. It was considered risky to bring together a film director and three big stars in an Irish tragicomedy. From a commercial viewpoint, the names of Maureen Stapleton, Walter Matthau and Jack Lemmon were fortuitous—the production sold out before opening. From an artistic viewpoint, the production was only partially successful.

The critics agreed that O'Casey's play was still quite relevant because the political situation was hardly changed since the play was written. They disagreed on the effectiveness of the production, although most found it lacked some element. The production reunited the comic team of Matthau and Lemmon (who had co-starred in the film of *The Odd Couple*) and the production therefore seemed to focus on the comic antics of Joxer and the Captain at the expense of the more tragic characters. Although individual performances were highly praised, the production seemed to lack human warmth or "heart" as one critic called it.

Stapleton received uniformly fine reviews. The actress' ability to connect with an audience is evident in this review which appeared in *Variety* (8 November 1974, 3): "Stapleton, who seems to have been left alone directorially, is such a strong stage actress that she carried off her role brilliantly, feeling all the pain, small joys and burdens of supporting her family. She does it with a resigned realness that bridges the gap between stage and auditorium and permeates deep into the audience, conveying the tone of the play exceedingly well on her own."

S25 *THE GLASS MENAGERIE*

Revival staged at the Circle in the Square Theatre, New York
Opened 18 December 1975
Closed 22 February 1976
Number of Performances: 77 (and 23 previews)

Credits
Playwright: Tennessee Williams. Director: Theodore Mann. Scenery:
Ming Cho Lee. Costumes: Sydney Brooks. Lighting: Thomas Skelton.
Incidental Music: Craig Wasson. Stage Managers: Randall Brooks and
James Bernardi. Company Manager: William Conn. Press: Merle
Debuskey and Susan L. Schulman.

Cast

The Mother	**Maureen Stapleton**
Her Son	Rip Torn
Her Daughter	Pamela Payton-Wright
The Gentleman Caller	Paul Rudd

Synopsis
See **S16**.

Reviews and Commentary
Stapleton portrayed Amanda Wingfield in this 1975 Broadway revival,
as she had done a decade before. The reviews of the production were mixed.
The critics approved of the acting and felt the play had held up
magnificently over its thirty-year life, but the overall effect of the production
at the Circle in the Square did not quite live up to memories of former
productions. Martin Gottfried, writing in the *New York Post,* focused his
dissatisfaction on the direction of Theodore Mann. Ed Wilson, writing in the
Wall Street Journal, felt that the production failed to catch the right
rhythms and nuances of the playwright.
Stapleton's critical response was, however, most positive. One critic
who loved the production, Clive Barnes, wrote in the *New York Times* "Miss
Stapleton plays pain close to the skin; her face is a map to a lifetime . . . . It
is a lovely, moving performance, all sad lavender tinged with tragic purple"
(19 December 1975, 52).

*****

S26 *THE CLUB CHAMPION'S WIDOW*

World premiere by the Robert Lewis Acting Company
Arena Theater, College of New Rochelle, New Rochelle, NY
Opened 24 January 1978
Closed 5 March 1978
Number of Performances: 14

Credits
Playwright: John Ford Noonan. Artistic Director: Robert Lewis. Designer: Beeb Salzer. Costumes: Joseph Manfredo. General Manager: Mitchell Maxwell. Stage Managers: John Fotia, Jerry Kissel and Jim Boutilier. Press: Bruce Cohen and Amy Sophia Marashinsky.

Cast

Gladys Boughton	**Maureen Stapleton**
Suzanne Boughton	Lisa Sloan
Dorson LaRue	John Braden
T.D. Boughton	Barry Jenner

Synopsis
Gladys Boughton is a widow living in Brookline, Massachusetts. Since the death of her husband (a golf professional), Gladys has been moving towards independence and away from the demands of family. Now she has met a man who she wants to marry. The action of the play centers on Gladys' transition to a new life. At the dining table we meet her "mama's boy" son, T.D., and his wife Suzanne. When Gladys arranges for her new companion, Dorson, to be introduced to T.D. and Suzanne, the son pretends his father is still alive and drinks too much. Suzanne tries to pull him together. As the charming Dorson pursues his suit with Gladys, she reveals the terrible truth that she never liked golf and was a widow long before her husband died. In the end she finds the courage to claim her own happiness.

Reviews and Commentary
The Club Champion's Widow was the premiere production of a new regional theatre, the Robert Lewis Acting Company, which opened in the arena theatre on the campus of the College of New Rochelle. Lewis describes this venture in detail in his book, *Slings and Arrows*. He had hoped to bring together the finest American actors to perform classics and new plays outside the rarified Broadway atmosphere. Maureen Stapleton, one of Lewis' favorite actresses, was his first choice for opening the theatre. Stapleton had been Lewis' student in the first class established at the Actors Studio in 1947 and he has always deeply admired her talent.

When the time came to select a vehicle for Stapleton, John Ford Noonan submitted *The Club Champion's Widow* which he had written specifically for Stapleton. The production had a successful run (although the theatre did not last past the first season). *New York Times* critic Mel Gussow, however, found weaknesses in the play which could not be surmounted by the excellent cast.

*****

S27   *THE GIN GAME*

Broadway premiere at the John Golden Theatre, New York
Opened 6 October 1977
Closed 31 December 1978
Number of Performances: 528
Stapleton and Marshall replaced the original cast 5 September 1978

Credits

Playwright: D. L. Coburn. Producers: Hume Cronyn and Mike Nichols. Director: Mike Nichols. Setting: David Mitchell. Costumes: Bill Walker. Lighting: Ronald Wallace. Production Supervisor: Nina Seely. Stage Manager: Brent Peek and William Chance. General Manager: McCann & Nugent. Company Manager: Maribeth Gilbert. Press: David A. Powers and Barbara Carroll.

Cast

Fonsia Dorsey	Jessica Tandy
	(replaced by **Maureen Stapleton**)
Weller Martin	Hume Cronyn
	(replaced by E. G. Marshall)

Synopsis

The setting is the sun porch of the Bentley Nursing and Convalescent Home for the Aged. Weller Martin is an elderly loner who hides out on the porch on visiting days. Fonsia Dorsey is a new resident of the home who also avoids the Sunday visitors. They meet and begin to get acquainted and Weller invites Fonsia to join him in a game of Gin Rummy. She claims to know little about the game, but accepts his offer to instruct her. She then has an amazing stroke of beginner's luck and beats him at several hands.

A week later they meet again and decide to play. They share information about their family histories and enjoy each other's company until Weller loses his temper at Fonsia's continual winning. In a fury, he stops the game, shouts at her and turns over the card table.

It gradually becomes clear that Weller and Fonsia have no friends or family to visit them, that they have cut themselves off from everyone and both are on fixed incomes. In spite of the apparent need for friendship between them, Weller's inability to accept that Fonsia plays Gin much better than he does causes him to alienate her with violent actions and language. The play ends in a furious argument as Weller lashes out at Fonsia and then limps away quietly and desperately.

Reviews and Commentary

The roles of Fonsia and Weller were created by the husband and wife team of Jessica Tandy and Hume Cronyn under the capable direction of Mike Nichols. The superior ensemble work of these remarkable actors made it difficult to judge the merit of Coburn's play. After more than a year's run E.G. Marshall and Maureen Stapleton were selected to replace Tandy and Cronyn. Nichols had directed Marshall and Stapleton on stage in *Plaza Suite* (see S18) and the actors had also performed together onstage in *The Crucible* (see S09) and on screen in the film *Interiors* (see F09).

The performance of Marshall and Stapleton was necessarily judged in comparison to the actors who had originated the roles. In spite of commendations for their work, the latter pair did not, in the opinion of *New York Times* critic Richard Eder, live up to the standard set by Tandy and Cronyn. Eder said that Stapleton and Marshall "lack the tragic ferocity of their predecessors . . . . [they] play them more enfeebled, softer and with less vitality" (22 November 1978, C9). Nevertheless, the play continued its run for a respectable period of time.

S28   *THE LITTLE FOXES*

Revival staged at the Eisenhower Theatre, John F. Kennedy Center
for the Performing Arts, Washington, D.C.
Opened 19 March 1981
Closed 25 April 1981
Moved to the Martin Beck Theatre, New York
Opened 7 May 1981
Closed 6 September 1981
Number of New York performances: 123 (and 8 previews)

Credits
Playwright: Lillian Hellman. Producers: Zev Bufman, Donald C. Carter
and Jon Cutler. Director: Austin Pendleton. Setting: Andrew Jackness.
Costumes: Florence Klotz. Lighting: Paul Gallo. Music Adapted by
Stanley Silverman. Hairstylist: Patrik D. Moreton. Sound: Jack Mann.
Stage Manager: Patrick Horrigan. General Management: Theatre Now,
Inc. Press: Charles Cinnamon, Fred Nathan, Patt Dale and Eileen
McMahon.

Cast

Addie	Novella Nelson
Cal	Joe Seneca
Birdie Hubbard	**Maureen Stapleton**
Oscar Hubbard	Joe Ponazecki
Leo Hubbard	Dennis Christopher
Regina Giddens	Elizabeth Taylor
William Marshall	Humbert Allen Astredo
Benjamin Hubbard	Anthony Zerbe
Alexandra Giddens	Ann Talman
Horace Giddens	Tom Aldredge

Synopsis
The play is set in a small Southern town in the year 1900. At the
outset the Hubbards (Oscar, Ben and their sister Regina) are entertaining a
businessman from Chicago (William Marshall). Marshall has presented a
proposition for a partnership in building a cotton mill in the town. Regina is
a forty-year-old, attractive but avaricious woman. Her brothers are older
than she and equally unscrupulous. The only barrier to their plans is
Regina's estranged husband, Horace, who commands her funds and is ill
in a hospital in Baltimore. Birdie, Oscar's timid wife is living proof of the
brutality of the Hubbard clan. Oscar married Birdie in order to lay claim to
her fortune and then so abused her that now, at age forty, she is alcoholic
and unbalanced.

In order to get Horace's approval for the deal to invest in the cotton
mill, Regina sends her teenage daughter, Alexandra, to go and bring her
father home. Alexandra is no match for her mother's will and so complies.
When Horace arrives home he reiterates his disgust for the Hubbards'
naked greed and refuses to cooperate. Oscar's son, Leo (who Regina hopes
to marry off to Alexandra) is a sly, insipid youth who works at the bank.

When Leo reveals that he can get into the bank box that holds Horace's fortune ($88,000 in bonds), Oscar and Ben agree to take the bonds and cut Regina out of the deal.

Horace learns of the theft and decides to make it Regina's only inheritance; he tells her he is changing his will so everything else will go to Alexandra. Regina expresses her hatred of Horace and goads him into a fatal attack. As Horace pleads for his medication, Regina calmly ignores him. When the brothers arrive Regina offers to keep the theft quiet in exchange for seventy-five percent of the cotton mill. Alexandra comes down to tell them her father has died. In spite of Regina's efforts to calm her, Alexandra announces that she is leaving the house and her mother in order to avoid becoming like Regina or Birdie.

Reviews and Commentary

The revival of *The Little Foxes* attracted a lot of attention because film star Elizabeth Taylor, at age forty-nine, chose the glamorous role of Regina as the vehicle for her American stage debut. The production previewed in Fort Lauderdale at the Parker Playhouse on 27 February 1981 where it played two weeks before it moved to the Kennedy Center in Washington.

The New York critics generally found merit in the production which received a Tony Award nomination for best reproduction of a play. Several critics faulted Austin Pendleton's direction of the play, saying it lacked shape and control and that the actors were allowed to do as they pleased. Nevertheless, he also received a Tony nomination for Best Director. Taylor was praised for her charisma if not her technique. The consensus was that she had chosen a good role with which to display her exceptional beauty and fiery spirit. Anthony Zerbe also received fine notices for his performance as Regina's older brother, Ben.

In many reviews, however, Maureen Stapleton was said to have stolen the show. *Time* critic T.E. Kalem said "without dimming Taylor's starshine, Stapleton pilfers top acting honors. As she portrays '22 years without a day of happiness,' she is not tearjerking but heartrending" (18 May 1981, 81). Douglas Watt said it was one of the finest performances of her career. Frank Rich said "Miss Stapleton is a wonder . . . this actress digs beneath the surface to give *The Little Foxes* a tragic, Chekhovian dimension . . . . Such is this actress's talent that she can conjure abject terror out of silence and thin air" (8 May 1981, C3). The actress received her fifth Tony Award nomination for her performance.

Following the New York engagement, the production toured two weeks in New Orleans and and two weeks in Los Angeles (Ahmanson Theater of the Music Center) before moving on to London. Stapleton stayed with the production until its Atlantic crossing, but did not continue because of her abject fear of flying.

George C. Scott and Maureen Stapleton share a moment in the 1968 Broadway hit, *Plaza Suite*. Each actor played three different roles. Photo by Martha Swope (© 1992).

Television Performances

In this section, **Television Performances**, the appearances of Maureen Stapleton are listed in chronological order. The heading gives the name of the program. If she appeared in a series, the name of the episode follows the name of the program on the second line. On the third line the date of the first broadcast is given, followed by the studio, the length of the program and pertinent information. A few programs are available on video cassette; this information is listed on the third line after the program name.

All the reviews from *Variety* cited here are available in *Variety Television Reviews* (see **B51**). This multi-volume set is not paginated; reviews appear under the dates indicated.

T01 *THE ACTORS STUDIO*
"Night Club"
3 October 1948; ABC TV; 30 minutes

Stapleton appeared in one episode of this distinguished dramatic showcase. The Peabody Award winning series was rehearsed two weeks and performed live for two seasons, 1948-49 and 1949-50. Actors were members of the influential theatre school, the Actors Studio.

Stapleton appeared in an episode entitled "Night Club." The cast also included Cloris Leachman and Lee Grant. The director was Sanford Meisner.

T02 *THE OLD KNICKERBOCKER MUSIC HALL*
"The Times Square Story"
8 October 1948; CBS; 30 minutes

"The Times Square Story" was a pilot for a series that did not develop. The concept for the show was a combination mystery and drama series to be broadcast live from the Old Knickerbocker Music Hall, a "gay nineties" revue in New York City. The patrons of the music hall were shown a dramatization of a crime and then they were asked to determine who committed the crime.

Bob Stevens and Robert Simon directed the pilot. The producer was Paul F. Moss and the writer was James Reach. The cast included Stapleton, Henry Lascoe, Darren McGavin, Sally Gracie, Jack Lemmon and Madeleine Lee. *Variety* praised the production as an interesting experiment (it was one of the first to use live, remote pick-ups), but criticized the melodramatic acting (13 October 1948).

T03 *WHAT HAPPENED?*
7-21 August 1952; NBC TV; 30 minutes

Ben Grauer was moderator for this short-lived quiz show which was patterned after *I've Got a Secret*. Stapleton was on a celebrity panel with Lisa Ferraday, Roger Price and Frank Gallop. The panel was introduced to a guest contestant and had to guess how the contestant had been involved with a recent news story. The stories included a Latin Quarter dancer who was allergic to mink, a man who had some birds build a nest in his pants, and a fortune teller whose crystal ball was stolen. Needless to say, *What Happened?* lasted a mere three weeks.

T04 *CURTAIN CALL*
"Carrie Marr"
19 September 1952; NBC TV; 30 minutes

This dramatization was presented for the Curtain Call series which telecast live plays from Hollywood during the summer of 1952. Stapleton co-starred with Frederic Tozere and Val Dufour.

T05 *PHILCO TELEVISION PLAYHOUSE*
"The Accident"
3 May 1953; NBC TV; 60 minutes

The Philco Television Playhouse was a highly regarded series of live television dramas. Both original scripts and material adapted for television were shown. The producer was Fred Coe.

The episode of "The Accident" was written by Paul Peters and directed by Vincent J. Donohue. Stapleton played a woman who becomes responsible for the care of her eleven-year-old nephew when his parents die. The drama shows the effect on the aunt and her family when the emotionally disturbed boy joins their household.

Clifford Tatum played the boy and Lee Graham played the woman's daughter. Other cast members included Jeffrey Lynn, Helen Ray, Joe DeSantis, Angela Adamides and Peter Hobbs.

Variety said that Stapleton "made the most of a most-human role, that of an understanding relative led to an unkind act by concern for her own twelve-year-old daughter" and commended the writing, directing and acting (6 May 1953).

T06 *PHILCO TELEVISION PLAYHOUSE*
"The Mother"
4 May 1954; NBC TV; 60 minutes

This episode on Philco featured an acclaimed script by Paddy Chayefsky. Delbert Mann directed a cast that included Maureen Stapleton, Cathleen Nesbitt, David Opatoshu, George L. Smith, Estelle Hemsley, Perry Wilson, Katherine Hynes, Dora Weissman, Anna Berger and Violetta Diaz.

Nesbitt played an elderly woman of Irish descent whose fierce independence is tested when her daughter (Stapleton) insists she move into their household.

T07 *PHILCO TELEVISION PLAYHOUSE*
"Incident in July"
10 July 1955; NBC TV; 60 minutes.

Stapleton's third appearance on the Philco Playhouse was in this drama by Calder Willingham. She played Mrs. Johnson, the wife of a counselor at a boy's day camp. Having no children of her own, Mrs. Johnson extends her maternal affections to one of the children. When those feelings are misunderstood, she suffers great humiliation.

The rest of the cast included Charles Dingle (Daddy Tom), Dick York (Andy), Peggy Maurer (Madeleine), Will West (Ham Ector), Allen Nourse (Mr. Johnson), Ethel Remey (Mrs. Mulberry), and Arthur Walsh (Jimmy McClain).

T08 *STAR TONIGHT*
3 February 1955 - 9 August 1956; ABC TV; 30 minutes

This series, produced by Harry Herrmann, ran for eighty episodes from 1955 to 1956. In each episode a well-known actor or actress was cast in a drama with an unknown performer. Stapleton was among the professionals who appeared in the series.

T09 *ARMSTRONG CIRCLE THEATRE*
"Minding Our Own Business"
1 November 1955; NBC TV; 60 minutes

John Cameron Swayze was the host/narrator for this drama anthology series which changed format in 1955 to emphasize dramas based on actual events. (In some sources this episode is listed under the title "Actual" because the *TV Guide* describes the story as "tonight's 'actual'.")

David Padwa adapted the story from a book by Charlotte Paul Grosshell which chronicled her experiences as the wife of a newspaperman. The drama tells of a Chicago newspaperman and his wife who relocate to a small town in Washington state and of their struggle to make new neighbors and start a local newspaper.

Stapleton played the role of Charlotte, Edward Andrews played Ed, Pat O'Malley played Walt Peden and Kenny Delmar played Peabody.

T10 *JUSTICE*
"Track of Fear"
11 December 1955; NBC TV; 30 minutes

This series also dramatized actual events—in this instance the stories were based on cases from the files of the National Legal Aid Society.

David Susskind was the producer of the series and William Prince played Richard Adams, an attorney and a recurring character. In this episode, written by Harold Gast, Stapleton co-starred with Theodore Bikel in a story about a man with a past. Faced with questions about that past, the man grows angry and seriously strains relations with his wife and friends.

T11 *ARMSTRONG CIRCLE THEATRE*
"H.R. 8438 - The Story of a Lost Boy"
12 June 1956; NBC TV; 60 minutes

This drama by Phil Reisman, Jr. tells the story of the reunion of an immigrant woman from Yugoslavia with the young son she left behind in Europe. The woman, however, is unaware that the boy she meets is actually an imposter who has stolen a passport to come to America.

Stapleton starred as Elizabeth Steigerwald, the mother. Voytek Dolinski played the role of the boy, Anton Steigerwald. Luis Van Rooten and Lola D'Annunzio were also in the cast.

T12 *STUDIO ONE*
"Rachel: A Love Story"
10 December 1956; CBS TV; 60 minutes

Studio One was another of the esteemed live drama series on television in its early years. This series developed from a radio series and produced nearly five hundred plays in its ten-year run.

Nevertheless, *Variety* saw little merit in this episode by Kathleen Lindsay and Robert Howard Lindsay. It dramatizes the story of Rachel, the wife of Andrew Jackson, who brought scandal to the President's name by marrying him before she had divorced her first husband. The plot revolves around Rachel's inner struggle over convincing Jackson to withdraw from the scandal and retire to his plantation. Jackson must decide between running for the Governorship of Tennessee, joining forces with Aaron Burr, or taking his wife's advice. The critic said that the overall effect was an overly long and thin plot in which Jackson himself never appeared (12 December 1956).

Stapleton's portrayal, along with that of the rest of the cast, was praised. The critic felt she brought warmth and compassion to the role and Everett Sloane gave a forceful performance as Aaron Burr, the man who tries to get Jackson to run his renegade army. The cast also included Edward Andrews (Henry Horne), Joanne Linville (Mary Sevier), Alma Hubbard (Moll), James E. Wall (Jed), Henderson Forsythe (John Overton), Mark Hyken and Edmond Glover.

T13 *THE ALCOA HOUR*
"No License to Kill"
1 September 1957; NBC TV; 60 minutes

A one-hour drama about a fatal car accident and the subsequent police investigation. Stapleton played Vi Miller who, with her husband and young son, is driving to Maine when their car collides with that of a businessman going to New York.

This was a re-make of a drama that originally aired in February 1957 and starred Hume Cronyn and Eileen Heckart. The production was re-filmed in cooperation with the Connecticut State Police and Aetna Casualty and Surety Company and aired over Labor Day Weekend. Governor Abraham E. Ribicoff narrated the film, which was intended to encourage driving safely.

Stapleton's co-star was Eddie Albert who played the role of the businessman, Ralph Grimes. The rest of the cast included Robert Strauss (Lt. Marchess), Frank Overton (Tyler), Hugh Reilly (Howard Miller), Cathleen Nesbitt (Mrs. Miller), Michael Strong (Resident Doctor), Frederick Rolf (Dr. Lane), Louis Badolati (Pollard), Norman Twain (Kirkland) and Stephen Chase (Buren).

T14 *THE SEVEN LIVELY ARTS*
"Blast in Centralia No. 5"
26 January 1958; NBC TV; 60 minutes

The Seven Lively Arts was a short-lived but impressive drama anthology series conceived and directed by John Houseman. This episode was dramatized by Loring Mandel from a story by John Bartlow Martin. George Roy Hill directed and John Crosby was the series host.

"Blast in Centralia No. 5" was highly acclaimed for its script, directing and acting. *Variety* described the drama as "a forceful and courageous presentation that scored with its very simplicity and pointed in a direction that has been barely explored by this medium" (29 January 1958).

Jason Robards, Jr. was the narrator of this drama, which was based on an account of a mine disaster in Illinois. Stapleton starred as the wife and mother of men killed in the explosion. The disaster had occurred following a long history of complaints about the dangerous working conditions in the mine—complaints that were routinely ignored by the authorities.

The cast included Stapleton, Milton Seltzer, Daniel Reed, Carl Low, Guy Raymond, Harry Gresham, John Hamilton, Walter Burke and Cliff James.

One specially haunting scene was the one in which the miner's wife talks to a reporter about the loss of her husband and son. This scene was featured on *CBS on the Air,* a 1978 retrospective of the best of CBS programming.

T15 *KRAFT TELEVISION THEATRE*
"All the King's Men"
Part I: 14 May 1958; Part II: 21 May 1958
NBC TV; 60 minutes each

Kraft Television Theatre was one of the preeminent live drama series in the Golden Age of television. In eleven years Kraft produced over 650 plays and "All the King's Men" was one of the finest dramas of the series. David Susskind was producer and Sidney Lumet directed.

Don Mankiewicz adapted Robert Penn Warren's Pulitzer Prize winning novel which dramatizes the rise to power and assassination of Louisiana Governor Huey Long. Long's fictional counterpart in the novel is Willie Stark. Neville Brand won raves for his portrayal of Stark, as did Maureen Stapleton for her performance as Stark's cunning lover, Sadie Burke. Stapleton garnered her first Emmy nomination for this role.

Also in the cast were Fred J. Scollay (Jack Burden), Anne Meacham (Anne Stanton), William Prince (Adam Stanton), Frank Conroy (Judge Irwin), John Fiedler (Sugar Boy), Perry Wilson (Lucy Stark) and Robert Emhardt (Tiny Duffy).

Variety gave the production an unqualified rave, calling it "tv drama at its very best . . . uncompromising in the wallop it packed and studded with a cast of principles who conveyed that they knew what they were about and were alerted to all the meaningful overtones and undertones of this ugly tale of Willie Stark" (21 May 1958).

T16 *PLAYHOUSE 90*
"For Whom the Bell Tolls"
Part I: 12 March 1959; Part II: 19 March 1959
CBS TV; 90 minutes each

Adapting Ernest Hemingway's epic novel to the screen was among the many ambitious projects of this highly acclaimed series. The three-hour film was not only an artistic challenge, its production budget also made history since the costs of making the two-part program surpassed almost any drama that had been made at that time.

Jason Robards, Jr. starred as Robert Jordan, the American who comes to Spain to fight in the Civil War. Maureen Stapleton played the gypsy, Pilar. Also in the cast were Maria Schell (Maria), Eli Wallach (Rafael), Nehemiah Persoff (Pablo), Steven Hill (Agustin), Vladimir Sokoloff (Anselmo), Milton Selzer (Fernando), Marc Laurence (El Sordo), Herbert Berghof (General Golz), Joseph Bernard (Primitivo), Nick Colossanto (Eladio) and Sydney Pollack (Andres). John Frankenheimer directed the script which A.E. Hotchner adapted from the novel.

Perhaps the critics felt a larger budget should yield a greater product. The gist of the reviews in *Variety* indicate that the film failed to handle the heroic scale of the war as well as it did the love story. Nevertheless, the acting (especially in peripheral roles) was greatly lauded. Stapleton again proved herself worthy of comparison, as the *Variety* critic's comments show: "Maureen Stapleton's Pilar, while not the 'old, ugly woman' the play refers to (and implanted in the minds of American audiences through Katina Paxinou's extraordinary performance in the Par film version), nonetheless was full of the fire and eloquence poured into her by Hemingway" (25 March 1959).

T17 *CBS TELEVISION WORKSHOP*
"Tessie Malfitano"
3 April 1960; CBS TV; 60 minutes

"Tessie Malfitano" was one of two plays by Emanuel Frachtenberg presented on this program. The other was "Anton Waldek." Albert McCleery was producer of the *CBS TV Workshop* and Murray Susskind was guest producer.

Stapleton played the title role in "Tessie;" Julie Bovasso (Sadie) and Albert Quinton (Dominick) also starred. The story is about a woman named Tessie who has a talent for getting involved in other people's lives. Her husband criticizes her for meddling, but the good-hearted Tessie feels she's just being helpful.

T18 *A QUESTION OF CHAIRS: THE CHALLENGE OF AMERICAN EDUCATION*
15 January 1961; CBS TV; 60 minutes

CBS and the Anti-Defamation League co-produced this docudrama which explored America's traditional resistance to educational change. The program consisted of dramatized scenes of American history focusing on the problems and issues in education.

Everett Sloane was narrator. The cast included Stapleton, Walter Abel, George Voskovec, Marc Richman, and Paul Lynde, among others. Don Kellerman was producer of the special; Mel Ferber was director and Lane Slate the writer.

T19 *PLAY OF THE WEEK*
"Four by Tennessee Williams"
6 February 1961; 120 minutes

Four one-act plays by Williams were adapted to the home screen: *I Rise in Flame, Cried the Phoenix*; *Hello from Bertha*; *The Lady of Larkspur Lotion*; and *The Purification*. Stapleton appeared with Eileen Heckart and Salome Jens in *Hello from Bertha*, which takes place in St. Louis on the wild side of town. Stapleton played Bertha, a woman of questionable reputation, whose life is on the down swing.

T20 *CAR 54, WHERE ARE YOU?*
"The Gypsy Curse"
12 November 1961; NBC TV; 30 minutes

Nat Hiken created and produced this wacky comedy of two Bronx police officers, Gunther Toody (played by Joe E. Ross) and Francis Muldoon (played by Fred Gwynne). In this episode Stapleton played Mrs. Lupesko, a revengeful gypsy. When a Mr. Kramer (Maurice Brennon) complains that the gypsy has conned him, Toody investigates and falls under the gypsy's curse.

T21 ***THE NAKED CITY***
"Oofus Goofus"
13 December 1961; ABC TV; 60 minutes

Mickey Rooney and Maureen Stapleton co-starred in this episode of the popular crime drama, *The Naked City*. The series was based on Mark Hellinger story and the 1948 movie of the same name.

Jo Pagano wrote the story which included series regulars Paul Burke (Detective Adam Flint), Horace MacMahon (Lt. Mike Parker), Nancy Malone (Libby) and Harry Bellaver (Sgt. Frank Arcaro). Rooney and Stapleton played George and Abbey Bick, who start a riot at the supermarket when George changes the price tags on the food and a carton of eggs sells for two cents and prime rib goes for four cents.

T22 ***THE NAKED CITY***
"Kill Me When I'm Young So I Can Die Happy"
17 October 1962; ABC TV; 60 minutes

Here Stapleton again portrays a character seeking revenge. This time she is retired policewoman Ruth Cullan who strikes back when police prevent her taking her own life. Carl Byrd and Rosetta Veneziam were the other guest artists. See **T21** for series regulars.

T23 ***THE DUPONT SHOW OF THE WEEK***
"The Betrayal"
21 October 1962; NBC TV; 60 minutes

Ernest Pendrell wrote this adaptation of Joseph Conrad's 1911 novel, *Under Western Eyes*. Jack Smight directed; Lewis Freedman produced. The story concerns the assassination of a Communist Party official behind the Berlin Wall. Franchot Tone played the East German Police Inspector and Stapleton portrayed a Nobel Prize-winning scientist and former Communist who is a leader in the East German underground. Margaret O'Brien, John Abbott, Burt Brinckerhoff and Blanche Yurka were also in the cast.

Variety found that the excellent acting could not save a flawed script which seemed dependent on atmosphere: " 'The Betrayal' was a mixture of melodramatics, spying, police state, skullduggery, and cardboard people" (24 October 1962).

T24 ***ROBERT HERRIDGE THEATER***
"Riders to the Sea"
29 November 1962; NET; 30 minutes

Robert Herridge was producer and host for this drama anthology series. This program was a television adaptation of Irish playwright John Millington Synge's one-act drama, *Riders to the Sea*. Karl Genus directed and Tom Scott created the music.

The play concerns a family on the Irish seacoast. At the outset of the story, the old widow of the family, Maurya, has lost five sons at sea. As the daughters wait to identify the remains of their brother, Michael, Maurya foretells the death of the last son, Bartley. Soon word comes that Barley has fallen from his horse into the waves and is dashed against the rock cliffs just as Maurya foreold. The old woman and her daughters are left to grieve their loss.

The cast included Maureen Stapleton, Helena Carroll, Liam Gannon and Katherine Willard.

T25 *EAST SIDE / WEST SIDE*
"One Drink at a Time"
27 January 1964; CBS TV; 60 minutes

This series only lasted one season but it effectively dramatized urban ills such as drug addiction, families struggling on welfare, and problems of the aged, in a stark realistic style. George C. Scott played Neil Brock, a young social worker in the New York ghetto. Other regulars were Cicely Tyson (Jane Foster) and Freida Hechlinger (Elizabeth Wilson). David Susskind produced the esteemed series.

"One Drink at a Time" was one of two episodes written for the series by Edward Adler, a New York cabbie. J.D. Cannon co-starred with Stapleton. They played Sam and Molly, two homeless people who have known one another for twenty years. An argument ensues between them when Molly tries to keep Sam from drinking wood alcohol. Other guest performers were John Karlen (Billy) and Tom Ahearne (Harry).

T26 *NEW YORK TELEVISION THEATRE*
"Save Me a Place at Forest Lawn"
7 March 1966; NET; 60 minutes

Lorees Yorby wrote this small screen adaptation of her own one-act play. Two accomplished character actresses, Eileen Heckart and Maureen Stapleton, co-starred as Clara and Gertrude, two elderly but feisty old friends who meet for dinner in a tawdry cafeteria to gossip and plan their burials. *Variety* praised the humor and compassion of Ms. Yorby's play and credited Heckart and Stapleton's performances for its successful realization (9 March 1966).

T27 *XEROX SPECIAL EVENT*
"Among the Paths to Eden"
17 December 1967; ABC TV; 60 minutes

Stapleton won the Emmy Award for her performance as Mary O'Meaghan in this story by Truman Capote. This program was one of three Capote stories filmed for television. The others were "Miriam" and "A Christmas Memory." All these stories were combined and released as a film, *Truman Capote's Trilogy* (see **F05** for details).

Capote was co-producer with Frank Perry and Eleanor Perry. The score was by Meyer Kupferman.

Martin Balsam co-starred as Ivor Belli, an ordinary-looking middle-age widower who visits his late wife's grave in a depressing urban cemetery. The dreary site is brightened by the arrival of a smiling, desperate spinster, Mary O'Meaghan. Mary sets out to alleviate Ivor's grief and so to find herself a husband.

The critic from *Variety* praised Balsam and Stapleton's performances, saying "their portrayals managed some genuine warmth and poignancy, and more humor than the script warranted" (20 December 1967).

T28 *JOHNNY CARSON'S REPERTORY COMPANY IN AN EVENING OF COMEDY*
12 November 1969; NBC TV; 60 minutes

Johnny Carson, George C. Scott, Maureen Stapleton and Marian Mercer starred in this hour of comedy skits. Rudy Tellez was producer, Bobby Quinn directed and Carson, Marshall Brickman and David Lloyd wrote the sketches.

It was, according to *Variety*, a cut above the usual comedy-hour fare due to the skills of the guest performers. Stapleton appeared in a sketch which lampooned an awards ceremony for underground movies. She also played a mother whose son is a filmmaker of adult movies and she portrayed a masculine actress starring in a film entitled *The Killing of Sister Bruce* (a parody of *The Killing of Sister George*). The final skit was a send-up of Tennessee Williams plays which the *Variety* critic felt was too burlesqued (19 November 1969).

T29 *MIRROR, MIRROR OFF THE WALL*
21 November 1969; NBC TV; 60 minutes

Stapleton once again co-starred with George C. Scott in this special which was produced for Prudential's *On Stage*. M.J. Rifkin and Murray Chercover were the executive producers. Producer was Alan Landsburg. Fielder Cook directed the script by David Shaw.

Scott played Max Maxwell, a down and out writer who turns to writing lurid adult fiction to pay the bills. He even takes on a pen name—N.Y. Rome—which develops into a full-fledged alter-ego who suddenly appears when his dirty book becomes a whopping success. Stapleton played Max's wife, Ruthie, who also develops an alter-ego. In their new roles, Ruthie and "Rome" go off to Hollywood to indulge in their new fantasies.

T30 *TENNESSEE WILLIAMS' SOUTH*
26 March 1973; Canadian Broadcasting Corporation TV

Harry Rasky's ninety-minute documentary was first aired on Canadian TV on the sixty-second birthday of playwright Tennessee Williams. Rasky produced, directed and wrote the script. Arla Saare was film editor; Lou Applebaum created the music; Stephen Finnie did the set decoration.

Williams himself appeared in the film talking about his life and taking viewers on a tour of the Southern towns where he grew up. In between these autobiographical segments, scenes from various Williams stories were performed by John Colicos, Colleen Dewhurst, William Hutt, Burl Ives, Maureen Stapleton, Jessica Tandy and Michael York. Ives recited the shoe salesman's monologue from "The Last of My Gold Watches," Dewhurst and Colicos played a scene from *Night of the Iguana*, Tandy performed her famous role of Blanche in *A Streetcar Named Desire*,

Hutt gave a monologue from *Small Craft Warnings,* and Michael York and Maureen Stapleton played Tom and Amanda from *The Glass Menagerie.*

Dan Sullivan reviewed the film in the *Los Angeles Times* when it aired on KCET-TV in Los Angeles, December 8, 1976. Sullivan said "Williams is in wonderful form here, the old possum who has got his health back and who has *not* lost his capacity for wonder" (8 December 1976).

T31 *GENERAL ELECTRIC THEATER*
"Tell Me Where It Hurts"
12 March 1974; CBS TV; 90 minutes

The teleplay for "Tell Me Where It Hurts" won an Emmy for its author, Fay Kanin. Stapleton starred in this story of a housewife, Connie Monone, who becomes dissatisfied with her life, so she forms a support group of her six closest friends; in so doing she brings about positive change for herself and her friends.

Roger Gimbel was the executive producer and Herbert Hirschmann the producer. Paul Bogart directed Kanin's teleplay. In addition to Stapleton, the cast included Paul Sorvino (Joe), Doris Dowling (Reva), Rose Gregorio (Agnes), Ayn Ruyman (Lynn), John Randolph (Lou), Louise Latham (Louise), Scottie MacGregor (Marge), Pearl Shear (Edna), and Fay Kanin (Jane).

The critic in *Variety* raved about Stapleton's peformance: "Fay Kanin has written one of the best roles for a woman in several years and Maureen Stapleton has interpreted it brilliantly." The same critic, however, faulted the teleplay for its one-dimensional male roles and its moral: "The play and its seeming endorsement of the inchworm approach to self-realization might not please the more militant advocates of feminine liberation" (20 March 1974).

T32 *QUEEN OF THE STARDUST BALLROOM*
13 February 1975; CBS TV; 120 minutes

This made-for-tv movie received numerous Emmy Award nominations, including a nomination for Stapleton as Best Actress in a Drama or Comedy Special. Following its success on the small screen, Michael Bennett adapted the script to the stage for the 1978 Broadway musical, *Ballroom.*

Stapleton starred in the role of Bea Asher, who struggles to cope with the sudden loss of her husband. She finds new reason for spending time at the local ballroom where she meets a shy postman, played by Charles Durning. They have a brief affair before she learns that he is married; nevertheless their gentle romance leads them to winning first prize in the dance contest.

Variety said that Stapleton and Durning's performances were "brilliant," especially in the ballroom sequences (19 February 1975). The film was enhanced by Marge Champion's award-winning choreography and its authentic atmosphere—it was filmed at Myron's, a famous ballroom dance hall in Los Angeles.

The production credits are as follows: Producers: Robert W. Christiansen and Rick Rosenberg. Director: Sam O'Steen. Teleplay:

Jerome Kass. Photography: David M. Walsh. Music: Billy Goldenberg. Original score: Billy Goldenberg, Alan Bergman and Marilyn Bergman. Choreography: Marge Champion. Editor: William H. Ziegler.

The cast included Stapleton (Bea Asher), Charles Durning (Al Green), Michael Brandon (Davis Asher), Elizabeth Berger (Jennifer), Lewis Charles (Johnny), Natalie Core (Pauline Krimm), Alan Fudge (Louis), Florence Halop (Sylvia), Danna Hansen (Martha), Jacquelyn Hyde (Angie), Holly Irving (Marie), Gil Lamb (Harry), Nora Marlowe (Emily), Charlotte Rae (Helen), Guy Raymond (Petie) and Beverly Sanders, Michael Strong, Claude Stroud, Ruth Warshawsky, Martha Tilton and Orin Tucker and his orchestra.

T33 CAT ON A HOT TIN ROOF
6 December 1976; Granada Television/NBC TV; 120 minutes

Laurence Olivier chose Tennessee Williams' Pulitzer Prize-winning play as the first offering in his *Tribute to American Theatre* series. Olivier played "Big Daddy" opposite Maureen Stapleton as "Big Mama." Natalie Wood and Robert Wagner starred as Maggie and Brick in an otherwise all-British cast.

Williams' play involves the conflicts in a Southern family that is dominated by the dying patriarch, Big Daddy. Gathered together to obstensably celebrate Big Daddy's birthday, his sons (Brick and Gooper) and their wives (Maggie and Mae) maneuver to get Daddy to name his heir. The shrewdest among the lot is Maggie "the cat," who must seduce her own disenchanted husband and become pregnant to influence Big Daddy to name Brick as heir to the estate.

Derek Granger and Laurence Olivier produced the program for Granada Television. Robert Moore directed Williams' teleplay. Michael Lankester did the music arrangements from the music of Henry Purcell. Set and costumes were by Peter Phillips and Jane Robinson, respectively. In addition to those already mentioned, the cast included Jack Hedley (Gooper), Mary Peach (Mae), Heidi Rundt (Dixie), Sean Saxon (Sonny), Mark Taylor (Buster), Elizabeth Caparros (Trixie), Jennifer Hughes (Polly), Sam Manseray (Lacey), Gladys Taylor (Daisy), Nadia Catouse (Brightie), George Harris (Sookie), Mel Taylor (Small), and David Healy (Doc Baugh).

Variety criticized the production for seeming dated and for falling into caricature. (The play was twenty-one years old when the telefilm was made.) Only Natalie Wood and Stapleton were commended for the credibility of their performances (8 December 1976).

T34 THERE'S ALWAYS ROOM
24 April 1977; CBS TV; 30 minutes

This was a pilot for a comedy series starring Maureen Stapleton. She played Madelyn Fairchild, a middle-aged woman who converts her Los Angeles home into a boarding house for eccentric friends. Other regulars were Conrad Janis, who played Stewart Dennis, the greeting card salesman, and Debbie Zip who played Annette Ederby, who resides with Madelyn while attending school. The rest of the cast on the pilot episode were Barry Nelson, Leland Palmer, Royce D. Appelgate and Woody Chambliss.

Although the series did not develop, *Variety* thought it showed real promise: "The concept has a *You Can't Take It with You* flavor that is all to its credit, with Stapleton presiding over the menage with a nice combination of whimsical flippancy and good commonsense" (27 April 1977).

T35 *THE GATHERING*
4 December 1977; ABC TV; 120 minutes
Video: Worldvision Home Video Inc.

The Gathering won the 1978 Emmy Award for Best Special, Drama or Comedy when it aired on *ABC Theatre*. Maureen Stapleton received an Emmy nomination as Best Actress as well. Critics raved about her performance in this drama about the reunion of a family at Christmas.

James Poe wrote this critically acclaimed teleplay, for which he received an Emmy nomination. Randal Kleiser also received a nomination for his direction of the telefilm and art director Jan Scott and set decorator Anne D. McCulley received an Emmy nomination for Outstanding Art Direction. Joseph Barbera was executive producer and Harry R. Sherman was producer.

The story is that of a self-centered executive (played by Edward Asner) who loses touch with his family. When he learns he is dying, he reunites with his estranged wife and family for a Christmas gathering. The film was highly regarded for its honest simplicity and moving drama. The critic in *Variety* wrote that "the triumph of the night must be credited to Maureen Stapleton as the wife who had been walked out on four years before for little apparent reason" (7 December 1977).

The cast was as follows: Edward Asner (Adam Thornton), Maureen Stapleton (Kate Thornton), Rebecca Balding (Julie Pelham), Sarah Cunningham (Clara), Bruce Davison (George Pelham), Veronica Hamel (Helen Thornton), Gregory Harrison (Bud Thornton), James Karen (Bob Block), Lawrence Pressman (Tom Thornton), John Randolph, (Dr. John Hodges), Gail Strickland (Peggy Thornton) and Edward Winter, Stephanie Zimbalist, John Hubbard, Mary Bradley Marable, Maureen Readinger, Ronald Readinger, Cynthia Longstreth and Priscilla Graham.

T36 *LETTERS FROM FRANK*
22 November 1979; CBS TV; 120 minutes

Art Carney and Maureen Stapleton co-starred in this drama based on a story by George Thompson. Carney played Frank Miller, who loses his job of thirty-five years to a computer. Frank's anger is tempered by the concerns of his wife, Betty (played by Stapleton), his son and the death of his older brother.

Letters from Frank was produced by Gerald W. Abrams (executive producer) and Ronald Shedlo (producer). Edward Parone directed the teleplay which was written by Stephen Karpf, Elinor Karpf and Larry Grusin.

The cast also included Mike Farrell (Richard Miller), Gail Strickland (Marlene), Mary Jackson (Edna Miller), Jenny O'Hara (Patty Miller), Lew Ayres (Dan Miller), Margaret Hamilton (Grandma Miller), Michael

Goodwin (Mr. Carstairs), Michael J. Fox (Ricky Miller), and Margaret Martin, Shirley Barkley, Guy Bannerman and Robert Stelmach.

T37 *THE GATHERING: PART II*
17 December 1979; NBC; 120 minutes
Video: Worldvision Home Video, Inc.

The popularity of the award-winning *The Gathering* (see **T35**) led to this sequel which focused on Kate Thornton, who was widowed in the first part. Part II aired on a different network, NBC, as part of its *Proud as a Peacock* offerings.

Once again the focus of the story is the gathering of the family at Christmas time. In this reunion, Kate Thornton has taken over the business of her husband following his death. When a handsome businessman (played by Efrem Zimbalist, Jr.) offers to buy her out, Kate finds a new love in her life which promises to alleviate her grief.

Charles S. Dubin directed the teleplay by Renee S. Longstreet and Harry S. Longstreet. Joseph Barbera was executive producer and Joel Rogosin was producer. Robert Prince created the music. The cast included Maureen Stapleton (Kate Thornton), Rebecca Balding (Julie), Patricia Conwell (Toni), Bruce Davison (George), Veronica Hamel (Helen), Jameson Parker (Bud), Lawrence Pressman (Tom), Efrem Zimbalist, Jr. (Victor Wainwright), Dennis Howard (Aaron), Jessica Hill (Tiffany), John Ine (Joey), Norman Goodman (Lee Rifkind), Anita Sangiolo (Lucille Rifkind) and Naomi Thornton, Edward C. Higgins, Rose Weaver and Father Frank Toste.

T38 *THE ELECTRIC GRANDMOTHER*
17 January 1982; NBC; 60 minutes
Video: Learning Corporation of America

This program was created for the *Peacock Showcase*, which presented programs for children. Jeffrey Kindley and Ray Bradbury created the teleplay, based on Bradbury's story, "I Sing the Body Electric." Stapleton played the part of a robot, an "electric grandmother," who is given a thirty-day trial in the home of a widower and his three children. One child rejects her and the grandmother is almost returned to the factory until a family crisis allows her to prove herself to the small child.

Linda Gottleib was executive producer; Doro Bachrach was producer. Noel Black directed the telefilm. In addition to Stapleton, the cast included Edward Herrmann, Tara Kennedy, Robert MacNaughton, Charles Fields, Paul Benedict, Madeleine Thornton-Sherwood, Truman Gaige, Richard Whiting, Dortha Duckworth, and Paula Trueman. Michael Pritchard and Sydney Penny were hosts.

T39 *LITTLE GLORIA ... HAPPY AT LAST*
Part I: 24 October 1982; Part II: 25 October 1982
NBC TV; 120 minutes each
Video: Prism Entertainment

Judith Crist included this telefilm in her list in *TV Guide* of the ten best movies of the year. She remarked that the drama "rises above its succulent domestic melodrama with taste, intelligence, a knock-out cast and opulence" (8 January 1983, 8). The four-hour special program was an adaptation of Barbara Goldsmith's popular novel about the 1934 trial for custody of ten-year-old heiress Gloria Vanderbilt. The program garnered six Emmy nominations and excellent reviews.

The star-studded cast included Martin Balsam (Nathan Burkan), Bette Davis (Alice Claypoole Vanderbilt), Barnard Hughes (Justice John Francis Carew), Glynis Johns (Laura Fitzpatrick Morgan), Angela Lansbury (Gertrude Vanderbilt Whitney), Christopher Plummer (Reginald Vanderbilt) and Maureen Stapleton, who played Nurse Emma Kieslich. Also in the cast were Michael Gross, John Hillerman, Rosalyn Landor, Joseph Maher, Leueen Willoughby and Kenneth Pogue. Jennifer Dundas played little Gloria.

The review in *Variety* was somewhat mixed. The critic found fault with the direction (it lacked subtlety) and the script (which was sensationalistic). Nevertheless, the brilliant cast and fascination of the story redeemed the film. The critic singled out Bette Davis for her role as the domineering Alice Vanderbilt, Angela Lansbury for her portrayal of Gloria's aunt, and Maureen Stapleton who "stalwartly played possessive, manipulative Nurse Kieslich" (27 October 1982).

Waris Hussein directed the teleplay written by William Hanley. Executive producers were Edgar J. Scherick and Scott Rudin. Producers were David Nicksay and Justine Heroux. Berthold Carriere did the music and Stuart Wurtzel designed the handsome production.

T40   *GREAT PERFORMANCES*
"Alice in Wonderland"
3 October 1983; NET; 90 minutes

In 1982 Eva LeGallienne and WNET-TV, the Public Broadcasting Network in New York, teamed up to produce a revival of LeGallienne's 1932 production of *Alice in Wonderland* on Broadway. It was a musical version with sets and costumes modeled after the classical Tenniel illustrations from Lewis Carroll's "Alice's Adventures in Wonderland" and "Through the Looking Glass." The Broadway production did not live up to its promise. Nevertheless, WNET took another gamble and put together a star-studded cast for the television production which aired on the *Great Performances* series.

Kate Burton, daughter of well-known British actor Richard Burton, played Alice in both the stage and television versions. Her father joined the television cast in the role of the White Knight. Maureen Stapleton was cast in the role played by LeGallienne on Broadway, that of the White Queen. The rest of the cast included Austin Pendleton (White Rabbit), Nathan Lane (Mouse), Fritz Weaver (Caterpillar), Kaye Ballard (Duchess), Geoffrey Holder (Cheshire Cat), André Gregory (Mad Hatter), Zeljko Ivanek (March Hare), Eve Arden (Queen of Hearts), Tony Cumming (Knave of Hearts), James Coco (King of Hearts), Swen Swenson (Gryphon), Donald O'Connor (Mock Turtle), Colleen Dewhurst (Red Queen), Alan Weeks (Tweedledee), Andre de Shields (Tweedledum), Richard Woods (Humpty Dumpty), and Richard Burton (White Knight).

John J. O'Connor, critic for the *New York Times,* applauded changes which "transformed a disastrous stage production of *Alice in*

Wonderland into a production of impressive charm" (3 October 1983). O'Connor credited executive producer Jac Venza for the condensation to a ninety-minute teleplay and expressed admiration for the score by Richard Addinsell and the costumes and settings by Patricia Zipprodt and John Lee Beatty, respectively. Others involved in the successful production were Ann Blumenthal (producer), Kirk Browning (director), Jonathan Tunick (arranger and composer of additional music), and Donald Saddler (choreographer).

T41 *FAMILY SECRETS*
13 May 1984; NBC; 120 minutes

Produced for the General Foods Golden Showcase, this telefilm originally was to have been entitled *Mother's Day*. It was aired to coincide with that holiday. Stapleton played a college dean, Maggie Lukauer, who has recently been widowed. Stefanie Powers played her daughter, Jessie Calloway, who is an aggressive career woman. Melissa Gilbert played Sara Calloway—Powers' illegitimate teenage daughter. The three women are reunited to pack up their belongings after the family home is sold. Memories and unresolved tensions flare up during the emotional reunion.

Variety panned this story as a "puffed-up women's magazine story about three generations of women [which] sheds light on their respective 'secrets' but doesn't do much in the drama department" (23 May 1984).

Executive producers were Raymond Katz and Sandy Gallin. Frank Brill was supervising producer. Stefanie Powers and Leonora Thuna produced the teleplay which Thuna also wrote based on a story by Powers. Director was Jack Hofsiss.

In addition to Stapleton, Powers and Gilbert, the cast included James Spader (Lowell Everall), Irene Tedrow (Mrs. Fenwick), Kimmy Robertson (Mickey), Gary Dontzig (Barry Haynes), Marion Ramsey (Linda Jones), and Gary Sinisie and Marlena Giovi.

T42 *SENTIMENTAL JOURNEY*
16 October 1984; CBS TV; 120 minutes

Jaclyn Smith and David Dukes co-starred in this tearful drama about a successful Broadway couple, Bill Gardner and Julie Ross-Gardner. She's a producer and he's a popular stage star. Following the wife's miscarriage, a young orphan enters their life, only to cause trouble when she returns the affection of Dukes but not that of Smith.

The telefilm was based on a story by Neila Gardner White. It had two former treatments—a 1946 film with Maureen O'Hara and John Payne and a 1958 version (*A Gift of Love*) with Lauren Bacall and Robert Stack. Darlene Craviotto and Frank J. Cavestani wrote the updated television version. James Goldstone directed. Gary Morton and Tony Richmond were executive producers. Harry R. Sherman and Lawrence Taylor-Mortoff were producers. Billy Goldenberg did the music.

Maureen Stapleton played Smith's loyal secretary, Ruthie. *Variety* approved of the production values of the film, but faulted it for excessive sentimentality and lack of credibility. The critic said that Stapleton "gives, along with Dukes, the telefilm any credibility it does have" (24 October 1984).

The rest of the cast included Jessica Rene Carroll (Libby), Elia Enid Cadilla (Alicia), Philip Levier (Steve), Russell Horton (Gregory), Sam Schachi (Roger), Robert Hill (Bookkeeper), Richmond Hoxie (Salesman), Michael P. Moran (Stagehand), Gerry Bamman (Artie) and William Andrews, Arthur French, Tom Bade, Michael Jeter, Tom Costello, Charles Duval and Shawn Elliott.

T43   *PRIVATE SESSIONS*
18 March 1985; NBC TV; 120 minutes

This pilot for a dramatic series was televised on the NBC *Monday Night at the Movies*. The series (which did not develop) was concerned with a divorced Manhattan psychotherapist, his teenage daughter, and the psycholanalyst who shares his suite of offices. Mike Farrell played the therapist, Dr. Joe Braden, and Maureen Stapleton played Dr. Liz Bolger, his co-worker. Critics found the premise of the series problematic because of the difficulty of making a psychiatrist's job dramatically interesting.

The pilot episode (in which Stapleton appeared only briefly) starred Kelly McGillis as Jennifer Coles, a patient of Doctor Braden who is driven to picking up strangers for casual sexual liaisons. The cast also included Denise Miller (Angie), Kathryn Walker (Claire Braden), Mary Tanner (Millie Braden), David Labiosa (Ramon), Tom Bosley (Harry O'Reilly), Robert Vaughn (Oliver Coles), Greg Evigan (Rick), Hope Lange (Mrs. Coles), Kim Hunter (Rosemary O'Reilly), Victor Garber (Jerry Sharma), John Cunningham (Paul Rodgers), Wendie Malick (Tippi), Elias Koteas (Johnny O'Reilly) and Paul Land, Davenia McFadden, Edmond Genest, Eevin Harisborough, John Horton, Kathryn Dowling, Jane Cronin, Raul Davila, John Capodice, Geoffrey Horne, Doug Sloan, William Converse Roberts, John Bentley and Lorraine Morin.

Michael Pressman directed the teleplay by Thom Thomas and David Seltzer. Executive producers were Deanne Barkley, Norman Gimbel and Philip Capice. Producer was Thom Thomas. Music was by Lalo Schifrin and production design by Charles Bennett.

T44   *THE THORNS*
January 1988; ABC TV; 30 minutes

This short-lived series was intended to be a mad-cap thirties-style sophisticated comedy, according to *Variety*, but it fell short of that mark (27 January 1988). The *New York Times* felt the series failed at the outset because the characters were quite unlikeable (15 January 1988).

The series revolved around a social climbing couple, the Thorns, and their family: Tony Roberts played the ambitious public relations man (Sloan Thorn), Kelly Bishop played his wife (Ginger), Marilyn Cooper was his mother (Rose), and Mary Louise Wilson played the French maid. Lori Petty, Adam Biesk, Lisa Rieffel and Jesse Tendler filled out the regular cast. Maureen Stapleton appeared in only one episode, entitled "The Maid."

Mike Nichols was executive producer of the series and John Bowab was director. Allan Leicht created the series and was chief writer and supervising producer. Music was by John Kander and Fred Ebb and Dorothy Loudon sang the theme song.

T45 *LIBERACE: BEHIND THE MUSIC*
9 October 1988; CBS TV; 120 minutes

This program, which aired on the *CBS Sunday Movie,* was one of two telefilms concerning the flayboyent Liberace. The other, entitled simply *Liberace* aired on ABC TV within a few weeks. *Variety* judged CBS's effort a sensationalistic travesty which emphasized Liberace's public image and self-indulgence. The critic singled out weak performances by Saul Rubinek, as the piano man's manager, and Paul Hipp as Elvis Presley, but said that "Maureen Stapleton, playing interfering mother Frances, does give her role bite and even credibility among the garish goings-on" (19 October 1988).

Victor Garber played Liberace. The cast also included Michael Wikes (Liberace's brother), Macha Grenon (Joanne Rio), Michael Dolan (Scott Thorsen) and Dianne Heatherington. David Greene directed; Linda Yellen and Nancy Bein were executive producers; Murray Shostak was producer; Gavin Lambert wrote the teleplay; and Hagood Hardy created the music.

T46 *B. L. STRYKER*
"Auntie Sue"
17 April 1989; ABC TV; 120 minutes

Maureen Stapleton made a guest appearance on this Burt Reynolds detective series. She played Reynolds' indomitable Aunt Sue who is determined to buy a magnificent old house for herself and her elderly friends.

Burt Reynolds led the cast in the title role. Other cast members included Ossie Davis (Oz), Dana Kaminski (Lyynda), Jack Gilford (Morrie Klein), Harry Carry, Jr. (Jim-Bob Jones), Douglas Fairbanks, Jr. (E.A.W.H. White), Ted McGinley (Mitch Slade) and Rita Moreno (Kimberly).

T47 *THE EQUALIZER*
"The Caper"
4 May 1989; CBS TV; 60 minutes

Edward Woodward starred in this dramatic series as crime investigator McCall. Chad Redding played Detective Shepherd. Stapleton made a guest appearance as an eccentric cleaning-woman who turns detective when she inadvertently witnesses a murder. Her actions jeopardize McCall's own investigation.

T48 *LAST WISH*
12 January 1992; ABC TV; 120 minutes

In 1991 the issue of a person's right to choose death over pain and illness came to the fore when a doctor helped a terminal patient commit suicide. *Last Wish* was thereore an important dramatization of a current social concern. This fact-based drama was adapted by Jerome Kass who had also written the 1975 teleplay of *Queen of the Stardust Ballroom* for which she received an Emmy nomination.

Last Wish is an dramatization of Betty Rollin's novel. Rollin is a news journalist who also wrote *First You Cry,* about her own victory over cancer. That book was adapted for television in 1978. *Last Wish* concerns Rollin's elderly mother, Ida, who also became a victim of cancer.

The story depicts Ida as an energetic senior who is thoroughly enjoying life until she learns she has cancer. She undergoes extensive treatment but in the end is unable to survive. When the chemotherapy makes her too ill to be able to eat she urges her daughter Betty to find her a graceful way to die. During a hiatus of the nausea Betty and her husband bring Ida a combination of pills that allows her to fall asleep and pass into a death with dignity.

Stapleton gave a bravura performance as the vital and stalwart Ida. Patty Duke matched that performance playing the daughter, Betty. The rest of the cast included Dwight Schultz (Ed), Lee Wallace (Alvin), Tresa Hughes (Shany), Patricia Englund (Rose), Ian D. Clark (Dr. Burns), Diane D'Aquila (Maryanne), Donna Goodhand (Freida), Marium Carvell (Belva) and Helen Hughes, Laura Press, Beth Berman, Glynis Davis, Tony de Santis, Craig Eldridge, Marc Gomes, Ellen Gould, Stephen Hunter, Patricia Idlette, Bill McIntyre, and Tom Melissis.

Jeff Bleckner directed. Executive producers were Joan Barnett and Jack Grossbart. David Shire created the music, Tony Hall was art director, Tod Feuerman was film editor, and François Protat was director of photography.

Film Performances

In this section, **Film Performances**, the films of Maureen Stapleton are listed in chronological order with the name of the studio, year of release, length in minutes and videotape distributor (if available on tape). Also listed are production credits, cast, a synopsis of the film and reviews and commentary on it. Minor film credits, such as home video and educational films, are incorporated into the **Biography** section.

F01 *LONELYHEARTS*
United Artists; 1958; 108 minutes

Credits
Based on the novella, *Miss Lonelyhearts*, by Nathanael West and the play by Howard Teichman. Producer: Dore Schary. Director: Vincent J. Donohue. Screenwriter: Dore Schary. Cinematographer: John Alton. Editors: Aaron Steele and John Faure. Music: Conrad Salinger. Music Director: Adolph Deutsch. Art Director: Serge Krizman. Set Decoration: Darrell Silvera. Costumes: Chuck Arrico and Angela Alexander. Make Up: Abe Haberman and Frank Laure.

Cast

Adam White	Montgomery Clift
William Shrike	Robert Ryan
Florence Shrike	Myrna Loy
Justy Sargent	Dolores Hart
Fay Doyle	**Maureen Stapleton**
Pat Doyle	Frank Maxwell
Ned Gates	Jackie Coogan
Frank Goldsmith	Mike Kellin
Mr. Sargent	Frank Overton
Don Sargent	Don Washbrook
Johnny Sargent	John Washbrook
Mr. Lassiter	Onslow Stevens
Edna	Mary Alan Hokanson

And John Gallaudet, Lee Zimmer, J. B. Welch, Charles Wagenheim, Frank Richards and Dorothy Neumann.

Synopsis

Dore Schary produced and wrote this screen adaptation of Nathanael West's cynical novel, *Miss Lonelyhearts*. The story is about an idealistic newspaper reporter (named Adam White in the film) and his hard-boiled editor, evocatively named Shrike.   In an effort to break down White's insistent belief in the goodness of man, Shrike challenges the reporter to become "Miss Lonelyhearts" and to write the paper's advice-to-the-lovelorn column.

As White takes on the identity of Lonelyhearts, he is deeply affected. Before long he is overwhelmed by the extreme pain and sorrow of the women who write to him for advice. Shrike presses White to become more personally involved with his readers to prove that most of them are really frauds. Faced with a chasm of human need, Lonelyhearts decides to try to help one soul. He betrays his own girlfriend by having a sordid affair with a reader named Mrs. Doyle. The woman seems at first to be a victim of a deadly marriage to a crippled and impotent husband but White soon learns that Mrs. Doyle is an unscrupulous nymphomaniac who is quick to play on his sympathy. This abortive attempt at compassion threatens his own future happiness and leads him into another affair with Shrike's alcoholic wife.

West's novel was set in the 1930s and ends violently with the murder of White at the hands of Mrs. Doyle's crippled husband. Schary, however, updated the novel, setting it in the 1950s and he revised the ending so that the reporter dramatically talks Doyle out of the murder and all the couples—the Doyles, the Shrikes, and White and his fiancée are reconciled.

Reviews and Commentary

The critics praised Montgomery Clift and a fine supporting cast but criticized Schary's adaptation. Although his version was much closer to West's novel than the first film adaptation (*Advice to the Lovelorn,* 1933), critics claimed that Schary backed away from the full tragedy of West's story and made it conform to the values of the day. In his critical essay, "Miss L Gets Married," Michael Klein wrote that the film demonstrated that "1950s values of pragmatic compromise and upwardly mobile suburbanite marriage [can] easily resolve the maddening contradictions that destroyed the obsessed figures of West's original work" (1978, 19). In *Time* West's novel was described as "a vision of hell on earth, a scream of anguish at the meaninglessness of human suffering," and Schary's version was termed "a snappy, sexy, phony little Horatio Alger story" (23 March 1959, 95).

Bosley Crowther, critic for the *New York Times*, praised the director and the cast but felt that Schary's script did not resolve the characters' crises in an effective way. He faults Schary for his rewriting of the final confrontation in which the irate husband threatens but does not go through with his violent intentions. Crowther found the film pretentious in that it infers a possible redemption for the characters that is impossible in their world.

Maureen Stapleton made an auspicious film debut in *Lonelyhearts*. She received her first Oscar nomination for her portrayal of Mrs. Doyle. Of her performance, Crowther said, "Miss Stapleton is harrowingly hectic as the hungry dame who deceives the young man" (5 March 1959, 35). The critic from *Time* called Stapleton "a gifted actress from Broadway who, in her first movie role, impersonates a revolting specimen discovered by Miss Lonelyhearts on a 'field trip' among his correspondents" (23 March 1959, 95).

*****

F02   *THE FUGITIVE KIND*
United Artists; 1960; 119 minutes

Credits
Based on a play by Tennessee Williams, *Orpheus Descending*. Producers: Martin Jurow, Richard A. Shepherd and the Pennebaker Company. Director: Sidney Lumet. Screenwriters: Meade Roberts and Tennessee Williams. Cinematographer: Boris Kaufman. Editor: Carl Lerner. Music: Kenyon Hopkins. Art Director: Richard Sylbert. Costumes: Frank Thompson.

Cast

Val Xavier	Marlon Brando
Lady Torrance	Anna Magnani
Carol Cutrere	Joanne Woodward
Vee Talbott	**Maureen Stapleton**
Jabe Torrance	Victor Jory
Sheriff Talbott	R.G. Armstrong
Uncle Pleasant	Emory Richardson
Ruby Lightfoot	Spivy
Dolly Hamma	Sally Gracie
Beulah Binnings	Lucille Benson
David Cutrere	John Baragrey
Dog Hamma	Ben Yaffee
PeeWee Binnings	Joe Brown, Jr.
Nurse Porter	Virgilia Chew
Gas Station Attendant	Frank Borgman
Attendant's Wife	Janice Mars
Lonely Girl	Debbie Lynch

Synopsis
   The Fugitive Kind is based on the stage play, *Orpheus Descending*. See **S13** for a synopsis of the plot.

Reviews and Commentary
   Meade Roberts collaborated with Tennessee Williams in the screen adaptation of his stage play which had suffered mixed reviews on Broadway.   Maurice Yacowar claims, in his essay on the film (in *Tennessee Williams and Film*), that the screenplay jettisoned much of the allegorical aspects of the play in favor of greater realism.   Indeed, the ending of the film is much more graphic in that Jabe not only shoots Lady but also torches the dry goods store and Val is pushed back into the flames by the force of the hoses wielded by the local vigilantes.   Thus, the burning

of the wine garden is repeated and this time takes Lady's life as it had her father's fifteen years before.

The title of the film is taken from a line at the end of the play. The local "bad girl," Carol Cutrere, retrieves Val's charred snakeskin jacket from the ashes of the store and says "wild things leave skins behind them, they leave clean skins and teeth and white bones behind them, and these are tokens passed from one to another so that the fugitive kind can always follow their kind."

This was a film that elicited strong feelings from critics, both positive and negative. Much was made of Marlon Brando's performance as Val Xavier and the parallels of the character with Elvis Presley. The filmscript managed to give more credibility to the characters' actions. For example, Lady's decision to refurbish the confectionary is seen as a result of her renewed interest in life following Val's appearance in the town. So there is more sense of cause and effect and less aimlessness in the film. Nevertheless some critics found the film long and pretentious. Hollis Alpert wrote in the *Saturday Review* that the cast was "up against some of the windiest writing Mr. Williams has ever perpetrated . . . replete with dreary symbolism, and ending with a message bound to give almost anyone a clammy sensation" (23 April 1960, 28). Bosley Crowther, critic for the *New York Times*, held a completely opposite view and found both the script and performances daring and admirable. Of Williams' drama Crowther writes that "it is the skill with which it is performed that sets one's senses to throbbing and feeling staggered and spent at the end" (15 April 1960, 13).

Although Stapleton had originated the role of Lady Torrance on Broadway, the role was given to Anna Magnani in the film version, thus establishing Stapleton's reputation as "the American Magnani." Instead Stapleton was cast as Vee Talbott whose dark visions of the brutality she has witnessed in the town find their way into her brooding paintings. Stapleton received kudos for her honest and sensitive portrayal.

*****

F03 *A VIEW FROM THE BRIDGE*

Transcontinental-Produzione Intercontinentali /
Continental Distributing; 1962; 110 minutes

Credits

Based on the play by Arthur Miller. Producer: Paul Graetz. Director: Sidney Lumet. Screenwriter: Norman Rosten. Cinematographer: Michel Kelber. Editor: Françoise Javet. Music: Maurice LeRoux. Art Director: Jacques Saulnier.

Cast

Eddie Carbone	Raf Vallone
Rodolpho	Jean Sorel
Beatrice Carbone	**Maureen Stapleton**
Catherine	Carol Lawrence
Marco	Raymond Pellegrin
Mr. Alfieri	Morris Carnovsky
Mike	Harvey Lembeck

Louis	Mickey Knox
Lipari	Vincent Gardenia
Longshoreman	Frank Campanella

Synopsis

"The bridge" in Miller's play is the Brooklyn Bridge and his story is set in the Brooklyn district of Red Hook. It is a gritty existence where Italian longshoremen struggle to survive in a new country. In the play the action is confined to the tenement rooms and stoop of Eddie Carbone. In the film the setting is extended to the docks where the immigrants earn their living.

The story revolves around Eddie, his wife Beatrice and his niece Catherine or Katie. It is a home of misplaced love where the brutish Eddie has distanced himself from a loving wife and has become too attached to the eighteen-year-old girl who has been brought up in his home. Eddie has kept Katie dependent on the family and has not allowed her to get a job or have a life of her own. Out of gratitude and sincere affection Katie has not questioned the situation until two of Beatrice's relatives arrive on the scene.

With the family's help, Marco and Rodolpho have entered the States illegally and are now "submarines"—illegal aliens laboring as dockworkers until they can obtain citizenship. They have fled an Italy where there is no work and little food. Marco is motivated by his need to support his family back in Italy. Rodolpho is a handsome, striking blond youth who desires to enjoy life in his adopted country. Eddie and Beatrice agree to shelter the men until they can get legal papers, but it is immediately apparent that the newcomers present a threat to Eddie's relationship with Katie. Rodolpho and Katie are strongly attracted to one another and fall in love.

Eddie struggles to hold on to Katie, becoming estranged from his own wife who encourages Katie's relationship with Rodolpho. Eddie even goes to a lawyer to prevent a marriage between the young lovers. When he fails to find legal recourse he tries to convince Katie that Rodolpho is only using her to gain legal citizenship and he will surely break her heart. It is now evident that Eddie's affection for Katie is more than fatherly and is obsessive in the extreme. Pushed by forces he cannot control, Eddie is devastated and moved to violence. He breaks the greatest taboo of the community when he reports Marco and Rodolpho to the immigration authorities. In so doing other "submarines" are found and Eddie is branded as the informer. Marco, who fears his family will now starve, vows to kill Eddie as he is taken off to jail.

Katie and Rodolpho decide to get married which will make him a legal citizen. Eddie forbids Beatrice to attend the wedding unless Marco (who is being released on bond) is made to apologize for his threat. Before the lovers can escape Eddie's fury, Marco arrives and in the ensuing brawl Eddie is killed.

Reviews and Commentary

The film adaptation of the play capitalized on the grim realism of the locale and characters and downplayed the metaphorical level of the play. The result was, for the most part, satisfying. The film was shot in Brooklyn (exterior scenes) and in Paris (interior scenes) and included an international cast of American, French and Italian actors. Italian film star Raf Vallone received extremely positive notices for his portrayal of the misguided, compulsive Eddie. Vallone's power and intensity carried the film with substantial support from a fine cast, especially French actor Jean Sorel as Rodolpho, Carol Lawrence as Katie and Morris Carnosvky as the lawyer, Alfieri.

Maureen Stapleton was admired by most of the critics for the warmth and desperation she engendered in the role of the wife, Beatrice. In *Films in Review* Henry Hart, however, lambasted director Lumet for casting Stapleton, saying: "Casting her in this part is inexcusable. She didn't dare hazard an Italian accent, and has nothing but her drab-dumpiness to carry her through a part that could and should have heightened the drama" (1962, 102). This seems a bit unfair, given the contrasting views of other critics and the fact that Stapleton's strength was playing this kind of matronly woman who struggled to support her man at any cost and she was extremely adept with accents—Italian, Irish, German, etc. So Hart's comments are suspect. The *Variety* critic found that Stapleton "still impresses in her expression of inner torment" (10 October 1962, 6).

Bosley Crowther faulted Miller's story, writing in the *New York Times* that the character of Eddie Carbone is pushed to such an extreme that we cease to care about him: "He is obviously stupid and stubborn. He merits no more sympathy. And the melodramatic climax comes not too soon or mercifully" (23 January 1962, 36). Nevertheless, Crowther and other critics praised Lumet's direction, the tangible realism of the film's atmosphere, and the many fine performances in the film so that those elements seem to have outweighed the film's shortcomings.

*****

F04   *BYE BYE BIRDIE*
Columbia Pictures; 1963; 120 minutes
Video: RCA/Columbia

Credits
Based on the musical comedy by Michael Stewart with music and lyrics by Charles Strouse, and Lee Adams. Producer: Fred Kohlmar. Director: George Sidney. Screenwriter: Irving Brecher. Cinematographer: Joseph Biroc (Panavision). Music: Charles Strouse. Music supervised, arranged and conducted by Johnny Green. Choreographer: Onna White. Production Design: Paul Groesse. Costumes: Pat Barto and Marjorie B. Wahl.

Cast

Rosie DeLeon	Janet Leigh
Albert Peterson	Dick Van Dyke
Kim McAfee	Ann-Margret
Mama	**Maureen Stapleton**
Hugo Peabody	Bobby Rydell
Conrad Birdie	Jesse Pearson
Ed Sullivan	Ed Sullivan
Mr. McAfee	Paul Lynde
Mrs. McAfee	Mary LaRoche
Claude Paisley	Michael Evans

Bob Precht	Robert Paige
Borov	Gregory Morton
Randolph	Bryan Russell
Mr. Maude	Milton Frome

And Ben Astar, Trudy Ames, Cyril Delevanti, Frank Albertson, Beverly Yates, Frank Sully and Bo Peep Karlin.

Synopsis

In a New York office, a love-lorn songwriter, Albert Peterson, is about to give up his fruitless career and get a straight job when his devoted and patient girlfriend, Rosie DeLeon, shows up to save the day. Rosie knows that one successful song will bring Albert the fame he craves and allow him to break away from his domineering mom and be free to get married. The highly motivated Rosie (she's been engaged for six years) concocts a plan for Albert to make his name. Having learned that the greatest rock and roll song idol of all time, Conrad Birdie, is being inducted into the Army, Rosie convinces Ed Sullivan to stage a farewell to Birdie on his television show which will include a symbolic kiss to an all-American girl (and, of course, Albert's soon-to-be-famous song).

To find the girl, Rosie holds a contest. The winner is the demure but dynamite Kim McAfee who is an outstanding member of the Conrad Birdie Fan Club in Sweet Apple, Iowa. The action shifts to Sweet Apple where the teenage girls are all aswoon over the imminent arrival of their idol, the Elvis-esque, hip-swinging, irreverent Birdie. The teenage boys are less than enthusiastic, however, and parades and protests fill the streets with song and dance.

While the town is reeling from the impact of Birdie's visit, Albert is trying to cope with his indomitable mother and persistent girlfriend. Kim, meanwhile, is coping with the fears of her parents and her boyfriend who wants her to call the whole thing off. Birdie takes over the whole town with his arrogant charm and fun-loving sexuality.

Just before the telecast Albert learns that the song will be cut in order to allow air time for a Russian ballet troupe which was also scheduled on the program. However, Albert's skill in chemistry solves the crisis by speeding up the orchestra conductor and condensing the long-winded ballet into a high-speed chase. Kim gives the symbolic kiss, Birdie is shipped off to the Army and Albert puts his mother on notice that he is getting married. Her reaction? "It's about time!"

Reviews and Commentary

This film gave Stapleton her first real opportunity to show her talent for comedy. Almost every role she had prior to this was intensely dramatic. In *Birdie* she played "Mama," the formidable mother of the songwriter played by Dick Van Dyke. Her first appearance reveals only her orthopedic shoes—they squeak—and the tail of her mink coat. We hear a voice crying "Albert!" It is a voice that could peel paint. She is a dumpy, frumpy, long-suffering widow who demands attention in every scene.

On the whole the film was a successful transition of a stage musical to the screen where the story retained the charm of youthful exuberance and the wacky comedy of the tribulations of the adults and never made the mistake of taking itself too seriously. The critics particularly enjoyed the sultry sleaze of Jesse Pearson's Birdie and the fetching sensuality of a very young Ann-Margret. Dick Van Dyke and Janet Leigh also earned kudos for their portrayals of the songwriter and his girl. Stapleton and Paul Lynde were similarly singled out for their efforts.

The *New York Times* critic faulted the screenplay for dwelling too long on the love story of the songwriter and thus removing Birdie from the screen for a large section of the film. However, *Variety* raved about the film for its entertainment value and gave the credit for its success to the director, screenwriter and cast, especially Ann-Margret: "Singer, hoofer, and cutie-pie, all wrapped up into one . . . this is one of the most exciting fresh personalities to take the cinematic stage in some time" and Maureen Stapleton, who was described as "a comedienne of the first order" (10 April 1963, 6).

*****

F05 *TRUMAN CAPOTE'S TRILOGY*
Allied Artists; 1969; 100 minutes

Credits
Based on three Truman Capote stories: "Miriam," "Among the Paths to Eden," and "A Christmas Memory." Producer and Director: Frank Perry. Screenwriters: Truman Capote and Eleanor Perry. Cinematographers: Joseph Brun and Vincent C. H. Sundby (Eastmancolor). Editors: Patricia Jaffe, Ralph Rosenblum and Sheila Bakerman. Music: Meyer Kupferman. Production Design: Peter Dohanos and Gene Callahan. Set Decoration: Leif Pedersen. Costumes: Frank Thompson and Anna Hill Johnstone.

Cast of "Miriam"
Miss Miller	Mildred Natwick
Miriam	Susan Dunfee
Miss Lake	Carol Gustafson
Emily	Robin Ponterio
Nina	Beverly Ballard
Mrs. Connolly	Jane Connell
Man in Theatre	Frederic Morton
Man in Automat	Richard Hamilton
Woman in Automat	Phyllis Eldridge
Dwarf	Tony Ross
Mr. Connolly	Brooks Rogers
Clerk in Shop	Niki Flacks

Cast of "Among the Paths to Eden"
Mary O'Meaghan	**Maureen Stapleton**
Ivor Belli	Martin Balsam

Cast of "A Christmas Memory"
Woman	Geraldine Page
Buddy	Donnie Melvin
First Aunt	Lavinia Cassels
Second Aunt	Christine Marler

Haha	Josep Elic
Woman in Car	Lynn Forman
Storekeeper	Win Forman
Narrator	Truman Capote

Synopsis

The three stories by Truman Capote\that make up this film all deal with loneliness. The first story, "Miriam," is about an elderly lady of that name who is a retired nanny now living alone in her Manhattan brownstone apartment. Her former charges are grown with children of their own but they want nothing to do with the old woman. The other people she meets (the neighbors in her building, the nursemaid in the park, the couple at the automat) all avoid her.

The elderly woman meets a strange young girl, also named Miriam, at the movies. The girl has long, silvery white hair and is dressed in a silk dress. She talks the woman into buying her a ticket and later shows up at her apartment door. She connives to be admitted to the woman's apartment and takes charge of the place. When the woman insists she leave, she deliberately breaks a vase that contained artificial flowers (because she hates flowers that are not real).

The woman grows frightened but the girl keeps appearing mysteriously, finally arriving with her box of clothes—all identical white silk dresses. The old woman seeks her neighbor's help to extricate the girl but their investigation finds nothing. The woman finally pushes the girl out the window, only to be confronted by her once again, cheerfully sitting at the foot of her bed. It is then clear that the girl is an abstraction of the woman's mind, an image of herself as a child who knows her innermost thoughts and feelings, even those she has hidden from herself.

The second story, "Among the Paths to Eden," brings together a lonely spinster and a middle-aged widower in a Queens cemetery. Mary O'Meaghan is a woman determined to find a husband with whom she may share her days. She is forty, matronly and congenial. Ivor Belli is an accountant who has dutifully come to put flowers on his wife's grave (although he is motivated more by responsibility than grief) when he is approached by Miss O'Meaghan. They have a pleasant encounter sparked by Mary's sense of hopefulness until it becomes evident that Ivor is not very interested in getting married again and if he does it will be to his long-time secretary. They part amiably as Mary sets her sights on another widower who is bearing flowers to a nearby grave site.

The final story, "A Christmas Memory," tells about the affection between a Southern boy, named Buddy, and an older woman, an adult cousin known only as "the woman." The story is told in narration as a memory of the special rituals the two create to experience the joy of Christmas. On that special cold morning, when the woman declares "Oh, my! It's fruitcake weather!" the two take their carefully saved pennies and nickles and buy the ingredients to make gifts for all their friends. The story relates the making of the fruitcakes, the handmade gifts, finding and decorating the tree, the flying of kites together. It is really a story of a special friendship which is curtailed when the boy is sent away to military school. Yet for Buddy the memory is an enduring sense of the deepest love and devotion.

Reviews and Commentary

These three Truman Capote stories were filmed as three television specials. Only "A Christmas Memory" and "Among the Paths to Eden" were aired but both received critical acclaim and Emmy Awards. Capote then packaged the three stories into a film which premiered at the Cannes Film Festival and was later made available to the educational market.

The critics were very impressed with the quality of the individual stories and the blending and adaptation into the film. As Howard Thompson wrote in the *New York Times,* "The cold fact is that *Trilogy* is all talk and little action. But it quietly says and conveys more about the human heart and spirit than most of today's free-wheeling blastaways on the screen. Delicately, it towers" (7 November 1969, 40).

Also commended were the fine performances by Geraldine Page, Mildred Natwick, and Maureen Stapleton. Stapleton's performance in "Among the Paths to Eden" had earned her an Emmy (Best Actress) when it was televised (see **T27**). The critic in *Variety* said "Maureen Stapleton, wonderfully counterpointed by Martin Balsam, is unforgettable as the plainjane spinster who seeks a husband among a cemetery's male visitors" (cited in *Variety Film Reviews 1968-70,* 5 November 1969).

*****

F06   *AIRPORT*
Universal Pictures; 1970; 137 minutes
Video: MCA

Credits
Based on the novel by Arthur Hailey. Producer: Ross Hunter. Associate Producer: Jacques Mapes. Director: George Seaton. Screenwriter: George Seaton. Cinematographer: Ernest Laszlo (Todd-AO, Technicolor). Editor: Stuart Gilmore. Music: Alfred Newman. Art Directors: E. Preston Ames and Alexander Golitzen. Set Decoration: Jack D. Moore and Mickey S. Michaels. Costumes: Edith Head.

Cast
Mel Bakersfeld	Burt Lancaster
Vernon Demerest	Dean Martin
Tanya Livingston	Jean Seberg
Gwen Meighen	Jacqueline Bisset
Patroni	George Kennedy
Ada Quonsett	Helen Hayes
D. O. Guerrero	Van Heflin
Inez Guerrero	**Maureen Stapleton**
Lt. Anson Harris	Barry Nelson
Cindy	Dana Wynter
Harry Standish	Lloyd Nolan
Sara	Barbara Hale
Cy Jordon	Gary Collins
Peter Coakley	John Findlater
Mrs. Harriet DuBarry Mossman	Jessie Royce Landis
Commissioner Ackerman	Larry Gates

And Peter Turgeon, Whit Bissell, Virginia Grey, Eileen Wesson, Paul Picerni, Robert Patten, Clark Howat, Lew Brown, Llana Dowding, Lisa Garritson, Patty Poulson, Jim Nolan, Malila Saint Duvall, Ena Hartman, Jodean Russo, Albert Reed, Sharon Harvey, Dick Winslow, Nancy Ann Nelson, Mary Jackson, Janis Hansen, Lou Wagner, Chuck Daniel, Shelly Novack and Charles Brewer.

Synopsis

Mel Bakersfeld is the beleaguered manager of Lincoln International Airport, a large metropolitan airport in the midwest. On the night of the year's worst winter storm the manager must cope with a myriad of problems—a 747 airliner stuck in the snow and the closing of one of the two runways, an angry Commissioner trying to get the airport closed to placate area residents who resent the noise, and a showdown with his socialite wife who is tired of playing second fiddle to Bakersfeld's career.

The airport is also the scene of several other dramas: a sweet little old lady stowaway who is trying to get to see her daughter in New York without buying a ticket (Ada Quonsett), a love triangle between Bakersfeld's sister, her pilot husband (Vernon Demerest) and the stewardess with whom he has been having an affair (Gwen), and a distraught ex-mental patient (Mr. Guerrero) who carries a bomb on board a flight to Rome so his wife may cash in on the travel insurance he has purchased.

These stories intersect when the stowaway, the pilot and his stewardess lover, and the man with the bomb all board Flight #2 to Rome. Meanwhile, on the ground, an astute customs official raises concern about the man with the attache case (Guerrero) just as the man's wife is found wandering the airport, almost paralyzed by fear that her husband may do something desperate. Bakersfeld and Tanya (the public relations agent for TransGlobal Airlines who has been carrying a torch for Bakersfeld), join forces to warn pilot Demerest of the stowaway and the bomber on his flight. Then Bakersfeld enlists the aid of maintenance chief Patroni to clear a second runway for the emergency landing of Flight #2.

All these efforts, however, fail to prevent Guerrero from setting off the bomb and blowing a huge hole in the fuselage of the plane, killing himself and seriously injuring the stewardess Gwen (who, it is revealed, is pregnant with Demerest's child). The pilot manages to return to the airport and land on the longer runway, which has been cleared only seconds before. By this time Bakersfeld's wife has walked out on him and he embarks on a more positive relationship with Tanya, Demerest goes off to the hospital with Gwen, and the traumatized passengers flood into the bustling airport terminal.

Reviews and Commentary

Airport was an adaptation of Arthur Hailey's best-selling novel of the same name. Most critics drew comparisons with *Grand Hotel* because the story is set in a public place and focuses on the numerous human dramas being played out in the place. Vincent Canby, critic for the *New York Times*, thought the film was old fashioned in its sentiment and construction but was also "so superficially contemporary . . . so breathlessly paced, so cheery, so chock-full of irrelevant facts, that *Airport* eventually comes to look and sound like the world's first 137-minute, 70-millimeter television commercial, with short, regular interruptions for entertainment" (6 March 1970, 34).

Canby also predicted, quite accurately, that the film would be enormously successful. In fact, the outrageous budget of the film (ten million dollars) brought a return of almost forty-five million, making it one of the most successful disaster movies of the day and led to two sequels and a parody (*Airplane*). The film received numerous Oscar nominations, including Best Picture and Best Screenplay.

Variety credited the success to the "sensitively scripted, strongly acted characterization of the principals" (18 February 1970, 17). The critics agreed that the star-studded cast, which included Burt Lancaster as the airport manager, Jean Seberg as Tanya, Dean Martin as Demerest and George Kennedy as Patroni, was the chief reason for the film's success. Helen Hayes was most impressive as the charming and cunning elderly stowaway.

Maureen Stapleton was cast as the desperate wife of the man who carries the bomb. She has only a few brief scenes to establish the character of a middle-aged waitress whose life with an incapacitated husband has caused her to give her children to a sister to raise and who is down to her last dollar. As the *Variety* critic observed, "for a less talented actress it would just be a bit part motivated by a plot need. By sheer emotional impact, Miss Stapleton transforms it into an Academy Award caliber supporting role" (18 February 1970, 17). In fact, both Stapleton and Hayes received Oscar nominations in the Best Supporting Actress category. Hayes won the award.

*****

F07   *SUMMER OF '42*
Warner Brothers; 1971; 102 minutes
Video: Warner

Credits
Producer: Richard A. Roth. Associate Producer: Don Kranze. Director: Robert Mulligan. Screenwriter: Herman Raucher. Cinematographer: Robert Surtees (Technicolor). Editor: Folmar Blangsted. Music/Music Director: Michel Legrand. Production Design: Albert Brenner. Set Decoration: Marvin March.

Cast

Dorothy	Jennifer O'Neill
Hermie	Gary Grimes
Oscy	Jerry Houser
Benjie	Oliver Conant
Aggie	Katherine Allentuck
Miriam	Christopher Norris
Druggist	Lou Frizzell
Dorothy's Husband	Walter Scott
Voice of Hermie's Mother	**Maureen Stapleton**
Narrator, Older Hermie	Robert Mulligan

Synopsis

Against the backdrop of a sun-washed New England seashore, a man's voice sets the scene for a nostalgic look at his own coming of age during the summer of 1942. We see him as a boy, crossing the dunes with his friends of the summer, Oscy and Benjie. The boy, Hermie, is fifteen years old and is both innocent and curious about sex and love and the relationship between them. His know-it-all friend Oscy, who has learned the little he knows about sex from a more experienced brother, is determined that this is the summer for the boys to become men. Oscy's crass ambition to "get laid" is counterpointed by Hermie's sensitivity and the confusion and abject fear of the least worldly of the three, Benjie. Benjie does, however, contribute to their collective education by smuggling a graphic sex manual out of the house so the boys can learn the basics.

Hermie is consumed with feelings he cannot define or comprehend as he watches an "older woman" who lives on the beach. The woman, Dorothy, is actually a young bride of twenty-two. Hermie sees her saying goodbye to her handsome husband when he is sent away to war. In time he meets Dorothy and begins a friendship, helping her to carry groceries or move boxes to the attic. Meanwhile the boys pick up two girls, Miriam and Aggie, at the movies. During the emotionally-charged romantic clips of Bette Davis in *Now, Voyager* the boys make advances to the girls.

Oscy is so encouraged by his success with Miriam he sets up a double date with the girls and Hermie to roast marshmallows on the beach. He then forces Hermie to make a trip to the local druggist to buy condoms. Somehow Hermie manages to survive the humiliation of the task and they make their date. While Hermie and the shy Aggie roast marshmallows Oscy is initiated by the more-experienced Miriam.

Hermie goes to visit Dorothy but she does not answer the door. He enters and finds the telegram reporting the death of her husband. She comes into the room, wracked with sorrow and he consoles her. In silence and gentleness she takes him into the bedroom and they make love. The next day Hermie returns to her door only to find a note saying goodbye and wishing him well.

Reviews and Commentary

The romantic setting of the 1940s seaside lends a credibility to this film. As Vincent Canby pointed out, "it is, perhaps, just a little too perfect, a little too symmetrical; not the way things really were, but the way they should have been" (19 April 1971, 51). One can ignore the blatant sexism of the film only because the historical setting softens it, as does the romanticized cinematography which baths the film in nostalgia. The juxtaposition of scenes (such as intercutting the famous *Now Voyager* scene—where the hero lights two cigarettes and gives her one of them—with the adolescent gropings in the back row) allows us to laugh at the silliness of it all while still understanding how serious it was to be fifteen.

The critics generally praised the film for taste. *Variety* said "the pitfalls in any film on this subject include the possibility of a too-adult treatment which sometimes patronizes, sometimes seems voyeuristic and sometimes a combination. In *Summer of '42* these stumbling blocks have been mitigated, though not entirely avoided" (21 April 1971, 17). The performances of all the cast were said to be excellent.

Maureen Stapleton was only heard and not seen in the film. She was the voice of Hermie's mother and, as such, represented a part of Hermie's life that seldom intruded on the screen. This was also the film debut of Stapleton's daughter, Katherine Allentuck, who received good notices for her portrayal of the plain, shy Aggie.

The film was a tremendous success at the box office, grossing more than twenty million dollars in its first release.

*****

F08   *PLAZA SUITE*
Paramount; 1971; 114 minutes
Video: Paramount

Credits
Based on the play by Neil Simon. Producer: Howard W. Koch. Director: Arthur Hiller. Screenwriter: Neil Simon. Cinematographer: Jack Marta (Technicolor). Editor: Frank Bracht. Music/Music Director: Maurice Jarre. Music and Lyrics to "Tangerine": Johnny Mercer and Victor Schertzinger. Art Director: Arthur Lonergan. Set Decoration: Reg Allen. Costumes: Jack Bear. Makeup: Gary Morris.

Cast
Sam Nash /Jesse Kiplinger /Roy Hubley	Walter Matthau
Karen Nash	**Maureen Stapleton**
Waiter	José Ocasio
Bellhop	Dan Ferrone
Miss McCormack	Louise Sorel
Muriel Tate	Barbara Harris
Norma Hubley	Lee Grant
Mimsey Hubley	Jennie Sullivan
Borden Eisler	Tom Carey

Synopsis
This film was adapted from the stage play. See **S18** for synopsis.

Reviews and Commentary
Several of Neil Simon's stage comedies have been adapted to film and this time the critics split into opposing camps. *Variety* gave the film a rave review, saying "if *Plaza Suite* can't break the film jinx on multiple-story features, there's no further point in trying . . . Many howls and a good undercurrent of pathos support what on the surface seems broad caricature" (12 May 1971, 19). Vincent Canby, however, writing in the *New York Times,* said "when a Broadway hit of the dimensions of Neil Simon's *Plaza Suite* is turned into an aggressively tiresome movie, the conventional thing to say . . . is that something's been lost in the play's translation to the screen" (14 May 1971, 46).

In this instance Stapleton shared in both the Broadway and Hollywood success of the play. Her role was diminished, however, because on Broadway she played all three female leads and on film she shared the spotlight with Barbara Harris and Lee Grant. The male role, however, was not split among three actors. Walter Matthau played the three characters originated onstage by George C. Scott. With Matthau as the unifying factor, the film presented the marital problems from a principally male perspective. Nevertheless, a reviewer in *The Motion Picture Guide* made this assessment: "This one made us laugh and cry at the same time and those are two emotions that are hard to come by in a single film" (Nash and Ross, 1985 vol. 6: 2418).

*****

F09   *INTERIORS*
United Artists; 1978; 93 minutes
Video: MCA/UA

Credits
A Jack Rollins-Charles H. Joffe Production. Producer: Charles H. Joffe. Director and Screenwriter: Woody Allen. Cinematographer: Gordon Willis (Technicolor). Editor: Ralph Rosenblum. Production Design: Mel Bourne. Costumes: Joel Schumacher.

Cast
Flyn	Kristin Griffith
Joey	Mary Beth Hurt
Frederick	Richard Jordan
Renata	Diane Keaton
Arthur	E. G. Marshall
Eve	Geraldine Page
Pearl	**Maureen Stapleton**
Mike	Sam Waterston

And Missy Hope, Kerry Duffy, Nancy Collins, Penny Gaston, Roger Morden and Henderson Forsythe.

Synopsis
The basic story of *Interiors* is very simple: a man decides to divorce his wife and the couple and their three adult daughters try to cope with the emotional upheaval as the father remarries and the first wife has a nervous breakdown. However, the actual action of the film is the interior struggle of each of the family members and its location is the psyche of the characters as much as the stark white rooms of the family's homes. Thus, the title of the film is most appropriate.

The father, Arthur, is a successful and wealthy lawyer. His wife, Eve, is an elegant and intelligent woman, an interior designer who has created interiors for her family that physically represent the absolute order and precision of her world view. Much of the film concentrates on the white rooms with bare floors, the mantle with five individual pale green stone vases and, most importantly, great areas of bare space, light and air.

Arthur and Eve are parents to three daughters who each have unresolved difficulties in their lives. Renata is the oldest and most successful—a poetess who has distanced herself from her mother and can therefore be encouraging and supportive when she undergoes crisis.

Renata is married to an unsuccessful writer, Frederick, who masochistically stays in the relationship with a woman who he cannot best. Joey is the daughter who most involves herself with Eve. Joey has her own crisis of identity. She lives with Mike, a social activist and filmmaker; but Joey has gone through various jobs as an actress, a photographer, and working at an ad agency. The third daughter, Flyn, is a film actress who is almost entirely self-centered and willfully absent from the fray.

Arthur announces one morning to Eve, Renata, and Joey that he is moving out and wants a trial separation. This precipitates a breakdown of order for Eve, who ends up in an institution for a while. Since the plot is presented in non-linear fashion, it is gradually revealed that Eve makes a slow comeback and begins to establish herself again as a designer but she refuses to give up on the marriage. Nevertheless, Arthur goes his own way and convenes the daughters to introduce them to Pearl, a woman he has decided to marry.

The idea of remarriage jolts the family, most of all Eve, who loses her frail grasp on hope and order. Renata quarrels with Frederick and Joey and she tells Mike (Joey's companion) that she plans to abort the baby she's carrying. The tensions between the family members rise to a crescendo when the daughters and their men return to the family home in Connecticut where Arthur and Pearl are married. Pearl is a lovely, buxom woman of great warmth and simplicity. She reads fortunes and eats, drinks, and dances with abandon. She has none of the intellectualism and pretension of Arthur's family, but she is sensitive enough to know they are loathe to welcome her.

Late that night, Joey rises to sift through her own confused feelings. She finds Eve standing in the entry and tells her she should not be there, not on the wedding night. Eve accepts that Arthur is lost to her and she quietly walks into the sea to her death. Joey goes after her and is almost killed herself, except for the intervention of Pearl and Mike. Finally, the family is convened once more for Eve's funeral. Each daughter is left to find her own path.

Reviews and Commentary

Critics and audiences alike experienced culture shock in this, Woody Allen's first dramatic film, or as Vincent Canby pointed out, "the first Woody Allen film that doesn't care to be funny" (2 August 1978, C15). An obvious homage to Bergman, the film is so interior that it has the aura of the analyst's office—a favorite Allen environment. Nevertheless, the film is one of great beauty. For example, Allen sets much of the film in cold white rooms with views of the sea; against these backdrops the characters wear muted tones of cream and grey. When the vibrant outsider, Pearl, enters the scene in a bright red dress—the viewer is jarred just as the family is shocked.

The film was more of an artistic success than a commercial one. Critics admired Allen's screenplay, direction and the art direction (all of which received Oscar nominations), and they highly praised the fine performances. Geraldine Page, as the severely attractive Eve, earned an Oscar nomination for Best Actress. Stapleton won the nomination for Best Supporting Actress for her moving portrayal of the new wife, Pearl. Vincent Canby said "Miss Page . . . is marvelous—erratically kind, impossibly demanding, pathetic in her loneliness and desperate in her anger. Miss Stapleton beautifully projects the tone and feelings of a sweet, robust, coarse woman who is never, never ridiculous" (2 August 1978).

*****

F10   *LOST AND FOUND*
Columbia Pictures; 1979; 106 minutes
Video: RCA/Columbia

Credits
Executive Producers: Arnold Kopelson. Producer/Director: Melvin Frank. Screenwriters: Melvin Frank and Jack Rose. Cinematographer: Douglas Slocombe (Panavision, Technicolor). Editor: Bill Butler. Music: John Cameron. Production Design: Trevor Williams. Art Director: Ted Tester. Set Decoration: Gerry Holmes. Costumes: Julie Harris.

Cast
Adam	George Segal
Tricia	Glenda Jackson
Jemmy	**Maureen Stapleton**
Eden	Hollis McLaren
Lenny	John Cunningham
Reilly	Paul Sorvino
Julian	Kenneth Pogue
Zelda	Janie Sell
Ellie	Diana Barrington
Jean-Paul	Leslie Carlson
Carpentier	John Candy
Gendarme	James Morris
Ski Patrol	Bruno Engler
French Doctor	David Bolt
Attendant	Richard Adams

And Mary Pirie, Nicole D'Amour, Denise Baillargeon, Roger Periard, Lois Maxwell, Douglas Campbell, John Anthony Robinow, Robert Goodier, Sandy Webster, Barbara Hamilton, Patricia Collins, Rob Garrison, Cecil Linder, James Hurdle, Martin Short, John Baylis and Dennis Strong.

Synopsis
Adam Watson is an English professor who is driving to a vacation at a French ski resort to lessen the pain of losing his wife eight months previously. Tricia, an Englishwoman whose husband has just ditched her for a twenty-year-old, is driving along the same road as Adam when their cars collide. At the hospital Tricia refuses to accept responsibility and Adam pursues her to get her to admit that she was driving on the wrong side of the road. He collides with her on the ski slopes, and they are both hospitalized with broken legs. There they become acquainted, fall in love and quickly marry.

Adam takes Tricia to America where he introduces her to Jemmy, his domineering mother. Jemmy runs Mother Watson's Subversive

Bookstore and makes it clear that she expects Adam to become a distinguished author.

Adam and Tricia arrive in the town where he teaches at the local college. Adam learns that he and his best friend, Lenny, are in competition for the one available tenure slot. The decision will hinge on whether Adam can finish the manuscript he has been working on for ages. Tricia, meanwhile, tries to adjust to her role as a faculty wife. She finds Adam has not removed his first wife's personal belongings from the house and she soon realizes that Adam is cutting her out of his most important life decisions. They argue furiously and make up frequently but Tricia cannot accept Adam's attention to Eden, his attractive graduate student, nor his negligence in completing his book.

Jemmy tries to help out Adam's tenure fight by getting a controversial film critic to come to the college to speak in Adam's class. At a dinner party Tricia gets drunk and humiliates the pretentious guests and her husband. At a loss to understand Adam's behavior, she finds and reads the former wife's diary. She then realizes that Adam is undercutting his own chances so that he will fail (and thus be free of Jemmy's expectations for him.) Although she still loves him, Tricia decides to leave Adam. In retaliation he stages a fake suicide which is almost successful. She saves him and walks out. At the last moment she relents and returns to find him sober and diligently working on his manuscript. They reconcile, happy with the knowledge that Adam is now his own man.

Reviews and Commentary

George Segal and Glenda Jackson made a successful comedy when they filmed *A Touch of Class* in 1973. *Lost and Found* brought these comedic pros together again but the critics found the later film lacked the charm and freshness of the first. Jackson again was cast as the acerbic British wit and Segal as an ineffective fellow, at the mercy of his mother's beck and call. Although *Lost and Found* was judged to be weak in some areas, the critics applauded the clever verbal sparring and slapstick comedy of Jackson and Segal.

The performances seem to have compensated for the shortcomings of the script. *Variety* said that the film "fortunately features two highly skilled performers who can play the material for more than it's worth" (12 June 1979, 18). *Variety* also commended the minor players, including Paul Sorvino for his exasperated cabbie and Maureen Stapleton whose interpretation of Jemmy, the "archetypal Jewish mother" was especially effective because "Stapleton, as usual, lends an endearing uniqueness to a character type that has been overdone."

*****

F11   *THE RUNNER STUMBLES*
Twentieth Century Fox; 1979; 99 minutes
Video: CBS/Fox

Credits
Based on the play by Milan Stitt. Producer/Director: Stanley Kramer. Screenwriter: Milan Stitt. Cinematographer: Laszlo Kovacs (CFI Color).

Editor: Pembroke J. Herring. Music: Ernest Gold. Production Design: Alfred Sweeney, Jr.

Cast

Father Rivard	Dick Van Dyke
Sister Rita	Kathleen Quinlan
Mrs. Shandig	**Maureen Stapleton**
Monsignor Nicholson	Ray Bolger
Erna	Tammy Grimes
Toby	Beau Bridges
Prosecutor	Allen Nause
Amos	John Procaccino
James	Billy J. Jacoby
Sister Immaculata	Sister Marguerite Morrissey
Sister Martha	Zoaunne LeRoy
Maurice	Don Riley
Sheriff	Ted D'Arms
Louise	Kendall Kay Munsey

And Casey Kramer, Jim Doyle, Katherine Kramer, Bill Dore, Jock Dove and Larry Buck.

Synopsis

This story of a love affair and a murder is told in flashbacks which move back and forth in time between the jail, the trial, and the events that led up to the crime. A young, spirited nun, Sister Rita, comes to an isolated community to teach in the parish school. Being the only young woman with two aging nuns, Sister Rita is drawn to the parish priest, Father Rivard. Sister Rita's vivacious personality disturbs the community and Father Rivard. Rita reminds Rivard of himself at a younger age—she is impulsive and has a personal relationship with God that is no longer possible for him.

When the older sisters are taken ill with consumption, Rivard allows Rita to stay with him, in spite of warnings from his housekeeper, Mrs. Shandig. Shandig is an illiterate woman who Rivard took in after she fled the mining camp where her husband worked until he disappeared. Fiercely protective of Rivard, Shandig accepts Rita's offer to teach her to read but she also tries to keep Rita from coming too close to Rivard.

Rivard tries to focus his energies on writing a book and keeping a professional distance from the young nun. One night there is a fire in the town and during the crisis Rita confesses her love to Rivard. Rivard struggles with his conflicting feelings for the woman and his God and discloses that he has already destroyed his book because he did not believe in it anymore. Rita insists they can find a way to be together but Mrs. Shandig intervenes. Rivard immediately leaves the town and the church. Only when he is arrested does he learn that Rita was murdered that night.

In the ensuing trial Rivard is assigned a lawyer with no trial experience, Toby Felker. Felker becomes fascinated with Rivard's story and vows to prove his innocence. He calls Mrs. Shandig to the stand and it is revealed that she followed Sister Rita out to the fire ditch, following Rivard's departure. Believing she was carrying out God's will, Mrs. Shandig buried the girl alive. Rivard is left to mourn the death of Sister Rita.

Reviews and Commentary

When playwright Milan Stitt wrote the play of *The Runner Stumbles*, he wrote the part of Mrs. Shandig for Maureen Stapleton. She did not play the role on Broadway but was cast in the film version. The critics declared that she turned in the best performance in the film.

Stitt's story is based upon an actual 1927 murder case. The play had a successful Broadway run before being adapted to the screen in a production starring Dick Van Dyke as Father Rivard and Kathleen Quinlan as Sister Rita. Critics were divided on the effectiveness of the film. Janet Maslin, reviewer for the *New York Times*, felt that Stitt's screenplay did not effectively dramatize the moral struggle of Rivard. The critic writing for *Variety,* on the other hand, judged the film to be "a powerful, thought-provoking film that manages to relate a simple love story and at the same time raise some severe moral questions" (4 April 1979).

Van Dyke, Quinlan and supporting actors Tammy Grimes, Ray Bolger, and Beau Bridges were applauded for strong performances, but it was Maureen Stapleton who, in the role of the illiterate housekeeper Mrs Shandig, turned in the finest performance. *Variety* said "it's Maureen Stapleton who almost walks away with the picture . . . . Stapleton's role is key to the development of the plot and it's because she's so convincing throughout that the film manages, in the end, to hold together so well" (cited in *Variety Film Reviews 1978-80*, 4 April 1979).

*****

F12   *THE FAN*
Filmways / Paramount; 1981; 95 minutes
Video: Paramount

Credits
Based on the novel by Bob Randall. Executive Producer: Kevin McCormick. Producer: Robert Stigwood. Director: Edward Bianchi. Screenwriters: John Hartwell and Priscilla Chapman. Cinematographer: Dick Bush (Technicolor).   Editor: Alan Heim.   Music/Lyrics to "Hearts, Not Diamonds" and "A Remarkable Woman": Marvin Hamlisch and Tim Rice. Music: Pino Donaggio. Musical Staging and Choreography: Arlene Phillips. Production Design: Santo Loquasto. Art Director: Paul Eads. Set Decorator: Leslie Bloom. Costumes: Jeffrey Kurland and Tom McKinley.

Cast

Sally Ross	Lauren Bacall
Jake Berman	James Garner
Belle Goldman	**Maureen Stapleton**
Inspector Ralph Andrews	Hector Elizondo
Douglas Breen	Michael Biehn
Emily Stolz	Anna Maria Horsford
David Branum	Kurt Johnson
Elsa	Feiga Martinez
Choreographer	Reed Jones
Douglas' Sister	Kaiulani Lee

John Vetta	Charles Blackwell
Director	Dwight Schultz
Saleswoman	Dana Delany
Young Man in Bar	Terence Marinan
Heidi	Lesley Rogers
Hilda	Parker McCormick
Pop	Robert Weil

And Ed Crowley, Gail Benedict, D. David Lewis, Griffin Dunne, Themi Sapountzakis, Jean DeBaer, Liz Smith, Haru Aki, Robin Albert, Rene Ceballos, Clif DeRaita, Edyie Fleming, Linda Haberman, Sergio Lopez-Cal, Jamie Patterson, Justin Ross, Stephanie Williams, Jim Wolfe, Thomas Saccio, Victoria Vanderkloot, James Ogden, Terri Duhaime, Donna Mitchell, Hector Osorio, Lionel Pina, Miriam Phillips, Jack R. Marks, George Peters, Esther Benson, Eric Van Valkenburg, Ann Pearl Gary, Madeline Moroff, Leo Schaff, James Bryson, J. Nesbit Clark, Tim Elliot, Paul Hummel and Jacob Laufer.

Synopsis

Sally Ross is an acknowledged star who is, at age fifty, preparing to make her debut in a Broadway musical. She is insecure about her talents, irritable and in constant need of reassurance. She is consoled by her former husband, Hollywood director Jake Berman. She is also protected and cared for by her devoted, down-to-earth secretary, Belle Goldman.

Among Sally's numerous fans is one psychotic young man named Douglas Breen. Douglas develops an obsessive desire for the star and writes wildly passionate letters to Sally but they are intercepted and discounted by Belle. Sally, meanwhile is preoccupied with her rehearsals and with Jake's relationship with Heidi, a much younger woman whom he intends to marry.

Douglas grows violent when his overtures are rejected and he begins a bloody series of murders and mayhem. He attacks Belle and horribly slashes her face with a straight razor and sends notes to Sally threatening more violence if she does not write him, but Sally does not have his name or address. Police Inspector Andrews arranges twenty-four-hour protection for the star. Douglas takes out his fury on David, a friend of Sally who accompanies her to parties (David is stabbed but survives). Douglas then kills Sally's maid and destroys her apartment.

Sally flees town, abandoning the show. Douglas picks up a man in a gay bar and murders him as well. By now Inspector Andrews has identified where Douglas lives and Sally feels safe enough to return to open in her Broadway musical. Belle, fully recovered, goes back to work for her and Jake decides to renew his relationship with Sally and give up Heidi.

On opening night Sally wows her audience and the show is a hit. Alone in her dressing room following her performance she is locked in the theatre with Douglas who has murdered the only other two persons there—the doorman and her dresser. Sally is chased at knifepoint into the empty theatre. There she stands up to the disturbed man and gains the upper hand so that she stops his violence by taking his life.

Reviews and Commentary
  The Fan is a predictable crime thriller based on Bob Randall's novel. It was unfortunately filmed just prior to the tragic murder of rock star John Lennon. By the time the film was released, that real-life drama made it all the more apparent that *The Fan* trivialized the very real dangers facing celebrities. Howard Kissel, writing in *Women's Wear Daily,* said "the wave of recent actual violence makes *The Fan*—a fairly routine attempt to commercialize and eroticize physical cruelty—particularly disgusting, but it would have been a shabby little picture under any circumstances" (18 May 1981, 24).
  The sterling cast, headed by a stylish Lauren Bacall in the role of Sally Ross, was overwhelmed by the mediocre material. Critics both applauded and decried Bacall's physical appearance—some thought she was glamorous as ever and others thought she looked haggard as the aging star. Michael Biehn, who played the murderous Douglas Breen, failed to strike the right chord but also had little chance, given the weaknesses of the script.
  Stapleton played Ross' pragmatic, fiercely loyal secretary. She looked younger than in other roles at this point in her career and she brought a gritty honesty to the part of Belle. She was especially effective in the scene where Belle and Sally argue about her handling of the offensive letters. In one scene the psychotic man stalks Belle through a darkened subway station and viciously (and graphically) slices up her face with a straight razor. It undoubtedly took great courage for Stapleton to film this scene because she had had to undergo therapy herself during her first Broadway run of *The Rose Tattoo* because she was terrified someone in the audience might shoot her while she was onstage.

*****

F13   *ON THE RIGHT TRACK*
  TDL-Zephyr / Twentieth Century Fox; 1981; 97 minutes
  Video: Fox

Credits
Producer: Ronald Jacobs. Director: Lee Phillips. Screenwriters: Tina Pine, Avery Buddy and Richard Moses. Cinematographer: Jack Richards (CFI Color). Editor: Bill Butler. Music: Arthur B. Rubenstein. Art Director: William Fosser.

Cast

Lester	Gary Coleman
Mary/Big Lady	**Maureen Stapleton**
Mayor	Norman Fell
Frank	Michael Lembeck
Jill	Lisa Eilbacher
Robert	Bill Russell
Sam	Herb Edelman
Felix	David Selburg
Shoeshine Concessioner	C. Thomas Cuncliffe
Lady with Suitcase	Belinda Bremner

Mario	Nathan Davis
Sean	Mike Bacarella
Vito	Jack Wasserman
Flower Lady	Fern Persons
Gerald	Arthur Smith
Louis	Mike Genovese
Harry	Harry Gorsuch
Bookstore Man	George Brengel
Mark	Corin Rogers
Sally	Page Hannah
IRS Man	I. W. Klein
Beauty Salon Boss	Muriel Bach

And Ronda Pierson, Linda Golla, Brenda Lively, John Mohrlein, Sally Benoit, Thom Brandolino, Jerry McKay, Mario Tanzi, Rick LeFevour, Edna Moreno, Bert Weineberg, James Hogan, Jr., Debbie Hall, Jamie Gertz, Steve Marmer, Gil Cantanzaro, Sr., Gil Cantanzaro, Jr., Chelcie Ross, Felix Shuman, James Andelin, Al Nuti, Mark Hutter and T. W. Miller.

Synopsis

Lester is a resourceful ten-year-old orphan who lives in an underground railway station beneath an ominous urban city. The little black boy lives in several rental lockers and ekes out a living shining shoes. He has a warm circle of friends who make him feel more at home down below than up on the streets of the real world. They include Mary, a sweet old bag lady, and Sam, the nice man who runs the station pizza parlor. There is also the fatherly Robert who works as a bathroom attendant and the pretty Jill who dreams of a singing career while she makes change in the game arcade.

Lester dispenses all kinds of advice to all comers and spends his time choosing winners from the Daily Racing Form. When the word gets out that Lester always chooses the winner, his friends place bets which bring them unexpected riches. A brash juvenile officer named Frank enters the story intent on putting Lester in an orphanage until he learns of the boy's special talents. He tries to exploit Lester (as the Mayor-up-for-re-election and the bookies also do).

Jill, meanwhile, wants to adopt Lester but cannot afford to do so. Lester's future is resolved when Jill and Frank fall in love and decide to adopt Lester. The talented boy, meanwhile, has convinced his chums to donate their money to the needy city. At the end Lester is led up to the street level of the city where he must learn to live.

Reviews and Commentary

This film generated very mixed reviews. The critics felt it depended on the appeal of the thirteen-year-old child star, Gary Coleman and a sitcom structure. For the director, Lee Phillips, and producer, Ronald Jacobs, this was their first feature film (their previous background was in television); but they did little to adjust to the larger format and screen. Critics were especially divided on the work of Phillips. Mildred Taffel (October 1981, 495) said that "Lee Phillips' direction is tasteless, spiritless and pedestrian, but not much could be done with so dull and unoriginal a tale." Whereas Kevin Thomas, writing for the *Los Angeles Times,* said

Phillips had made the film "handsome, energetic and even, at times, lyrical" (23 August 1981, calendar 33),

Although Coleman was judged to be overly cute (in the pejorative sense), the supporting cast garnered better reviews, especially Lisa Eilbacher as Jill and Maureen Stapleton as Mary or "Big Lady." Thomas observed "you can't help but wish that Maureen Stapleton had a part worthier of her, but she has fun with what there is to it."

*****

F14   *REDS*
Paramount; 1981; 200 minutes
Video: Paramount

Credits
Producer and Director: Warren Beatty. Executive Producers: Simon Relph and Dede Allen. Associate Producer: David L. MacLeod. Screenwriters: Warren Beatty and Trevor Griffiths. Cinematographer: Vittorio Storaro (Technicolor). Editors: Dede Allen and Craig McKay. Music: Stephen Sondheim and Dave Grusin. Production Design: Richard Sylbert. Art Director: Simon Holland. Costume Design: Shirley Russell.

Cast

John Reed	Warren Beatty
Louise Bryant	Diane Keaton
Max Eastman	Edward Herrmann
Grigory Zinoviev	Jerzy Kosinski
Eugene O'Neill	Jack Nicholson
Louis Fraina	Paul Sorvino
Emma Goldman	**Maureen Stapleton**
Paul Trullinger	Nicolas Coster
Speaker at the Liberal Club	M. Emmet Walsh
Mr. Partlow	Ian Wolfe
Mrs Partlow	Bessie Love
Carl Walters	MacIntyre Dixon
Helen Walters	Pat Starr
Mrs. Reed	Eleanor D. Wilson
Floyd Dell	Max Wright
Horace Whigham	George Plimpton
Maurice Becker	Harry Ditson
Ida Rauh	Leigh Curran
Crystal Eastman	Kathryn Grody
Marjorie Jones	Brenda Currin
Jane Heap	Nancy Duiguid
Barney	Norman Chancer
Big Bill Haywood	Dolph Sweet
Police Chief	Ramon Bieri
Pinkerton Guard	Jack O'Leary
Pete Van Wherry	Gene Hackman
Dr. Lorber	Gerald Hiken
Julius Gerber	William Daniels

Allan Benson	Dave King
Joe Volski	Joseph Buloff
Alex Gomberg	Stefan Gryff
Interpreter	Denis Pekarev
Vladimir Lenin	Roger Sloman
Leon Trotsky	Stuart Richman
A. Kerensky	Oleg Kerensky

And Nikko Seppala, John J. Hooker, Shane Rimmer, Jerry Hardin, Jack Kehoe, Christopher Malcolm, Tony Sibbald, R. G. Armstrong, Josef Sommer, Jan Triska, Ake Lindman, Pertti Weckstrom, Nina Macarova, José DeFillippo and Andres La Casa.

The Witnesses: Roger Baldwin, Henry Miller, Adela Rogers St. Johns, Dora Russell, Scott Nearing, Tess Davis, Heaton Vorse, Hamilton Fish, Isaac Don Levine, Rebecca West, Will Durant, Will Weinstone, Oleg Kerensky, Emmanuel Herbert, Arne Swabeck, Adele Nathan, George Seldes, Kenneth Chamberlain, Blanche Hays Fagen, Galina Von Meck, Art Shields, Andrew Dasburg, Hugo Gellert, Dorothy Frooks, George Jessel, Jacob Bailin, John Ballato, Lucita Williams, Bernadine Szold-Fritz, Jessica Smith, Harry Carlisle and Arthur Mayer.

Synopsis

Reds is the story of the personal and political lives of journalist/ activist John Reed and writer Louise Bryant. Their relationship to each other and to history is shown through an extended montage of scenes showing how they met, fell in love, and became inextricably connected with the social and political movements from 1915 to 1921. Their personal history is set in perspective with recurring scenes of "witnesses"—aged faces of contemporary figures filmed in a black void—who recount their actual memories of Reed and Bryant.

Reed, a notable liberal journalist, first meets Bryant, the free-thinking wife of a conservative dentist, in Portland, Oregon in 1915. Reed agrees to let her interview him for a small magazine for which she writes and they talk through the night. When he leaves for New York, she abandons her husband to follow him.

In the bohemian atmosphere of Greenwich Village, Bryant and Reed's love affair catches fire as she is introduced to his imposing circle of friends: the dignified, devout anarchist Emma Goldman, the radical Max Eastman, and poet-playwright Eugene O'Neill. Bryant finds it difficult to establish herself as an author or individual while Reed becomes more deeply involved with politics. After an argument they join O'Neill and other artists in Provincetown where they plan to write experimental plays and poetry.

Reed, however, finds he cannot resist leaving her to go to the Democratic Convention as America veers towards war and Bryant falls into an affair with the cynical, attractive O'Neill. When Reed returns he pretends not to notice his lover's infidelity and instead forsakes their vow of free love and proposes marriage, which she accepts. Their marriage is overshadowed as Reed, encouraged by the Russian revolution, gets more involved with the American Socialist Party. Bryant tires of being marginalized and left at home and goes off to Europe to become a war correspondent.

Reed becomes ill and loses a kidney. In spite of his doctors' warnings, he follows Bryant to France where he convinces her to go with him to Russia. Bryant agrees to go along as a peer, not a lover, and together they travel to Petrograd to write about the revolution there. At a meeting of the workers, Reed comes forward and assures the cheering crowds that the workers of America will support their revolution. Bryant and Reed renew their marriage and each drafts a book on the political developments in Russia.

In 1918 Reed and Bryant return to New York to complete their books. Reed gains notoriety from his account, *Ten Days That Shook the World*. He visits Emma Goldman in jail before she is deported to Russia. Reed once again becomes more involved in politics and neglects Bryant. When his faction of the Socialist Party splits away from the main one, he is elected to go to Russia to get recognition for his faction, the Communist Labor Party.

This time Bryant refuses to go along and makes it clear she may not be waiting for Reed if he comes back. Still, he goes to Russia and is one of the very few that are able to be smuggled into the country. When Reed is told by the party leader, Zinoviev, that the factions of his party must be merged together before they will be recognized, Reed tries to leave but is denied permission. Anxious to return to Bryant, he tries to escape and is imprisoned in a Finnish jail.

Reed grows very ill in jail and sends word to Bryant. She determines to get him out and smuggles herself aboard a freighter and works her way to Finland. Meanwhile, Reed is released in a prisoner exchange by Lenin and is returned to Russia. He meets up again with Emma Goldman who tells him Bryant would never come to his rescue because she is not really a revolutionary. She also tells him that she is disillusioned, that the dream is over and that she is leaving. Reed agrees to work for Zinoviev and is sent to Baku to stir up the populace there.

Meanwhile Goldman and Bryant meet in Russia and Goldman admits that she had misjudged Bryant. On his return from Baku (where he was astonished by the anti-American sentiments and where his speeches were significantly changed by Zinoviev) the train is attacked by a White Army faction. Disillusioned, seriously ill, and battered from the fierce encounter, Reed staggers off the train to Bryant's waiting arms. Their loving reunion is fleeting as Reed is taken off to a hospital where, with Bryant at his bedside, he sinks into death.

Reviews and Commentary

Reds was an artistic and critical success, although its commercial appeal was adversely affected by the conservative mood sweeping the country in the first year of Ronald Reagan's presidency. Warren Beatty's fascinating screen epic garnered Oscars for Beatty's direction, Storaro's lush cinematography and for Maureen Stapleton's incisive portrait of Emma Goldman.

The critics were divided on some issues and agreed on others. Some criticized Beatty (who co-authored the screenplay with Trevor Griffiths) for changing historical fact for dramatic effect (such as delaying the reunion of the lovers until after the attack on the train from Baku, although Bryant and Reed in fact had made contact prior to that time). Some felt that the story should have focused on the revolution and put the romance in the background. Many faulted either the characterization of Louise Bryant or Diane Keaton's interpretation of her. Critic Carolyn Porter, however, writing in *Film Quarterly* (Spring 1982, 43), suggests that "if we look closer at the film's treatment of the Reed-Bryant affair, I think it becomes clear that the film's charge comes from a plot development focused not on the story of John Reed, but on the story of Louise Bryant." Porter goes on to trace the transformation of Bryant from a woman of no clear self-image who has little understanding of her place in the world into a whole individual, as devoted to her own principles as Reed is to his own. Porter adds: "What has made this transformation possible is a combination of her refusal to abandon the struggle to prove herself capable of living beyond Reed's margins, and Reed's capacity to understand and be patient with that struggle."

Beatty's decision to use the "witnesses" was universally recognized as innovative and effective. The contemporary voices of such people as Henry Miller, George Jessel and Oleg Kerensky (Kerensky's actual grandson) personalized the memories of Reed and Bryant and showed how quickly our perceptions blur in time. Even for those who offered adverse criticism, the film was acknowledged to be an impressive work. Beatty attempted the near impossible and he succeeded in establishing himself as a serious filmmaker with this film.

Much of the richness of *Reds* was due to the superb performances of the supporting cast. Although Beatty and Keaton received mixed but generally positive reviews for their portrayals of Reed and Bryant, Jack Nicholson was highly praised for his portrait of the cold, intellectual Eugene O'Neill, Jerzy Kosinski made an admirable screen debut as Grigory Zinoviev and Edward Herrmann was impressive as Max Eastman. Maureen Stapleton gave one of her most memorable performances in the role of Emma Goldman. Although she only appears in a few brief scenes, Stapleton created a character of great depth which rang true both dramatically and historically—a woman of profound conviction and dedication.

Vincent Canby, film critic for the *New York Times*, said "*Reds* is an extraordinary film, a big romantic adventure movie, the best since David Lean's *Lawrence of Arabia,* as well as a commercial movie with a rare sense of history . . . . [it is a] large, remarkable rich, romantic film that dramatizes—in a way no other commercial movie in my memory has ever done—the excitement of being young, idealistic and foolish in a time when everything still seemed possible" (4 December 1981, C8).

*****

F15   *JOHNNY DANGEROUSLY*
Twentieth Century Fox; 1984; 89 minutes
Video: CBS/Fox

Credits
Executive Producers: Bud Austin and Harry Colomby. Producer: Michael Hertzberg. Director: Amy Heckerling. Screenwriters: Norman Steinberg, Bernie Kukoff, Harry Colomby and Jeff Harris. Cinematographer: David

M. Walsh (DeLuxe Color). Editor: Pam Herring. Music: John Morris. Lyrics to "Dangerously": Norman Gimbel. Title song written and performed by "Weird Al" Yankovic. Choreographer: Tony Stevens. Production Design: Joseph R. Jennings. Set Decoration: Rick Simpson. Costume Design: Patricia Norris.

Cast

Johnny Dangerously	Michael Keaton
Vermin	Joe Piscopo
Lil Sheridan	Marilu Henner
Ma Kelly	**Maureen Stapleton**
Dundee	Peter Boyle
Tommy Kelly	Griffin Dunne
Sally	Glynnis O'Connor
The Pope	Dom DeLuise
Maroni	Richard Dimitri
Burr	Danny DeVito
Pat	Ron Carey
Vendor	Ray Walston
Arthur	Dick Butkus
Young Johnny	Byron Thames
Desk Sergeant	Alan Hale
Charley	Scott Thomson
Cleaning Lady	Sudie Bond
Dutch	Mark Jantzen
Manny	Gary Watkins
Vito	Mike Bacarella

And Hank Garrett, Leonard Termo, Troy W. Slaten, Alexander Hertzberg, Georg Olden, Cynthia Szigeti, Elizabeth Arlen, Doris Grossman, Richard Warwick, Mike Finneran, Paul B. Price, Will Seltzer, Dick Dalduzzi, Gordon Zimmerman, Katie La Bourdette, Norman Steinberg, Frank Slaten, Dean R. Miller, Neal Israel, Edward C. Short, Shelley Pogoda, Jerome Michaels, Russell Forte, Jack Nance, Joy Michael, Richard L. Rosenthal, Carl A. Gottleib, Paula Dell, Harvey Parry, Jeffrey Weissman, Richard A. Roth, Chuck Hicks, Bob Eubanks, Mert Rich, Hal Riddle, Trisha Long and Claudia Kim.

Synopsis

Johnny Dangerously is a comic spoof of 1930s gangster films. The story begins in a pet shop where shop owner Johnny Kelly apprehends a small boy stealing a puppy. Johnny tells the boy crime does not pay and illustrates his point with his own life story. We flashback to 1910 where Johnny is a paperboy on the lower east side of New York. He lives with his mother, Ma Kelly, and his little brother, Tommy, in a tenement filled with the mounds of laundry Ma washes to support them.

When his ever-ailing mom needs an operation, Johnny does a job for the crime boss Jocko Dundee and earns the name "Johnny Dangerously." The years pass and Johnny stays out of trouble until Ma Kelly needs another operation (a "thyroid search") and Johnny goes to work for Dundee on a regular basis. He becomes a folk hero in his neighborhood but keeps his new identity from his mom and goody-two-shoes brother (who he is putting through law school).

Dundee's family-style gang is at war with rival gangster Maroni when Johnny's old nemesis, Danny Vermin, joins the Dundee gang. Dundee is nearly killed when Maroni plants a bomb in his toilet and so he turns over the reins to Johnny. By now brother Tommy has completed law school and joined the DA's office. When the DA (on the take from Johnny) cannot deter Tommy's crusade to rid the city of gangs, Tommy's car is deprived of brakes. Tommy survives and gets the DA's job.

Johnny, meanwhile, has fallen in love with torch singer Lil Sheridan. While they dream of settling down, Vermin plots to take over the gang. Vermin manages to frame Johnny for the murder of the Crime Commissioner and almost succeeds in killing Tommy but Johnny breaks out of the Big House and exposes Vermin, earning himself a pardon. In the final scene Johnny is back in his cozy little shop where he has convinced his young thief that crime does not pay. He then steps into a limousine with a gorgeously dressed Lil as if to say "maybe it does pay, a little."

Reviews and Commentary

The critics agreed that *Johnny Dangerously* got off to a hilarious start and went downhill to a disappointing end. Along the way, however, the film had its moments—many fine comedic exchanges in which the humor ranged from sophisticated parody to puerile silliness. The final result was an extended sitcom skit that failed. The positives were the performances of Michael Keaton as the jaunty, Cagney-esque Johnny Dangerously and Maureen Stapleton as the ever-ailing Ma Kelly.

Kevin Thomas, critic for the *Los Angeles Times,* said the film should have been titled *Johnny Disastrously* but he also said that "fast, funny, slyly self-mocking and as limber as the classic screen comics, Keaton has an Irish-looking mug and a cocky air that's perfect for the Cagney-like street kid turned sleekly groomed racketeer" (21 December 1984, calendar 4).

Johnny Dangerously was Stapleton's first film appearance since winning the Oscar for *Reds* three years earlier. Her roles could not have been more different. In *Johnny Dangerously* she is white-haired and dumpy—a caricature of an Irish washer-woman with the language of a guttersnipe. *Newsweek* said Stapleton's portrayal "is the movie's most successful creation, a worthy, weather-beaten, Warner-Bros. cliché condensed to its hilarious essence" (Ansen 14 January 1985, 53). *Time* said "only the redoubtable Maureen Stapleton, listening to some wild pulse of her own, finds something she can dance to" (Schickel 14 January 1985, 66).

*****

F16   *COCOON*

Twentieth Century Fox; 1985; 117 minutes
Video: CBS/Fox

Credits

Producers: Richard D. Zanuck, David Brown and Lili Fini Zanuck.
Director: Ron Howard. Screenwriter: Tom Benedek, from a story by David

Saperstein. Cinematographer: Don Peterman (DeLuxe Color). Editors:
Michael Hill and Daniel Hanley. Music: James Horner. Music: "Gravity"
performed by Michael Sembello. Special music and dance coordination:
Gwen Verdon. Production Design: Jack T. Collis. Set Decoration: Jim
Duffy. Costume Designer: Aggie Guerard Rodgers. Makeup: Robert
Norin and Kevin Haney. Special Effects: Greg Cannom, Rick Baker and
Industrial Light & Magic.

Cast

Art Selwyn	Don Ameche
Ben Luckett	Wilford Brimley
Joe Finley	Hume Cronyn
Walter	Brian Dennehy
Bernie Lefkowitz	Jack Gilford
Jack Bonner	Steve Guttenberg
Mary Luckett	**Maureen Stapleton**
Alma Finley	Jessica Tandy
Bess McCarthy	Gwen Verdon
Rose Lefkowitz	Herta Ware
Kitty	Tahnee Welch
David	Barret Oliver
Susan	Linda Harrison
Pillsbury	Tyrone Power, Jr.
John Dexter	Clint Howard
Pops	Charles Lampkin
Doc	Mike Nomad
Lou Pine	Jorge Gil
DMV Clerk	Jim Ritz
Smiley	Charles Rainsbury
Aliens	Wendy Cooke
	Pamela Prescott
	Dinah Sue Rowley
	Gabriella Sinclair

And Cindi Vicino, Russ Wheeler, Harold Bergman, Ivy Thayer, Fred
Broderson, Mark Cheresnick, Bette Shoor, Mark Simpson, Robert Slacum,
Jr., Rance Howard, Jean Speegle, Charles Voelker, Irving Krone, Clarence
Thomas and Ted Science.

Synopsis

The setting is Sunny Shores Villas, a retirement community in St.
Petersburg, Florida. Three elderly residents, Art Selwyn, Ben Luckett and
Joe Finley, gain entry to a vacant estate to go swimming in the enclosed
pool. The seniors struggle with the reality of age—Ben's failing eyesight
causes him to lose his driver's license and Joe learns he is losing his battle
with cancer.

Meanwhile, a couple from out of town named Walter and Kitty rent a
boat from Jack Bonner, a young man eking out a living by taking tourists on
fishing trips. Walter and Kitty offer Jack a month's contract and they also
show up at the estate, which they rent for a month. Soon they are filling the
estate pool with "cocoons"—huge ovoid rocks—which they have brought up
from the ocean floor and transported via Jack's vessel.

The seniors find the cocoons but continue their private swims. Soon they realize they are feeling terrific. Joe and Ben show renewed interest in their wives (Alma and May) and Art begins courting Bess, the attractive villa resident who teaches dance to the other seniors. In a short time the fellows are like teenagers. Joe's cancer is in complete remission and Ben passes a new eye test. The three of them take their ladies on the town, dancing, bowling and partying.

Jack becomes suspicious about his strange clients and is horrified to discover they are aliens who have taken human form. They have come from a planet called Antarea to recover twenty members of a ground crew who were left on earth ten thousand years previously. They convince Jack to help them save the crew, entombed in the cocoons.

The stories converge when the seniors are caught by the aliens and are denied access to the pool. The problems of age resume until Ben asks Walter for permission for them to use the pool and they once more grow youthful, but the secret gets out and the residents from Sunny Shores storm the pool. By the time they are discovered they have absorbed the life force from the cocoons, making it impossible for Walter and Kitty to take them home.

Ben recruits the seniors to help Walter return the cocoons to the ocean floor so they can be salvaged at a later date. Walter then offers the elderly folks the opportunity to go with the aliens and to thus escape the ravages of age. At night about fifty people steal away from the home and board Jack's boat to rendezvous with the mother ship. They are discovered and pursued by the coast guard but in the end all make it to the mother ship, except Jack who chooses to stay home.

Reviews and Commentary

Ron Howard directed *Cocoon* following his successful direction of the fantasy about a mermaid, *Splash*. *Cocoon* is a fantasy with similar charm and the critics conceded that Howard had again managed to tug the heartstrings and tickle the funnybone. Janet Maslin complimented the older cast which "functions as a graceful ensemble, with a warmheartedness that seems genuine without getting out of hand" (21 June 1985, C5).

The harshest criticism was that the film was too derivative, combining as it did elements from *E.T.*, *Close Encounters of the Third Kind, The Man Who Fell to Earth*, and *Peter Pan*. Perhaps this was unavoidable since the special effects were handled by George Lucas' Industrial Light & Magic.

The critics were unanimous in their praise of the principle actors, especially Hume Cronyn and Jessica Tandy, Wilford Brimley, Don Ameche, Gwen Verdon, and Maureen Stapleton as the oldsters who grow young. Tahnee Welch, daughter of Raquel Welch, made an auspicious debut as the lovely alien Kitty. Brian Dennehy gave a subtle but strong portrait of Walter. The film was quite popular for what *Los Angeles Times'* critic Sheila Benson described as its "wit, against-expectation situations, tenderness, humanity, a collection of brilliantly fine actors, plus this admittedly all-stops-out-ending, which works because we so nakedly want it to" (21 June 1985, calendar 1).

F17   *THE MONEY PIT*
Amblin Entertainment / Universal Pictures; 1986; 91 minutes
Video: MCA

Credits

Executive Producers: Stephen Spielberg and David Giler. Producers: Frank Marshall, Kathleen Kennedy and Art Levinson. Director: Richard Benjamin. Screenwriter: David Giler. Cinematographer: Gordon Willis (DeLuxe Color). Editor: Jacqueline Cambas. Music Composed and Conducted by Michel Colombier. Music/Lyrics: Michel Colombier, Kathleen Wakefield, White Lion, Johann Sebastian Bach, Walter Marks, Julian Bargas, Giorgio Moroder, Deborah Harry, Bill Monroe, Gaetano Donizetti, Salvatore Cammanrano, Peter Alsop and Ritchie Valens. Production Design: Patrizia von Brandenstein. Art Director: Steve Graham. Set Decoration: George de Titta, Sr. Costume Design: Ruth Morley. Makeup: Mickey Scott. Special Effects: Michael Wood.

Cast

Walter Fielding	Tom Hanks
Anna Crowley	Shelley Long
Max Beissart	Alexander Godunov
Estelle	**Maureen Stapleton**
Art Shirk	Joe Mantegna
Curly	Philip Bosco
Jack Schnittman	Josh Mostel
Shatov	Yakov Smirnoff
Brad Shirk	Carmine Caridi
Ethan	Brian Backer
Benny	Billy Lombardo
Marika	Mia Dillon
Carlos	John van Dreelen
Walter Fielding, Sr.	Douglass Watson

And Lucille Dobrin, Tetchie Agbayani, Scott Turchin, Radu Gavor, Grisha Dimant, Lutz Rath, Joey Balin, Wendell Pierce, Susan Browning, Henry Baker, Mary Louise Wilson, Irving Metzman, Frank Maraden, Mike Russo, Joe Ponazecki, Michael Hyde, Mike Starr, Frankie Faison, Jake Steinfeld, Matthew Cowles, Nestor Serrano, Michael Jeter, Afemo Omilami, Bruno Iannone, Ron Foster, Alan Altshuld, Tzi Ma, Cindy Brooks, Leslie West, White Lion, Robey and The Fabulous Heavyweights: Tom Filiault, Doug Plavin, Chris Tuttle and Ed Vadas.

Synopsis

Walter Fielding is a young New York lawyer whose partner (and father) has just skipped town with all the firm's assets and has run off to Rio to marry a girl half his age. Walter, bravely trying to pay off his father's debts, negotiates with his clients which include recording artists and rock bands such as White Lion, Cheap Girls and Robey. Walter's girlfriend, Anna, is a violinist for the symphony who has recently divorced Max, the symphony's egotistical, world-class conductor. She and Walter are living in Anna and Max's old apartment but Max suddenly returns to New York and they are evicted. Walter tells Anna that he wants to marry her and get a little house and enjoy a simple life.

Unable to find an apartment, Walter and Anna are lured to the country where they find a one-million dollar house on the market for only $200,000. They take the train to see the house and meet Estelle—the flamboyant, aging, red-haired owner who tearfully shows them the mansion. Drinking heavily, she tells them she is desperate for money because her beloved husband, Carlos, has been picked up by Israeli intelligence and she needs cash immediately to save him. Forced to decide on the spot, Walter and Anna combine their meager fortunes and buy the house.

Disaster ensues the minute they arrive. The front door falls out of its frame, the bathtub spouts mud and the entire central staircase collapses, leaving no access to the upstairs except up a ladder. As the lovers try to cope, they sink more and more money into their "money pit." They find there is no running water, an electrical fire guts the kitchen, and the bathtub falls through the rickety floor to shatter in the foyer.

After a tremendous effort they get the only carpenter and plumber willing to work for them—the "Shirk" brothers—to bring in a crew that seems to consist of heavy metal bikers and tawdry circus performers. The problems escalate as the crew digs up the yard, cuts huge holes in the building facade and then leave because Walter has not secured the building permits.

Four months later an army of construction workers are on hand and things have improved; the house is actually partially habitable. Anna and Walter continue their jobs although Anna has to fend off Max's charming attempts to get her to come back to him. When Walter goes out of town for one night Anna succumbs to Max's offer of a hot meal and a hot bath. To her horror she wakes up in his bed and Max provides details of their passionate night together. When Walter discovers this he and Anna have a huge fight and decide to leave each other—as soon as the house is finished.

The house is finally fully restored to its glory but Walter and Anna are going their separate ways. Even when Max tells Anna that she did not sleep with him that night, Anna is too hurt by Walter's mistrust to tell him. Just before she walks out the door Walter relents and forgives her even before he learns the truth. They are married in the garden of their fabulous estate.

The final scene shifts back to Rio where Walter's father, with his own young bride, is turning over a suitcase of cash to buy an immense villa that "only needs a little work." The sellers are the red-haired Estelle and her husband Carlos!

Reviews and Commentary

The performances of Tom Hanks as Walter Fielding and Shelley Long as Anna Crowley were filled with charm and appeal is this yuppie disaster film. However, critics felt that the Spielberg special effects displaced the potential comedy inherent in the characters. As critic Kevin Thomas observed in the *Los Angeles Times*, "*The Money Pit* grows increasingly mechanical, both in its content and in the resolution of its plot, as the effects start overwhelming this essentially modest little romantic comedy" (26 March 1986, calendar 1).

The film was a marvel of technical know-how with several outstanding "Rube Goldberg" episodes in which everything that could go wrong did in an elaborate ballet of deconstruction. Vincent Canby noted that "the spectacle is so impressive that you hesitate to laugh" (26 March 1986, C19). That seems to be the consensus of the critical opinion.

In spite of this flaw, the critics enjoyed a bevy of fine performances. In addition to Hanks and Long, Joe Mantegna was an oily Art Shirk, Boris Godunov was a charismatic conductor who never took himself too seriously, and Maureen Stapleton was the lovable crook, Estelle. Canby particularly favored Ms. Stapleton who, he said, "provides the film with a high style that gets lost in between her appearances" (26 March 1986, C19).

*****

F18   *HEARTBURN*
Paramount Pictures; 1986; 108 minutes
Video: Paramount

Credits
Producers: Mike Nichols and Robert Greenhut. Director: Mike Nichols. Screenplay by Nora Ephron, based on her novel. Cinematographer: Nestor Almendros (Technicolor). Editor: Sam O'Steen. Music: Carly Simon. Production Design: Tony Walton. Art Director: John Kasarda. Set Decoration: Susan Bode. Costume Design: Ann Roth. Makeup: J. Roy Helland and Lee Halls.

Cast

Rachel	Meryl Streep
Mark	Jack Nicholson
Richard	Jeff Daniels
Vera	**Maureen Stapleton**
Julie	Stockard Channing
Arthur	Richard Masur
Betty	Catherine O'Hara
Harry, Rachel's Father	Steven Hill
Dmitri	Milos Forman
Annie	Natalie Stern
Thelma Rice	Karen Akers
Juanita	Aida Linares
Della	Anna Maria Horsford
Detective O'Brien	Ron McLarty
Dr. Appel	Kenneth Walsh
Subway Thief	Kevin Spacey
British Moderator	John Wood
Contractor Laszlo	Yakov Smirnoff
Eve	Mercedes Ruehl
Diana	Joanna Gleason
Dan	R. S. Thomas
Ellis	Jack Gilpin
Sidney	Christian Clemenson

And Sidney Armus, Caroline Aaron, Lela Ivey, Tracey Jackson, Libby Titus, Angela Pietropinto, Cynthia O'Neal, Susan Forristal, Dana Ivey, John Rothman, Elijah Lindsay, Jack Neam, Kimi Parks, Salem Ludwig, Patricia Falkenhain, Margaret Thomson, Charles Denney, Greg Almquist, Garrison Lane, Ryan Hilliard, Dana Streep, Mary Streep, Cyrilla Dorn, May Pang, Michael Regan, Ari M. Roussimoff and Luther Rucker.

Synopsis

Rachel Samstat and Mark Forman meet at a wedding. She's an attractive magazine writer and food critic in her thirties from New York. He's a Washington reporter in his forties. As the wedding ceremony commences, Rachel asks her friend and editor, Richard, who Mark is and if he is single. She is told "he's famous for it." For his part, Mark is just as intrigued by Rachel and they get together at the reception and fall in love almost immediately.

Although they have both been through failed marriages, they decide to try again. Rachel, however, gets cold feet on the big day. As the wedding party awkwardly stands about or falls asleep Rachel is closed up in her room, tormented with her fears of making a mistake. Friends, family, her therapist, Vera, even strangers come in to shore up her courage. Finally, Mark comes in to see her and she puts aside her apprehensions and the wedding takes place.

She gives up the job she loves and moves to Washington where Mark has bought a dilapidated brownstone which has been gutted by fire. They hire a Hungarian contractor to renovate and begin their marriage bliss under the dripping ceilings and dust covered walls. Rachel makes some friends but the pretentious and boorish social crowd and the living conditions at home strain the marriage.

Coming home from a party one night, Rachel and Mark scrap about the inept contractor (the renovation is more like demolition at this point), but their argument dissipates when Rachel reveals to Mark that she is pregnant. They split a pizza and sing "baby" songs to each other. The couple finds delight in their first child, a little girl, Annie. Rachel soon is pregnant again and thoroughly relishes her life as a mother, wife and homemaker.

Her dream is, however, short-lived. As she finds fulfillment in her new baby, Mark becomes more distant. Through one of the gossips who inhabits their social orb, Rachel learns that Thelma Rice, a tall, attractive Washington socialite, is having an affair. She does not give it much thought until she overhears her hairdresser discussing the tell-tale signs of cheating. Rachel bolts from the chair, her hair still half-combed, and rushes home to check Mark's desk. There she finds ample proof of her husband's dalliance, including extravagant expenditures on flowers, meals and gifts.

Rachel confronts Mark who admits the adultery. In a fury she packs up Annie and flies back to New York. She gets her old job back but secretly hopes Mark will come to make amends. Living at her father's house, she fantasizes that her troubles have become the subject of a *Masterpiece Theatre* series. She returns to her therapy with Vera. One day on her way to group therapy a man on the subway takes note of the expensive ring that Mark has given her. He follows her to the group and robs them all of their valuables, including the ring.

After a short time Mark arrives in New York and he and Rachel reconcile and return to Washington. Still, Rachel cannot help watching for indications that Mark may be cheating on her. In a vengeful mood she tells her gossipy friend that Mark's lover, Thelma, had developed a sexual disease. When Mark confronts Rachel with her lie, she learns that Thelma has come to their house. Rachel becomes furious but goes into labor. With the birth of their second child, the couple maintain an awkward peace until Rachel gets her stolen ring back from the New York police. She takes the love token to the jeweler for repair and finds out that Mark has bought a fabulously expensive necklace and it is not for her.

This time Rachel plans her exit carefully. At a dinner party she and Mark participate in a discussion about marriage and what it should be. Rachel then prepares the key lime pie she has brought for dessert and carefully smashes it in Mark's face. Collecting the children, she takes the first plane back to New York, leaving Mark for good.

Reviews and Commentary

Heartburn is based on Nora Ephron's novel which bitterly chronicled the breakup of her marriage with the noted Washington journalist, Carl Bernstein (who, with Bob Woodward, broke the Watergate Scandal). The novel caused a tremendous stir in Washington because of its stinging indictment of the private life of a very public couple. However, Ephron's screenplay considerably muted the force of her attack and the result is a film which divided the critics.

Richard Combes, writing in *Monthly Film Bulletin*, said "*Heartburn* is a wonderfully smooth dovetailing of the particular and the general, of specific social and domestic circumstances with a still-life of Every Affair" and that Nichols direction "makes *Heartburn* the best American comedy of the decade" (February 1987, 49). However, David Denby of *New York Magazine* found much less value in the screen adaptation, saying "it's a skillful movie, but very, very small, and often precious—the story of a marriage told entirely from one side, and told with great knowingness but very little real understanding . . . . *Heartburn* is perhaps the most naggingly detailed view of an American upper-bourgeois marriage ever put on film" (4 August 1986, 62).

Most of the critics sided with Denby, feeling that the shortcomings in the script were cleverly disguised with an impressive cast and confident direction by Mike Nichols. Critics lauded the performances of Meryl Streep and Jack Nicholson in the roles of Rachel and Mark as well as those of Jeff Daniels as Richard, Stockard Channing as Rachel's friend Julie, and Maureen Stapleton in the cameo role of Vera, Rachel's therapist.

*****

F19   *SWEET LORRAINE*
Autumn Pictures / Angelika Films, 1987, 91 minutes
Video: Paramount

Credits
Executive Producers: Angelika Saleh and Joseph• Saleh.   Producer/
Director: Steve Gomer. Screenwriters: Michael Zettler and Shelly Altman.

Based on a story by Michael Zettler, Shelly Altman, George Malko. Cinematographer: Rene Ohashi. Editor: Laurence Solomon. Music: Richard Robbins. Production Design: David Gropman. Art Director: Karen Schulz. Set Decoration: Richard Hoover. Costume Designer: Cynthia Flynt.

Cast

Lillian Garber	**Maureen Stapleton**
Molly	Trini Alvarado
Sam	Lee Richardson
Jack	John Bedford Lloyd
Phil Allen	Freddie Roman
Howie	Giancarlo Esposito
Karen	Edith Falco
Leonard of Great Neck	Todd Graff
Bobby	Evan Handler
Sarah	Mindy Morgenstern
Julie	Tamara Tunie
Ivan	Boris Sichkin
Tony, the Chinese Cook	Ben Lin

And Marcel Rosenblatt, Don Moore, Mark Lewis, Jerry Lott, Paula Trueman, Bill Alton, Robyn Finn, Annie Karzen, Maurice Brenner, Marcella Warner, Bernie Cove, Bernie Barrow, Joan Kaye, David Lipman, Domingo and Sylvia Alvarado, Michael Baskin, James Wexler and Philip Gittelman.

Synopsis

The Lorraine is an aging summer resort hotel in the Catskills run by Lillian Garber, a charming senior citizen who treats her guests as her extended Jewish family. Sam, her dear friend and companion, returns each summer from his job in the Bronx to work as the salad chef in the Lorraine's kosher kitchen. Lil has lived her whole life at the Lorraine but she questions whether she should sell it to developers. The eighty-year-old estate is in bad need of repairs, the guests are superannuated, and the atmosphere is but a tawdry reflection of a once sophisticated, chic hotel.

Lil's college-age granddaughter, Molly, arrives unexpectedly from Phoenix. Molly is fleeing her parents who are going through a messy divorce. She goes to work in the kitchen where Sam teaches her the art of making cole slaw and how to command respect from the rowdy college kids who work as waiters and kitchen help. Molly gets to know the guests and Phil Allen, the obnoxious "social director" and stand-up comic who specializes in "Borscht Belt" humor and leads the Jewish aerobics on the lawn each day.

Sam urges Lil to take a generous offer for the Lorraine and to retire with him to the Bronx but Molly insists that she would like to stay and help Lil hold onto the hotel. Molly also has a summer romance with Jack, the handsome, aloof handyman. When Jack shows her just how badly run-down the hotel is, Molly realizes that Lil needs to sell it while she can.

Labor Day arrives and the guests and staff celebrate the end of summer. Sam and Lil (who has now sold the hotel) prepare to head for their new life together in the Bronx. With a promise that Jack will visit for

Christmas, Molly sadly goes back to finish her senior year at college. They board up the Lorraine for the last time where it will wait to be torn down to make room for the condominiums the new owners will build there.

Reviews and Commentary

This film was the directing debut of Steve Gomer and it was, apparently, a labor of love. The film was shot at the Heiden Hotel in Fallsburg, New York, and, like the hotel in the film, the Heiden was torn down soon after. Gomer's personal connections to the Heiden enrich the film with a genuine nostalgia that never rings false. Gomer's grandfather was an employee at the Heiden and he thus spent many summers at the hotel (and later married a granddaughter from the family that built it). The director's eye for detail is apparent in every frame of *Sweet Lorraine.*

Maureen Stapleton starred as another Jewish matron in this film. In the role of Lillian Garber, Stapleton created the warmth and wisdom that permeated throughout the film and was essential to its success. Particularly effective was Stapleton's portrayal of Lil's loving relationship with Sam. As *Los Angeles Times* critic Michael Wilmington observed, "you expect Maureen Stapleton and Lee Richardson to be better than good. They don't disappoint you; their scenes together have an old-pro silkiness and deft interplay" (24 June 1987, calendar 5).

It is, however, the ensemble playing of a well-chosen cast that hold our attention throughout this pleasant, gentle film. Jami Bernard, writing in the *New York Post*, says that "one of the things that makes this movie a standout is the many levels on which the characters relate to one another. The extended family of the Lorraine is a complex, interdependent web. Sweet, but never saccharine" (1 May 1987, 33).

*****

F20   *MADE IN HEAVEN*
Lorimar Pictures, 1987, 102 minutes
Video: Lorimar Home Video

Credits
Producers: Raynold Gideon, Bruce A. Evans and David Blocker. Director: Alan Rudolph. Screenwriters: Bruce A. Evans and Raynold Gideon. Cinematographer: Jan Kiesser. Editor: Tom Walls. Music Director: Mark Isham. "We Never Danced" written by Neil Young, performed by Martha Davis. Production Design: Paul Peters. Art Director: Steven Legler. Set Designers: David Boatright and Gershon Ginsburg. Set Decorators: Rosemary Brandenburg and Lynn Wolverton. Costumes: April Ferry. Make-up: Edward Ternes and Annie Menassian. Special Effects: Doug DeGrazzio and Max W. Anderson.

Cast
Mike Shea/Elmo Barnett	Timothy Hutton
Annie Packert/Ally Chandler	Kelly McGillis
Mike's Aunt Lisa	**Maureen Stapleton**
Annette Shea, Mike's Mother	Ann Wedgeworth

Emmett Humbird	as Himself
	(Debra Winger, uncredited)
Steve Shea, Mike's Father	James Gammon
Brenda Carlucci	Mare Winningham
Ben Chandler	Don Murray
Tom Donnelly	Timothy Daly
Lucille	Ellen Barkin
Donald Sumner	David Rasche
Wiley Foxx	Amanda Plummer
Giu Blanchard/Brian Dutton	Willard Pugh
Lyman McCray	Vyto Ruginis
Truck Driver	Neil Young
Stanky, Mechanic	Tom Petty
Shark	Ric Ocasek
Mrs. Packert	Marj Dusay
Mr. Packert	Ray Gideon
Billy Packert	Zack Finch
Orrin	Rob Knepper
Mr. Bjornstead	James Tolkan
Sam Morrell	Gailard Sartain
Angel with Tophat	John Considine
Woody, Talent Coordinator	Elliot Rabinowitz
Mario the Toymaker	Tom Robbins
Miss Barnett	Debra Dusay
Mrs. Burwell	Patricia Earnest
Reginald/TV Interviewer	Leon Martell
TV Interviewers	Dave Miachaels
	Billy Jo Rucker

And Paul Sloan, Larry Sloan, Lauren Hill, Ann Owens, Tom Walls, Mark Isham, Matraca Berg, Pee Wee Ellis, Michelle Graybael, Patrick O'Hearn, Colin Chin, Carol Veto, Iris Farmer, Theresa Hightower, Robert Gould, Chester Clark, Elliot Street, Michael Klastorin, Meeghan Ochs, Henry Sanders, David Bethany, Pete Munro, Johnny Popwell, Alveda King Beale, Stuart Manne, Randy Cash, Christen Childers, Jim L. Gassman, Jack Hager, Jennifer Deer Johnson, Irv Gorman, Rick West, Jon Kohler, Danielle Aubuchon, Amy Van Nostrand, Kelly Wellman, Ed Yousefian, Denise Stephens, Doug De Grazzio, Gladys Lavitan, Kerry Lyn McKissick, Sonya Maddox, John Rosenberg, David Paradis, Paul A. Simmons, J. Vaganek, George Pappas, Kerrie Cullen, Carrie Paddock and Matthew Paddock.

Synopsis

In a movie theatre in a small American town in the 1940s a young ex-soldier, Mike Shea, sits with his girlfriend, Brenda, watching the ending of Hitchcock's *Notorious*. They join Mike's parents for a bite after the movie and Brenda and Mrs. Shea advise Mike, who has been laid off, on how to find another job. When Mike is turned down for a job at the bank and Brenda informs him that she is getting married to her boss, Mike hits the road for California. He only gets a hundred miles when he comes upon an accident. A car has plunged off a bridge and is sinking with a mother and two children in it. Mike saves the family but loses his own life.

He comes to in a palatial, empty room and is greeted cheerfully by his Aunt Lisa. She is his closest relative in heaven and has come to give him clothes and introduce him to life on the other side. Here one only has to imagine where you want to go and you are there. Aunt Lisa is now a painter (her reward for being without artistic talent on earth). So she paints in her atelier in Paris or Florence, depending upon her mood. Mike adjusts to his new world after he meets Emmett Humbird, a mysterious red-headed man who drinks whiskey, smokes and evidently "runs things" in heaven.

Mike soon meets Annie, a soul who was born in heaven. They fall in love and Mike imagines them a house and they plan a wedding. However, their plans cease when Mike learns from Emmett that Annie is due for an incarnation on earth. Unable to accept her loss, Mike strikes a deal with Emmett to incarnate as well and he is given thirty years in which to find Annie or be miserable forever.

Annie (now Ally Chandler) is born to a loving family. Her father becomes a successful toy manufacturer and Annie goes into the business, writing a children's book about her imaginary friend named Mike. Over the thirty years she marries a filmmaker (Tom Donnelly), takes over her father's business at his death, is divorced by Tom and left unhappily on her own. Mike, meanwhile, has been reborn as Elmo Barnett and suffers a miserable childhood and becomes a sixties drifter, a soldier in Nam, and finally a successful musician.

Throughout the thirty years Annie and Mike almost come together and then stray far from one another. Annie meets other men and Mike is almost snared by an evil seductress who involves him in a robbery. With no memory of their heavenly existence, they are filled with inexplicable yearning for something that they cannot define. With a little help from Emmett and from the Shea's (Mike's former parents), their paths converge on the final day just in time to have them fall in love on sight.

Reviews and Commentary

Made in Heaven is a unique film with the personal stamp of director Alan Rudolph who had previously created the low-budget but critically acclaimed films *Choose Me* and *Trouble in Mind*. For this film Rudolph got studio backing but accepted only half the budget offered so that he could restrict the emphasis on special effects and concentrate on the story. The film is therefore described in *The 1988 Motion Picture Guide Annual* as "a deeply poetic fantasy masquerading as a Hollywood film" and Rudolph is said to be "a visionary working in a land of business deals and power lunches" who has "still managed to come up with a wholly personal film" (Nash and Ross, 1989, 171).

Critic Janet Maslin said *"Made in Heaven* has a disarming gentleness and a light, buoyant charm, not to mention a penchant for surprises" (6 November 1987, C16). Moreover, there are considerable surprises, not the least of which is a remarkable, uncredited performance by Debra Winger as the inexplicable Emmett Humbird. In a short, chopped-off red wig, chain-smoking with a husky, gravelly voice, Winger is unrecognizable. Timothy Hutton, (who was married to Winger at the time the film was made) also received acclaim for his multi-faceted portrayals of Mike and Elmo as did Kelly McGillis for her very angelic Annie and fetching Ally.

There were more surprises in the numerous cameo performances that sustain an otherwise disjointed screenplay. Maureen Stapleton created the delightful Aunt Lisa who paints her garish canvasses and serenely takes heaven in stride. Ellen Barkin and Amanda Plummer livened up the screen with portrayals of the road-house slut Lucille and the rock group promoter Wiley Foxx. There were also brief appearances by rock musicians Neil Young, Tom Petty and Ric Ocasek and novelist Tom Robbins.

Although critics quibbled about various elements of the film, they seemed to agree that Rudolph had created something original and entertaining. *Newsday* critic Mike McGrady said that "a combination of first-rate talents has created a featherweight concoction that is charming in its innocence—also silly, wacky, goofy and pleasantly enjoyable" (6 November 1987, C5).

*****

F21 *NUTS*

Barwood Films / Warner Brothers; 1987, 116 minutes
Video: Warner Home Video
(Also available in Spanish under title *Me Quieren Volver Loca*)

Credits

Based on the play by Tom Topor. Executive Producers: Teri Schwartz and Cis Corman. Producer: Barbra Streisand. Director: Martin Ritt. Screenwriters: Tom Topor, Darryl Ponicsan and Alvin Sargent. Cinematographer: Andrzej Bartkowiak (Technicolor). Editor: Sidney Levin. Music: Barbra Streisand. Music Conducted and Arranged by Jeremy Lubbock. Production Design: Joel Schiller. Art Director: Eric Orbom. Set Decoration: Anne McCulley. Costume Design: Joe Tompkins.

Cast

Claudia Draper	Barbra Streisand
Aaron Levinsky	Richard Dreyfuss
Rose Kirk, Claudia's Mother	**Maureen Stapleton**
Arthur Kirk	Karl Malden
Dr. Herbert A. Morrison, Psychiatrist	Eli Wallach
Francis MacMillan, Prosecuting Attorney	Robert Webber
Judge Stanley Murdoch	James Whitmore
Allen Green	Leslie Neilsen
Clarence Middleton	William Prince
First Judge	Dakin Matthews
Harry Harrison	Paul Benjamin
Saul Kreiglitz	Warren Manzi
Dr. Johnson	Elizabeth Hoffman
Dr. Arante	Castulo Guerra

And Stacy Bergman, Hayley Taylor-Block, Matt Rivald, John Wesley, Sarina Grant, Tyra Ferrell, Nicole Burdette, Valentina Quinn, Carlos Cervantes, Ron Cummins, Gerry Okuneff, Conni Marie Brazelton, Roydon Clark, Dana Dru Evenson, Bruce Barbour, Noel Walcott III, Tony Rolon,

Pamela Seamon, Tina Lifford, Stephannie Howard, Rocco Karega, Armando Diaz, Alphonse V. Walter, Joseph Romeo, Ernest-Frank Taylor, Edward Blackoff, Darryl Ponicsan, Billy Kane, Lavelle Roby, Shirley Jo Finney, Sharon Barr, Annie LaRussa, Babbie Green, Barbara Ann Grimes, Cecilia Garcia, Leontine Guilliard and Suzanne Kent.

Synopsis

Aaron Levinsky is an overworked Legal Aid attorney who is assigned to represent Claudia Draper, a high-price call girl who is charged with manslaughter for killing one of her clients. Claudia's mother, Rose, and step-father, Arthur, have decided to have her committed rather than endure a trial but Claudia fears being locked up without reprieve for years to come. Levinsky is charged with convincing the court that Claudia is not "nuts" and is competent to stand trial.

As Levinsky painstakingly wins the trust of the angry, emotionally volatile Claudia, he gains insight into his client's past and his own capacity for compassion. He goes to Claudia's apartment (the scene of the crime) and finds that the rooms reflect an intelligent, sensitive, sophisticated woman—an image which is radically different from the irrational, hostile "hooker" Levinsky visits in her cell on Rikers Island.

Levinsky discusses Claudia's mental health with Dr. Herbert A. Morrison, the state-appointed psychiatrist who has declared Claudia incompetent to stand trial, but Morrison himself is incompetent and predisposed to interpret Claudia's fury as mental instability.

As Levinsky prepares his case, Claudia experiences flashbacks which reveal how she met the client, Allen Green, how he refused to leave after their sexual encounter, how he viciously attacked her and how she stabbed him in self-defense, using a shard of a broken mirror.

During the court hearing Claudia's mother and step-father take the stand and tell how her natural father had deserted the women when Claudia was only a child and that Claudia's own marriage ended in divorce. Further examination reveals the causes of Claudia's deep-seated anger and how it led to her decision to become a prostitute. Levinsky takes note of grotesque cartoons Claudia draws during the hearing, of her reluctance to have her mother questioned, and of inferences that Claudia was always unstable. It is discovered that Claudia's step-father, Arthur, had sexually abused her since her childhood and that her husband physically abused her as well. The revelation sends Claudia into hysterics and her mother is struck mute in horror.

Levinsky has by now developed a deep understanding and compassion for his client. He puts her on the stand where she defends her choices to leave her husband and turn to prostitution, becoming a five hundred dollar an hour call girl. She also proves her understanding of the law, refuses further psychiatric examination, and states her determination to stand trial.

During a recess, Claudia and her mother are finally reconciled (Arthur is no longer present). The judge returns, agrees to let Claudia stand trial, and frees her on bail. A final caption says that Claudia Draper did go to trial and was acquitted of the murder charge.

Reviews and Commentary

Richard Corliss, writing in *Time,* said this movie was "very mixed *Nuts*" (30 November 1987, 104) and certainly the critics paid many double-edged compliments to Streisand, the film's producer and unquestioned star. *Nuts* was directed by Martin Ritt whose repertoire of social dramas includes *Norma Rae* and *Sounder.* The screenplay was adapted by Tom Topor, Darryl Ponicsan and Alvin Sargent from Topor's impressive 1980 Broadway drama. That collaboration produced a script which critics considered obvious and static—Claudia is never really crazy enough to warrant serious consideration of mental incapacity and it is apparent at the outset that she is smarter and saner than the doctors and lawyers who imprison her. *New York Post* critic Roger Ebert said "*Nuts* is essentially just a futile exercise in courtroom clichés, surrounding a good performance that doesn't fit" (20 November 1987, 33).

Nevertheless, Streisand received high praise for a bravura performance in a meaty, demanding role and for skillful choices in her supporting cast. Richard Dreyfuss gave an incisive performance as the lawyer Levinsky and Eli Wallach and James Whitmore added solid support as the hospital psychiatrist and presiding judge. Stapleton played the mother who never really knew her own daughter. J. Hoberman wrote in the *Village Voice* "*Nuts* is a rowdy convention of grizzled pros . . . . It's sour fun to watch Wallach play dumb or Stapleton milk her material as ruthlessly as any Lady Macbeth" (1 December 1987, 78).

*****

F22   *HELLO ACTORS STUDIO*
Copra-Productions / Nanouk Films; 1987; 165 minutes

Credits
Executive Producer: Alain Guesnier. Producer (Montreal): Anouk Brault. Director: Annie Tresgot. Cinematographers: Michel Brault, Serge Giguere, Peter Reniers and Chris H. Leplus. Editor: Variety Mosznyski. Music: Luc Perini. Sound: Dominique Chratand and Philippe Scultety.

Cast
Paul Newman
Ellen Burstyn
Eli Wallach
Shelley Winters
Harvey Keitel
Maureen Stapleton
Lee Grant
Gene Wilder
Rod Steiger
Sally Kirkland
Arthur Penn
Elia Kazan
Sydney Pollack

Synopsis

The documentary film is a three-hour investigation into the history of the most celebrated acting school in America, the Actors Studio. The film offers a retrospective of the establishment and development of the Studio. It presents testimony of many of the Studio's accomplished members (see the cast list, above) and also shows exercises with young students to demonstrate some of the famous techniques taught and developed there.

Reviews and Commentary

This documentary, directed by Annie Tresgot, was a cooperative venture of production companies in Paris and Montreal. Filmed about five years after the death of the Studio's guru and guiding light, Lee Strasberg, the film lacks that special voice. *Variety* found the film rambling and diffuse. *New York Times* critic Walter Goodman thought the film was overly long, especially the exercise sessions with the younger students and he found many of the testimonials to be hackneyed or self-serving. Nevertheless, Goodman appreciated such reminiscences as Eli Wallach's comments on Marilyn Monroe's work at the Studio and "Gene Wilder's funny and touching account of how he persuaded himself to fall in love with a male sheep" for a Woody Allen film (9 November 1988, C19).

It is unfortunate that this film is not currently available on videotape. The testimony of Maureen Stapleton and her many colleagues at the Studio provide a valuable oral history of an important institution of the American theatre.

*****

F23   *COCOON: THE RETURN*
Zanuck-Brown / Twentieth Century Fox; 1988; 116 minutes
Video: CBS/Fox

Credits

Producers: Richard D. Zanuck, David Brown and Lili Fini Zanuck. Director: Daniel Petrie. Screenwriter: Steven McPherson. Based on a story by Stephen McPherson, Elizabeth Bradley and characters created by David Saperstein. Cinematographer: Tak Fujimoto (DeLuxe Color). Editor: Mark Roy Warner. Music: James Horner. Music Editor: Jim Henrikson. Production Design: Lawrence G. Paull. Set Decoration: Frederick C. Weiler and Jim Poynter. Costumes: Jay Hurley. Special Effects: J. B. Jones, Greg Cannom and Robert Short. Animation: Gordon Baker, Tim Berglund and Sean Turner. Visual Effects: Industrial Light & Magic.

Cast

Art Selwyn	Don Ameche
Ben Luckett	Wilford Brimley
Sara	Courteney Cox
Joe Finley	Hume Cronyn
Bernie Lefkowitz	Jack Gilford
Jack Bonner	Steve Guttenberg
David	Barret Oliver

Mary Luckett	**Maureen Stapleton**
Ruby	Elaine Stritch
Alma Finley	Jessica Tandy
Bess McCarthy	Gwen Verdon
Kitty	Tahnee Welch
Susan	Linda Harrison
Pillsbury	Tyrone Power, Jr.
Doc	Mike Nomad
Phil/Antereans	Wendy Cooke
Rose	Herta Ware

And Brian C. Smith, Fred Buch, Harold Bergman, Glenn Scherer, Tom Kouchalakos, Alan R. Jordan, Fritz Dominique, Iris Acker, Will Marchetti, Shelley Spurlock, Ted Milford, Chris Fuxa, Bill Wohrman, Jay Smith, Tony Vila, Jr., Brian Jay Andrews, David Easton, Matt Ford, Jack McDermott, Darcy Shean, Barrie Mizerski, Madeline Lee, Mal Jones, Patricia Rainier, Richard Jasen, Patricia Winters, Rachel Renick, Ryan Szurgot, Anthony Finazzo, Kelly Jasen, Stephanie Oldziej, Priscilla Ashley Behne, Glenn L. Robbins, Bruce McLaughlin, Buddy Reynolds, Carlos Gonzalez, Kevin Corrigan, Robert Gwaltney and Robert Short.

Synopsis

Cocoon: The Return is the sequel to the enormously successful film *Cocoon* (see **F16**). The story begins five years later and brings back the aliens from Antarea and six of the senior citizens who elected to go into outer space rather than give themselves over to the vicissitudes of old age. Art and Bess, Mary and Ben, and Alma and Joe return to earth for a four day visit while the Antareans work to collect the cocoons from the sea. The cocoons, which are shelters for Antareans left on earth in the last episode, are now in danger because of seismic activity on the ocean floor.

The seniors are radiantly healthy but discover they must weigh that vigor against earthly joys. Several plot lines are woven together through the film. Mary and Ben are reunited with their daughter and grandchildren and find that one grandson, David, desperately needs their guidance and support. Alma is tempted to stay on earth when she is hired to work with foster children at a day care center; but her husband, Joe, is confronted with a resurgence of cancer. Art and Bess are thrilled to be back in the social whirl on earth which they relish until life takes a surprising turn when Bess learns she is pregnant.

The seniors also renew their friendship with Bernie, their stodgy friend who chose to remain on earth. They find him miserable, hooking rugs in a rest home and spending his days visiting his beloved wife's grave. Art and Joe introduce him to Ruby, the vivacious manager of a local hotel, but it takes some convincing for Bernie to break free from the past.

Meanwhile, Jack Bonner is again recruited to help the Antareans. He is now captain of a glass-bottom tour boat and is pleased to see the prettiest Antarean, Kitty, again. The plot thickens when Jack discovers that one of the cocoons has been discovered by the Oceanographic Institute where scientists cut it open and imprison its ethereal inhabitant. Sara, a beautiful doctor at the Institute, learns to communicate with the alien, but cannot protect it from the military men who would dissect it.

When Alma runs into the street to save a child she is critically injured. Joe makes the ultimate sacrifice when he gives her his life force and succumbs to cancer. Alma recovers and decides to stay on earth to work with the children. Ben and Mary also decide to stay, feeling that watching their family grow is more important than immortality.

Art, Ben and Kitty are almost prevented from recovering the frail Antarean from the Institute but Sara helps them get away. The mother ship comes to pick up the remaining cocoons and Kitty, Bess and Art. Alma, Ben and Mary join Bernie (now dating the lively Ruby) and they all come to say their goodbyes to their departing friends. Jack coincidentally meets up with Sara who he has seen in a vision conjured up by Kitty—that vision foretold that Sara and Jack would happily marry.

Reviews and Commentary

The critical response for this sequel was one of general disappointment. The critics faulted the director (Daniel Petrie) and the screenwriter (Stephen McPherson) for creating a disjointed and sentimental film that rather awkwardly strung together a number of subplots around the banal plot of experiment-happy scientists pursuing lovable aliens. Janet Maslin said "*Cocoon: The Return* is so tired, in fact, that it can barely recapitulate the winning formula of the original hit . . . . the net effect is one of being on a cruise ship to hell" (23 November 1988, C15).

Nevertheless, the film is not without charm. All the critics agreed that the strength of both the original and the sequel was their casts of distinguished actors. Elaine Stritch, in the role of the indomitable Ruby, was a notable addition to the cast of the latter film. Jack Gilford was still irascible as Bernie. Hume Cronyn and Jessica Tandy shared a touching bedside farewell. Maureen Stapleton and Wilford Brimley warmly demonstrated the simple pleasures of home and family and Don Ameche and Gwen Verdon lit up the ballroom with their stylish sophistication. Courteney Cox also made a charming appearance as the sympathetic Sara. *Variety* (25 November 1987, 15) also praised the quality of the production values, including James Horner's jazzy score, the marvelous sun-drenched cinematography and the special magic created by Industrial Light & Magic.

Appendix:
Nominations, Awards,
and Honors

Maureen Stapleton has garnered the highest honors for her work on the stage, in film and on television. The nominations, awards and honors Stapleton has earned are listed below in chronological order under the categories of Tony Awards, Oscars, Emmys and Grammys, followed by a listing of miscellaneous awards. Cross references refer the reader to detailed descriptions of that performance in the main text of this book.

TONY AWARDS
(ANTOINETTE PERRY AWARDS)

The Rose Tattoo
1951—see S06

<u>Win for Stapleton</u>
   Best Actress, Supporting or Featured (Dramatic)

<u>Other Wins</u>
   Best Play: Tennessee Williams
   Best Actor, Supporting or Featured (Dramatic): Eli Wallach
   Best Producer (Dramatic): Cheryl Crawford
   Best Scenic Designer: Boris Aronson

The Cold Wind and The Warm
(1959—see S14)

<u>Nomination for Stapleton</u>
   Best Actress (Dramatic)

Toys in the Attic
(1960—see S15)

<u>Nomination for Stapleton</u>
   Best Actress (Dramatic)

<u>Wins</u>
      Best Actress, Supporting or Featured (Dramatic): Anne Revere

<u>Other Nominations</u>
      Best Play: Lillian Hellman
      Best Actor (Dramatic): Jason Robards, Jr.

Plaza Suite
(1968—see S18)

<u>Nomination for Stapleton</u>
      Best Actress (Dramatic)

<u>Wins</u>
      Best Director: Mike Nichols

<u>Other Nominations</u>
      Best Play: Neil Simon

The Gingerbread Lady
(1971—see S20)

<u>Win for Stapleton</u>
      Best Actress (Dramatic)

The Little Foxes
(1981—see S28)

<u>Nomination for Stapleton</u>
      Best Actress, Featured Role (Dramatic)

<u>Other Nominations</u>
      Best Director (Dramatic): Austin Pendleton
      Best Reproduction of a Play or Musical: Zev Bufman, Donald C.
      Carter, John Cutler

EMMY AWARDS

All the King's Men
(1958/1959—see T15)

<u>Nomination for Stapleton</u>
      Best Single Performance by an Actress

Among the Paths to Eden
(1967/1968—see T27)

Win for Stapleton
> Best Single Performance by an Actress

Queen of the Stardust Ballroom
(1974/1975—see T32)

Nomination for Stapleton
> Best Actress in a Drama or Comedy Special

Wins
> Best Special Musical Material: Alan Bergman, Marilyn Bergman, Billy Goldenberg
> Best Photography: David Walsh
> Best Choreography: Marge Champion

Other Nominations
> Best Special, Drama or Comedy: Robert W. Christiansen, Rick Rosenberg
> Best Director, Special Program, Drama or Comedy: Sam O'Steen
> Best Actor in a Drama or Comedy Special: Charles Durning
> Best Supporting Actress, Single Performance, Drama or Comedy Special: Charlotte Rae
> Best Writing, Special Program, Drama or Comedy Original Teleplay: Jerome Kass
> Best Music Composition, Special: Alan Bergman, Marilyn Bergman, Billy Goldenberg
> Best Costume Design: Bruce Walkup

The Gathering
(1977/1978—see T35)

Nomination for Stapleton
> Best Actress in a Drama or Comedy Special

Win
> Best Special, Drama or Comedy: Joseph Barbera, Harry R. Sherman

Other Nominations
> Best Director: Randal Kleiser
> Best Writing, Special Program, Drama or Comedy Original Teleplay: James Poe
> Best Art Direction for a Dramatic Special: Jan Scott (Art Director) and Anne D. McCulley (Set Decorator)

ACADEMY AWARDS
(OSCARS)

Lonelyhearts
(1958—see F01)

Nomination for Stapleton
>   Best Supporting Actress

Airport
(1970—see F06)

Nomination for Stapleton
>   Best Supporting Actress

Wins for the Film
>   Best Supporting Actress: Helen Hayes

Other Nominations
>   Best Picture
>   Best Screenplay: George Seaton
>   Best Cinematography: Ernest Laszlo
>   Best Art Decoration/Set Decoration: Preston Ames and Alexander
>   Golitzen; Jack D. Moore and Mickey S. Michaels
>   Best Sound: Ronald Pierce and David Moriarty
>   Best Film Editing: Stuart Gilmore
>   Best Original Score: Alfred Newman
>   Best Costumes: Edith Head

Interiors
(1978—see F09)

Nomination for Stapleton
>   Best Supporting Actress

Other Nominations
>   Best Actress: Geraldine Page
>   Best Direction: Woody Allen
>   Best Screenplay Written Directly for the Screen: Woody Allen
>   Best Art Direction: Mel Bourne; Daniel Robert

Reds
(1981—see F14)

Win for Stapleton
>   Best Supporting Actress

Wins for the Film
    Best Direction: Warren Beatty
    Best Cinematography: Vittorio Storaro

Other Nominations
    Best Picture
    Best Actor: Warren Beatty
    Best Actress: Diane Keaton
    Best Supporting Actor: Jack Nicholson
    Best Screenplay: Written Directly for the Screen: Warren Beatty and
        Trevor Griffiths
    Best Art Direction: Richard Sylbert, Michael Seirton
    Best Sound: Dick Vorisek, Tom Fleischman, Simon Kay
    Best Film Editing: Dede Allen, Craig McKay
    Best Costumes: Shirley Russell

GRAMMY AWARDS

To Kill a Mockingbird
(1975)

Nomination for Stapleton
    Best Spoken Word, Documentary or Drama Recording

OTHER AWARDS AND HONORS

1951 **Mademoiselle Award**
Stapleton was among the recipients of this annual award, given by
Mademoiselle Magazine, honoring outstanding career achievement.

1965 ***Variety's* Poll of New York Drama Critics**
Stapleton won the award as Best Actress, Dramatic Star for her
performance of Amanda Wingfield in *The Glass Menagerie* (see **S16**).

1971 **Golden Globe Award**
Stapleton nominated as Best Actress in a Supporting Role for her
performance in the film *Airport* (see **F06**).

1971 **Drama Desk Award**
Stapleton won an award for Outstanding Performance for her
portrayal of Evy Meara in *The Gingerbread Lady* on Broadway (see
S20).

1971 ***Variety's* Poll of New York Drama Critics**
Stapleton won the award as Best Female Lead in a Straight Play for
her portrayal of Evy Meara in *The Gingerbread Lady* on Broadway
(see **S20**).

1978   **New York Film Critics Circle Award**
Stapleton won the Best Supporting Actress award for her performance in the film *Interiors* (see **F09**).

1978   **Los Angeles Film Critics Association Award**
Stapleton won the Best Supporting Actress award for her performance in the film *Interiors* (see **F09**).

1980   **Actors Studio Award**
Stapleton was among the members of the studio who were given this once in a lifetime award for their contributions to the theatre.

1981   **Theatre Hall of Fame**
Stapleton was inducted into the Theatre Hall of Fame on 5 April 1981.

1981   Volume 37 of *Theatre World 1980-81* was dedicated to Stapleton. She appears on the cover and the book presents a photo retrospective of her career.

1981   The Theatre at the Hudson Valley Community College in Troy, New York, was named after Maureen Stapleton.

1982   **National Society of Film Critics Award**
Stapleton won the Best Supporting Actress award for her performance as Emma Goldman in *Reds* (see **F14**).

1982   **British Academy Award**
Stapleton won the Best Supporting Actor Award for her performance in *Reds* (see **F14**).

Bibliography

The **Bibliography** is divided into two sections. Section One includes interviews, archival sources, photographic essays, biographical and general references for Stapleton's career. Section Two includes selected reviews of individual film, television or stage productions.

Section I—Books, Articles and Archives

B01 Adelson, Susan. *People Weekly.* 17 (3 May 1982): 51. Interview.

B02 Arnold, Christine. "Stapleton Takes Acting Successes in Stride." *Miami Herald*, 7 June 1981. Interview during run of *The Little Foxes*.

B03 Bell, Arthur. "Bell Tells." *Village Voice.* 7 May 1979.

B04 Black, Charlotte. "No 'stardust' for Maureen's Eyes." *Albuquerque Tribune.* 25 Oct. 1976. Profile of Stapleton during rehearsals for *Waiting for Godot.*

B05 Blum, Daniel. *Great Stars of the American Stage, A Pictorial Record.* New York: Greenberg, 1952. A brief profile plus a two pages of photos from Stapleton's childhood and very early career.

B06 Blum, Daniel. *A Pictorial History of the American Theatre, 100 Years—1860-1985.* New York: Crown, 1985. Has photos of several of Stapleton's best-known roles.

B07 Bordman, Gerald, ed. *The Oxford Companion to American Theatre.* New York: Oxford University Press, 1984. Biographical profile.

B08 Brooks, Tim and Earle Marsh. *The Complete Directory to Prime Time Network TV Shows, 1946-Present.* 3rd ed. New York: Ballantine Books, 1985.

B09 Brown, Peter. "Maureen Stapleton in *Waiting for Godot.*" *Viva Magazine*, 25 Apr. 1976, 10. Profile.

B10 Burke, Tom. "And a Terrific Tap Dancer." *New York Times.* Sunday, 3 Jan. 1971, sec. 2. Personal profile written during the run of *The Gingerbread Lady.*

B11 Cantwell, Mary. "Simplicity Is the Key to Her Art." *New York Times,* Sunday, 21 June 1981, sec. 2. Interview during *The Gingerbread Lady.*

B12 Entry skipped

B13 Entry skipped

B14 Capote, Truman, Eleanor Perry and Frank Perry. *Trilogy, An Experiment in Multimedia.* Introduction by John M. Culkin, S. J. New York: Macmillan Co., 1969. This college text accompanied the release of the film, *Truman Capote's Trilogy* (see **F05**). The text includes Capote's short stories and the scripts of their television and film adaptations, film credits, and pictures of the film shoots.

B15 Clurman, Harold. *All People Are Famous.* New York: Harcourt, Brace, Jovanovich, 1974.

B16 Clurman, Harold. *Lies Like Truth, Theatre Reviews and Essays.* New York: Macmillan Publishing Co., 1958. Has several references to Stapleton.

B17 *Contemporary Theatre, Film and Television.* Vol. 4. Detroit: Gale Research, 1987.

B18 *Entertainers, The.* Foreword by John Gielgud. New York: St. Martins/ Harrow House, 1980, 254 and 266. Conceived, edited and designed by Harrow House Editions, Ltd., London. Clive Unger-Hamilton, gen. ed. Brief biographical profile and photographs of Stapleton.

B19 Funke, Lewis and John E. Booth. *Actors Talk About Acting.* New York: Random House, 1961. Brief biography and in-depth interview in which Stapleton talks about her acting technique.

B20 Gam, Rita. *Actors: A Celebration.* New York: St. Martin's Press, 1980. Maureen Stapleton wrote the foreword to this book of interviews with actors.

B21 Gam, Rita. *Actress to Actress.* Preface by Robert Whitehead. New York: Nick Lyons Books, 1986. Seven page interview with Stapleton; a highly personal, chatty account.

B22 Garfield, David. *The Actors Studio, A Player's Place.* New York: Macmillan Publishing Co., 1984. Several references to Stapleton's work at the Studio.

B23 Gianakos, Larry James. *Television Drama: Series Programming: A Comprehensive Chronicle, 1947-1959*. Metuchen, NJ: Scarecrow Press, 1980.

B24 Gianakos, Larry James. *Television Drama: Series Programming: A Comprehensive Chronicle, 1959-1978*. Metuchen, NJ: Scarecrow Press, 1978.

B25 Giosa, Sue. *Maureen Stapleton: The Life of an Actress*. Master's thesis, Queens College, New York, June 1978.

B26 Gruen, John. "Maureen Stapleton Is Terribly Tired." *New York Magazine*, 20 May 1988, 49-50. Interview of Stapleton during the run of *Plaza Suite*.

B27 Hansen, Patricia King and Stephen L. Hansen, eds. *Film Review Index*. Vol. 2: 1950-1985. Phoenix: Oryx Press, 1987. Extensive bibliographic index for film reviews.

B28 Henderson, Mary C. *Theater in America*. New York: Harry N. Abrams, Inc. 1986. Has photos of several of Stapleton's best-known roles.

B29 Kaplan, Mike, ed. *Variety's Directory of Major U.S. Show Business Awards*. New York: R.R. Bowker, 1989.

B30 Katz, Ephraim. *The Film Encyclopedia*. New York: Thomas Y. Crowell, 1979. Has a short film biography on Stapleton.

B31 Keating, J. "No Maribou for Maureen." *Cue* 20-11 (17 Mar. 1951): 12.

B32 Kimmel, Melody. "Maureen Stapleton. An Interview by Melody Kimmel." *Films in Review* 33 (Feb. 1982): 71-75. Interview conducted around the time of the film *Reds*.

B33 Lewis, Robert. "Discovering 'The Life of Our Times'." *American Theatre* 3 (Apr. 1986). Lewis discusses The Method; short reference to Stapleton.

B34 Lewis, Robert. *Slings and Arrows, Theater in My Life*. New York: Stein and Day, 1984. Lewis talks about his work with Stapleton on *The Club Champion's Widow*.

B35 Lincoln Center Performing Arts Research Library, New York, New York. Has clipping and photo files on Stapleton's productions.

B36 Marill, Alvin H. *Movies Made for Television, The Telefeature and the Mini Series 1937-1973*. New York: Zoetrope, 1986.

B37 McGill, Raymond D., ed. *Notable Names in the American Theatre*. Clifton, NJ: James T. White & Co., 1976. Biographical profile.

B38 McNeil, Alex. *Total Television, A Comprehensive Guide to Programming from 1948 to the Present.* 2nd ed. New York: Penguin Books, 1984. Many references to Stapleton's credits, including awards.

B39 Millstein, G. "Theatre Arts Gallery." *Theatre Arts* 44 (July 1960): 10-12.

B40 Moritz, Charles, ed. "Maureen Stapleton" in *Current Biography Yearbook 1959*, 424-426. New York: H.W. Wilson Co., 1960. Early biographical profile.

B41 Museum of Television and Radio, New York, NY. This museum has several of Stapleton's television performances available for public viewing. The collection includes: parts 1 and 2 of "All the King's Men" (**T15**), "Queen of the Stardust Ballroom" (**T32**), "Cat on a Hot Tin Roof" (**T33**), "CBS on the Air: A Celebration of 50 Years," and "The Kennedy Center Honors . . . "

B42 Nash, Jay Robert and Stanley Ralph Ross. *The Motion Picture Guide.* Chicago: CineBooks, 1985-89. Ten volume set plus annual supplements and two volume index that provide extensive information on films from 1927 through 1988. Cast, production credits, synopsis and critical opinion are included.

B43 "New Star." *New Yorker* 27 (24 Feb. 1951): 19-20.

B44 *New York Theatre Critics' Reviews.* New York: Critics' Theatre Reviews. Weekly publication that reprinted reviews of major New York newspapers. These reviews are compiled into annual volumes that provide a rich source of critical opinion of New York stage productions. Volumes from 1949 to 1981 are excellent sources for reviews of Stapleton's stage work.

B45 *New York Times Film Reviews.* New York: New York Times and Arno Press, 1970-73. Six volume set and index of film reviews published in the *New York Times* from 1913 up to 1972.

B46 *New York Times Theatre Reviews, 1920-1980.* New York: New York Times Books. Set of 13 vols. and 2-vol. index that reprints theatre reviews that appeared in the *New York Times.*

B47 *Notable Names in the American Theatre.* Clifton, NJ: James T. White & Co., 1976.

B48 Okon, May. "Her Loss Is Broadway's Gain." *New York Sunday News,* 1 Jan. 1967. Interview that traces Stapleton's weight problems.

B49 Ozer, Jerome S., ed. *Film Review Annual.* 7 vols. Englewood, NJ: Ozer Publishing, Inc. 1982-88. Excellent source for reprints of film reviews from a wide variety of publications.

B50 Parish, James Robert and Vincent Terrace. *The Complete Actor's Television Credits: 1948-1988.* Vol. 2, *Actresses.* 2nd ed. Metuchen, NJ: Scarecrow Press, 1990.

B51 Proutz, Howard H., ed. *Variety Television Reviews.* New York: Garland Publishing, Inc. 1988-1991. Fifteen volume set with index covering weekly reviews in *Variety* for the years 1923 to 1988.

B52 Reed, Rex. *People Are Crazy Here.* New York: Delacorte, 1974.

B53 Rice, Vernon. "Curtain Cues, Stapleton Claims a Special Talent." *New York Post,* 8 June 1951.

B54 Rollyson, Carl E. Jr. *Marilyn Monroe, A Life of the Actress.* Ann Arbor, MI: UMI Research Press, 1986. Brief discussion of Stapleton's performance in a scene with Monroe at the Actors Studio.

B55 Rosen, Esther. *Maureen Stapleton, American Actress.* Master's thesis, University of Arizona. Ann Arbor, MI: University Microfilms, 1983. Photocopy. Focuses on Stapleton's stage career; a personal interview with Stapleton is included in the thesis.

B56 Ross, Lillian. "Maureen Stapleton." *New Yorker* 37 (28 Oct. 1961): 120. Personal profile of the actress and her early career; reprinted in *The Player: A Profile of an Art.*

B57 Ross, Lillian and Helen Ross. "Maureen Stapleton" in *The Player: A Profile of an Art,* 297-303. New York: Simon and Schuster, 1962. Reprint of the article above.

B58 Rouse, Sarah and Katharine Loughney, comps. *Three Decades of Television.* Washington: Library of Congress, 1989. This is a catalog of programs acquired by the Library of Congress for the years 1949-1979. The catalog includes one film of Stapleton's, the 1962 television production of *Riders to the Sea.* This program can be viewed at the Library of Congress.

B59 "Salute of the Week: Maureen Stapleton." *Cue Magazine.* 40-5 (30 Jan. 71): 1.

B60 Shale, Richard, comp. *Academy Awards.* Rvsd. 2nd ed. New York: Frederick Ungar Publishing, 1982.

B61 Sharp, Christopher. "Jeepers, Creepers, Maureen, Where'd You Get Those Peepers?" *Women's Wear Daily,* 27 Feb. 1974. Interview with Stapleton at the time her television special, "Tell Me Where It Hurts" aired.

B62 Spoto, Donald. *The Kindness of Strangers, The Life of Tennessee Williams.* Boston: Little Brown & Co., 1985.

B63 Stahl, Bob. "A Prisoner of Emotion." *TV Guide* 11 (6 July 1963): 26-28.

B64 Stang, Joanne. "Maureen into Amanda." *New York Times*, 16 May 1965. Interview during the run of *The Glass Menagerie*.

B65 Stapleton, Maureen. "Is It Wrong for Serious Actors To Do Commercials?" *New York Times*, 9 May 1971. Stapleton and Sioban McKenna express their opinions on this subject; Stapleton sees no conflict between commercial and artistic aims.

B66 Stapleton, Maureen. *Reminiscences of Maureen Stapleton: Oral History, 1960*. An unpublished, 79-page transcript of an interview with Stapleton by John E. Booth and Lewis Funke. Popular Arts Project, part V; located at Columbia University, Oral History Research Office, Box 20, Room 801, Butler Library, New York. Stapleton's permission is required to read, reproduce or quote. It is probable that this transcript is the source for the 1961 interview published by Funke and Booth, listed above (see **B19**).

B67 "A Star in Spite of Herself." *Long Island Newsday*, 7 June 1981. Interview with Stapleton during run of *The Little Foxes*.

B68 Stitt, Milan. "Games Maureen Plays." *Horizon Magazine*, Dec. 1978, 25.

B69 Sullivan, Dan. "Comedy Success No Joke to Miss Stapleton." *New York Times*, 16 Feb. 1968. Personal profile written during her run of *Plaza Suite*.

B70 Tallmer, Jerry. "The Icing on the Gingerbread." *New York Post*, 3 Apr. 1971. Interview with Stapleton after winning Tony Award.

B71 "Tennessee Williams' Most Recent Design." *Cue Magazine,* 3 Feb. 1951. Photo essay of the Broadway premiere of *The Rose Tattoo*.

B72 Terrace, Vincent. *Encyclopedia of Television Series, Pilots and Specials 1937-1973*. New York: Zoetrope, 1986.

B73 Terrace, Vincent. *Television 1970-1980*. San Diego: A.S. Barnes & Co., 1981.

B74 *Variety Film Reviews*. 20 vols. New York: R.R. Bowker, Inc., 1991.

B75 *Variety's Complete Home Video Directory*. New York: R.R. Bowker, 1989. Provides information on television and films and their availability on video.

B76 Walter, Claire. *Winners: The Blue Ribbon Encyclopedia of Awards*. Rvsd. ed. New York: Facts on File, Inc., 1982. Lists Stapleton's awards.

B77 Wasserman, Debbi. "People Who Make Theatre, Maureen Stapleton: Connecting with a Role." *New York Theatre Review*, Mar. 1978, 23. Interview in which Stapleton discusses how she chooses her roles.

B78 *Who's Who of American Women 1991-92*. 17th ed. Wilmette, Ill: Marquis Who's Who, 1991, 952.

B79 Williams, Tennessee. *Memoirs*. Garden City, NY: Doubleday & Co., 1975. Several references to Stapleton's work and friendship with Williams.

B80 Williams, Tennessee. *Papers 1911-1983*. Columbia University, Rare Book and Manuscript Library, Butler Library, New York, NY. Correspondence, manuscripts, photographs, set designs, programs, playbills and other printed materials and sound recordings. Manuscripts include *Orpheus Descending, The Rose Tattoo* and *A Lovely Sunday for Creve Coeur*. There is also a playbill of *The Rose Tattoo's* opening performance, signed by Stapleton and the cast.

B81 Willis, John. *Theatre World, 1980-81*. Vol. 37. New York: Crown, 1982. This volume is dedicated to Maureen Stapleton. She is featured on the cover and a photo retrospective is printed at the beginning of the book. Other volumes of *Theatre World* contain cast and production credits and statistical information on the actress's Broadway productions.

B82 Woods, Jeannie M. "Maureen Stapleton" in *Notable Women in the American Theatre, a Biographical Dictionary*. Alice M. Robinson, Vera Mowry Roberts and Milly S. Barranger, eds. New York: Greenwood Press, 1989. Biographical profile focusing on Stapleton's theatre career.

B83 Young, William C., ed. *Famous Actors and Actresses on the American Stage. Documents of American Theater History*. 2 vols. New York: R.R. Bowker Co., 1975.

Section II—Reviews of Major Stage and Film Productions

Listed below are only a few of the many hundreds of reviews of Stapleton's performances. For additional critical opinion, the reader is also referred to those references listed above that provide a broad selection of reprinted reviews or provide an extensive listing of reviews on specific productions: **B27, B42, B44, B45, B46, B49, B51,** and **B74.**

Stage:

The Bird Cage
B84   Atkinson, Brooks. *New York Times,* 23 Feb. 1950.
B85   Watts, Richard Jr. *New York Post,* 23 Feb. 1950.

The Club Champion's Widow
B86   Gussow, Mel. *New York Times,* 30 Jan. 1978.

The Cold Wind and the Warm
B87   Atkinson, Brooks. *New York Times,* 9 Dec. 1958.
B88   Kerr, Walter. *New York Herald Tribune,* 9 Dec. 1958.
B89   Tynan, Kenneth. *Curtains.* New York: Atheneum Books, 1961.

The Country Girl
B90   Gottfried, Martin. *Women's Wear Daily,* 17 Mar. 1972.
B91   Kalem, T.E. *Time,* 27 Mar. 1972.

The Crucible
B92   Atkinson, Brooks. *New York Times,* 2 July 1953.
B93   Watts, Richard Jr. *New York Post,* 23 Jan. 1953.

The Emperor's Clothes
B94   Atkinson, Brooks. *New York Times,* 10 Feb. 1953.
B95   Hawkins, William. *New York World-Telegram,* 10 Feb. 1953.
B96   Kerr, Walter. *New York Herald Tribune,* 10 Feb. 1953.

The Gin Game
B97   Eder, Richard. *New York Times,* 22 Nov. 1978.

The Gingerbread Lady
B98   Barnes, Clive. *New York Times,* 14 Dec. 1970.
B99   Watts, Richard. *New York Post,* 14 Dec. 1970.

The Glass Menagerie
(1965 and 1975 productions)
B100   Barnes, Clive. *New York Times,* 19 Dec. 1975.
B101   Gottfried, Martin. *New York Post,* 19 Dec. 1975.
B102   Taubman, Howard. *New York Times,* 5 May 1965.
B103   Wilson, Ed. *Wall St. Journal,* 23 Dec. 1975.

Juno and the Paycock
B104   *Variety,* 8 Nov. 1974.

The Little Foxes
B105 Kalem, T.E. *Time,* 18 May 1981.
B106 Rich, Frank. *New York Times,* 8 May 1981.
B107 Watt, Douglas. *Daily News,* 8 May 1981.

Norman, Is That You?
B108 Barnes, Clive. *New York Times,* 20 Feb. 1970.
B109 Gottfried, Martin. *Women's Wear Daily,* 20 Feb. 1970.

Orpheus Descending
B110 Atkinson, Brooks. *New York Times,* 22 Mar. 1957.
B111 Watts, Richard Jr. *New York Post,* 22 Mar. 1957.

Playboy of the Western World
B112 Nathan, George Jean. *The Theatre Book of the Year, 1946-47.* New York: Alfred A. Knopf, 1947.

Plaza Suite
B113 Cooke, Richard P. *Wall St. Journal,* 16 Feb. 1968.
B114 Gottfried, Martin. *Women's Wear Daily,* 15 Feb. 1968.

Richard III
B115 Atkinson, Brooks. *New York Times,* 10 Dec. 1953.
B116 Hawkins, William. *New York World-Telegram,* 10 Dec. 1953.

The Rose Tattoo
B117 Atkinson, Brooks. *New York Times,* 5 Feb. 1951.
B118 Guernsey, Otis L. Jr. *New York Herald Tribune,* 5 Feb. 1951.
B119 Hawkins, William. *New York World Telegram,* 5 Feb. 1951.
B120 Mishkin, Leo. *New York Morning Telegraph,* 22 Oct. 1966.
B121 Sullivan, Dan. *New York Times,* 21 Oct. 1966.

The Seagull
B122 Kerr, Walter. *New York Herald Tribune,* 12 May 1954.

The Secret Affairs of Mildred Wild
B123 Kroll, Jack. *Newsweek,* 27 Nov. 1972.

Toys in the Attic
B124 Atkinson, Brooks. *New York Times,* 26 Feb. 1960.
B125 McClain, John. *New York Journal American,* 26 Feb. 1960.

Twenty-Seven Wagons Full of Cotton
B126 Watts, Richard Jr. *New York Post,* 20 Apr. 1955.

Television

"Alice in Wonderland"
B127 O'Connor, John J. *New York Times,* 3 Oct. 1983.

"All the King's Men"

B128   *Variety*, 21 May 1958.

"Among the Paths to Eden,"

B129   *New York Times*, 18 Dec. 1967.
B130   *Variety*, 20 Dec. 1967.

"Blast in Centralia No. 5"

B131   *Variety*, 29 Jan. 1959.

"Cat on a Hot Tin Roof"

B132   *Variety*, 8 Dec. 1976.

"The Cosmic Eye"

B133   *Variety*, 13 Nov. 1985.

"The Electric Grandmother"

B134   *The Magazine of Fantasy and Science Fiction* 62 (June 1982): 118.
B135   *English Journal* 73 (Feb. 1984): 110.

"For Whom the Bell Tolls"

B136   *Variety*, 25 Mar. 1959.

"The Gathering"

B137   *Variety*, 7, Dec. 1977.

"Little Gloria . . . Happy at Last"

B138   Crist, Judith. *TV Guide*, 8 Jan. 1983.
B139   *Variety*, 27 Oct. 1982.

"Queen of the Stardust Ballroom"

B140   *Variety*, 19 Feb. 1975.

"Save Me a Place at Forest Lawn"

B141   *Variety*, 9 Mar. 1966.

"Tell Me Where It Hurts"

B142   *Variety*, 20 Mar. 1974.

Film

Airport

B143   Canby, Vincent. *New York Times*, 6 Mar. 1970.
B144   *Variety*, 18 Feb. 1970.

Bye Bye Birdie

B145   *New York Times*, 5 Apr. 1963.
B146   *Variety*, 10 Apr. 1963.

Cocoon
B147 Benson, Sheila. *Los Angeles Times,* 21 June 1985.
B148 Maslin, Janet. *New York Times,* 21 June 1985.

Cocoon: The Return
B149 Maslin, Janet. *New York Times,* 23 Nov. 1988.
B150 *Variety,* 23 Nov. 1988.

The Fan
B151 Kissel, Howard. *Women's Wear Daily,* 18 May 1981.

The Fugitive Kind
B152 Alpert, Hollis. *Saturday Review,* 23 Apr. 1960.
B153 Crowther, Bosley. *New York Times,* 15 Apr. 1960.
B154 Yacowar, Maurice. *Tennessee Williams and Film.* New York: Frederick Ungar Publishing, 1977.

Heartburn
B155 Combes, Richard. *Monthly Film Bulletin* (Feb. 1987): 49.
B156 Denby, David. *New York* (4 August 1986): 62.

Hello Actors Studio
B157 Goodman, Walter. *New York Times,* 9 Nov. 1988.
B158 *Variety,* 25 Nov. 1987.

Interiors
B159 Canby, Vincent. *New York Times,* 2 Aug. 1978.
B160 *Variety,* 2 Aug. 1978.

Johnny Dangerously
B161 Ansen, David. *Newsweek,* 14 Jan. 1985.
B162 Thomas, Kevin. *Los Angeles Times,* 21 Dec. 1984.
B163 Schickel, Richard. *Time,* 14 Jan. 1985.

Lonelyhearts
B164 Crowther, Bosley. *New York Times,* 8 Mar. 1959.
B165 Klein, Michael. "Miss L Gets Married." In *The Modern American Novel and the Movies,* Gerald Peary and Roger Shatzkin, eds., 19-28. New York: Frederick Ungar Publishing, 1978.
B166 *Time,* 23 March 1959.

Lost and Found
B167 *Variety,* 12 June 1979.

Made in Heaven
B168 Maslin, Janet. *New York Times,* 6 Nov. 1987.
B169 McGrady, Mike. *Newsday,* 6 Nov. 1987.

The Money Pit
B170 Thomas, Kevin. *Los Angeles Times,* 26 Mar. 1986.
B171 Canby, Vincent. *New York Times,* 26 Mar. 1986.

Nuts
B172   Corliss, Richard. *Time,* 30 Nov. 1987.
B173   Ebert, Roger. *New York Post,* 20 Nov. 1987.
B174   Hoberman, J. *Village Voice,* 1 Dec. 1987.

On the Right Track
B175   Taffel, Mildred. *Films in Review* (October 1981): 495.
B176   Thomas, Kevin. *Los Angeles Times,* 23 Aug. 1981.

Plaza Suite
B177   Canby, Vincent. *New York Times,* 14 May 1971.
B178   *Variety,* 12 May 1971.

Reds
B179   Canby, Vincent. *New York Times,* 4 Dec. 1981.
B180   Kauffmann, Stanley. *Field of View, Film Criticism and Comment.* New York: PAJ Publications, 1986.
B181   Porter, Carolyn. *Film Quarterly* (Spring 1982): 43.

The Runner Stumbles
B182   Maslin, Janet. *New York Times,* 4 Apr. 1979.
B183   *Variety,* 4 Apr. 1979.

The Summer of '42
B184   Canby, Vincent. *New York Times,* 19 Apr. 1971.
B185   *Variety,* 21 Apr. 1971.

Sweet Lorraine
B186   Bernard, Jami. *New York Post,* 1 May 1987.
B187   Wilmington, Michael. *Los Angeles Times,* 24 June, 1987.

Truman Capote's Trilogy
B188   Thompson, Howard. *New York Times,* 7 Nov. 1969.
B189   *Variety,* 5 Nov. 1969.

A View from the Bridge
B190   Crowther, Bosley. *New York Times,* 23 Jan. 1962.
B191   Hart, Henry. *Films in Review* 13 (1962): 102-103.
B192   *Variety,* 10 Oct. 1962.

Index

About the Author

JEANNIE M. WOODS is Assistant Professor of Theatre in the Department of Theatre and Dance, School of Visual and Performing Arts, at Winthrop University in Rock Hill, South Carolina. Dr. Woods is an actor, director, and theatre historian. She is also the author of the forthcoming *Theatre to Change Men's Souls: The Artistry of Adrian Hall.*

Titles in
Bio-Bibliographies in the Performing Arts

Milos Forman: A Bio-Bibliography
Thomas J. Slater

Kate Smith: A Bio-Bibliography
Michael R. Pitts

Patty Duke: A Bio-Bibliography
Stephen L. Eberly

Carole Lombard: A Bio-Bibliography
Robert D. Matzen

Eva Le Gallienne: A Bio-Bibliography
Robert A. Schanke

Julie Andrews: A Bio-Bibliography
Les Spindle

Richard Widmark: A Bio-Bibliography
Kim Holston

Orson Welles: A Bio-Bibliography
Bret Wood

Ann Sothern: A Bio-Bibliography
Margie Schultz

Alice Faye: A Bio-Bibliography
Barry Rivadue

Jennifer Jones: A Bio-Bibliography
Jeffrey L. Carrier

Cary Grant: A Bio-Bibliography
Beverley Bare Buehrer

Maureen O'Sullivan: A Bio-Bibliography
Connie J. Billips

Ava Gardner: A Bio-Bibliography
Karin J. Fowler

Jean Arthur: A Bio-Bibliography
Arthur Pierce and Douglas Swarthout

Donna Reed: A Bio-Bibliography
Brenda Scott Royce

Gordon MacRae: A Bio-Bibliography
Bruce R. Leiby

Mary Martin: A Bio-Bibliography
Barry Rivadue

Irene Dunne: A Bio-Bibliography
Margie Schultz

Anne Baxter: A Bio-Bibliography
Karin J. Fowler

Tallulah Bankhead: A Bio-Bibliography
Jeffrey L. Carrier

Jessica Tandy: A Bio-Bibliography
Milly S. Barranger

Janet Gaynor: A Bio-Bibliography
Connie Billips

James Stewart: A Bio-Bibliography
Gerard Molyneaux

Joseph Papp: A Bio-Bibliography
Barbara Lee Horn

Henry Fonda: A Bio-Bibliography
Kevin Sweeney

Edwin Booth: A Bio-Bibliography
L. Terry Oggel

Ethel Merman: A Bio-Bibliography
George B. Bryan

Lauren Bacall: A Bio-Bibliography
Brenda Scott Royce

Joseph Chaikin: A Bio-Bibliography
Alex Gildzen and Dimitris Karageorgiou

Richard Burton: A Bio-Bibliography
Tyrone Steverson

www.ingramcontent.com/pod-product-compliance
Lightning Source LLC
Chambersburg PA
CBHW070443100426
42812CB00004B/1192